Subsequent chapters examine the emergence of such nationwide senior-advocacy organizations as the American Association of Retired Persons, the National Council of Senior Citizens, and the Gray Panthers; the development of a productive coalition between this "gray lobby" and organized labor; and the impact of organized old-age politics in achieving such key legislation as Medicare and the Older Americans Act in the 1960s. The institutionalization of the senior rights movement, which reached critical mass in the mid 1960s and early 1970s, is covered in depth, as are the social forces, such as the conservative New Right, which could conceivably lead to the fragmentation and demise of the movement in coming decades.

The authors ultimately predict that future efforts to control the direction of the public debate will continue to center on competing definitions of what would constitute an equitable relationship between generations and classes in American society. Whatever scenario does unfold, they project, it will be the success of the politically influential in selling one of these interpretive packages to the American public, rather than any objective demographic or economic trends, that will primarily determine the direction of American old-age policies over the next several decades.

THE AUTHORS

Lawrence Alfred Powell is assistant professor of political science at the University of Texas at San Antonio, John B. Williamson is professor of sociology at Boston College, and Kenneth J. Branco is associate professor of sociology at Stonehill College.

THE
SENIOR RIGHTS
MOVEMENT

Framing the Policy Debate in America

SOCIAL MOVEMENTS PAST AND PRESENT

Irwin T. Sanders, Editor

THE SENIOR RIGHTS MOVEMENT

Framing the Policy Debate in America

Lawrence Alfred Powell,
Kenneth J. Branco,
and John B. Williamson

Twayne Publishers
An Imprint of Simon & Schuster Macmillan
New York

Prentice Hall International
London Mexico City New Delhi Singapore Sydney Toronto

The Senior Rights Movement: Framing the Policy Debate in America
Lawrence Alfred Powell, Kenneth J. Branco, and John B. Williamson

Twayne Publishers
An Imprint of Simon & Schuster Macmillan
1633 Broadway
New York, NY 10019

Library of Congress Cataloging-in-Publication Data

Powell, Lawrence A.
  The senior rights movement: framing the policy debate in America
  / Lawrence Alfred Powell, John B. Williamson, Kenneth J. Branco.
      p.   cm.—(Social movements past and present)
  Includes bibliographical references and index.
  ISBN 0-8057-9710-6 (cloth). — ISBN 0-8057-9746-7 (paper)
  1. Aged—United States—Social conditions.   2. Aged—Government
  policy—United States. I. Williamson, John B. II. Branco,
  Kenneth J.   III. Title.   IV. Series.
HQ1064.U5P67   1996
305.26'0973—dc20   95-42917
                                                                   CIP

The paper used in this publication meets the minimum requirements of American
National Standard for Information Sciences—Permanence of Paper for Printed Library
Materials. ANSI Z39.48-1984. ∞™

10 9 8 7 6 5 4 3 2 1 (hc)
10 9 8 7 6 5 4 3 2 1 (pb)

Printed in the United States of America

To
Lucian W. Pye,
Murray Edelman,
and William Gamson,
for teaching us the importance of symbolism
in politics

Contents

Preface

This book is a history of the struggle for old-age justice in America as it has unfolded since colonial times. Worthy scholars have traversed portions of this terrain before us; we have derived much inspiration and insight from the works of W. Andrew Achenbaum, Henry Pratt, Jill Quadagno, Ann Orloff, John Myles, Robert Binstock, and David Hackett Fischer, among others. This volume seeks to extend and further integrate those pioneering efforts, adding a fresh perspective of our own, which focuses on how struggles to advance "senior rights" have revolved around the framing of public debates between progressives and conservatives over appropriate definitions of what would constitute equity or justice in old age. Using examples of political rhetoric and media images from colonial days to the present, the analysis in this volume highlights the ongoing importance of political symbolism in constructing the "realities" of old-age politics in America.

Our goal throughout the production of this work has been to achieve a rich interdisciplinary synthesis across diverse areas of knowledge that bear on old-age politics in America. We hope that the product of these integrative efforts will provide, for the general reader, a palatable history of the "senior rights movement" that is accessible to students of sociology, history, politics, and public policy, while at the same time stimulating some new ideas within the professional scholarly literatures on social movements, symbolic politics, and gerontology.

Like the history of old-age politics, this volume is a complex social construct, reflecting the creative contributions of many persons. Lawrence Alfred Powell is the primary author of chapters 1–8. Kenneth Branco and John Williamson made contributions throughout the book and to all phases of the work. For their patient help in locating historical materials for use in this work, we are grateful to the reference staffs of Dewey and Rotch libraries at the Massachusetts Institute of Technology, Widener Library at Harvard University, Mugar Memorial Library of Boston University, the Boston Public Library, the O'Neill Library at Boston College, the Cushing-Martin Library at Stonehill College, the Archives of Labor History and Urban Affairs of Walter Reuther Library at Wayne State University, Krannert and HSSE libraries of Purdue University, the libraries of the University of Texas at Austin, and Elizabeth Coates Maddux Library at Trinity University. Rosemary Frey contributed to the preparation of this manuscript in a number of ways, including playing a major role in the preparation of the extensive bibliography and in securing permissions for use of the political cartoons. The authors wish to acknowledge the assistance and support of Charles Derber, Eunice Doherty, Darlene Epstein, Maureen Eldredge, Eden Fergusson, Sheri Grove, Elizabeth Johnson, David Karp, Keith Neisler, Lisa Pelletier-Branco, Robert Winston Ross, Adrian Saenz, Ben Sargent, and Sheryl Zettner. The authors also wish to acknowledge the financial support of the Purdue Research Foundation, Boston College, Stonehill College, and the University of Texas, in the form of funding for research expenses, summer stipends, and released time from teaching to work on this research project. Finally, the authors are especially indebted to Irwin Sanders, Robert Benford, Carol Chin, John Martin, Athenaide Dallett, Anne Davidson, Barbara Sutton, and Mary Reed at Twayne Publishers for their tireless editorial assistance and moral support in the preparation of this volume.

Chapter One

Old-Age Equity as a Social Construct

*The Symbolic Politics of Reality Definition and
Mass Persuasion*

> The critical element in political maneuver for advantage is the cre-
> ation of meaning: the construction of beliefs about the significance of
> events, of problems, of crises, of policy changes, and of leaders. The
> strategic need is to immobilize opposition and mobilize support. . . .
> Allocations of benefits must themselves be infused with meanings.
> Murray Edelman, "Political Language and Political Reality"[1]

On 14 August 1935 President Franklin D. Roosevelt signed into law a
landmark piece of legislation designed to provide retirement benefits
for the nation's elder citizens. Over the course of the next half century, "Social Security" was to become the most popular and successful
federal program of the American welfare state. In recent years, however, a renewed public debate has emerged over the future of the
Social Security system and whether that future will prove fair to
younger generations. Poised on one side of the debate, conservative
intellectuals, economists, and politicians have advanced a pessimistic
view of the future of Social Security. Widely disseminated through
the national media, this image of "impending crisis" suggests that as
the American population "grays" over the next several decades
owing to low fertility rates, the Social Security program and
Medicare are destined to "go bankrupt," because there will be so
many older people collecting their benefits relative to a much smaller number of younger workers paying into the system.[2] A closely

1

related argument, championed by lobby groups such as "Lead . . . or Leave" and "Americans for Generational Equity," holds that as the large post–World War II "baby boom" generation reaches retirement age it will place such a heavy financial burden on those still in the labor force that younger workers of a future era—say in about the year 2030—will balk and "refuse to pay." They argue that the huge generation of aged baby-boomers will consume so much of the nation's health-care resources, housing resources, and so on, that a dramatic reduction in the standard of living for the rest of the population will inevitably result—a reduction that will provoke an indignant "age war" against these "greedy geezers" and the "expensive" federal programs that serve them (Kotlikoff 1992; Longman 1987; Barringer 1993).

On the other side of the public debate, defenders of the social rights of elderly Americans counter that to formulate this emerging policy dilemma strictly in terms of issues of cost-containment, generational inequity, and "getting Big Government off the taxpayer's back" is misleading, not to mention heartless to the aged. They argue for a "humane" federal agenda that would instead give primacy to issues of elderly "needs," citizen "rights" to old-age support, the "common stake" that exists between generations, and "equity between rich and poor" (Minkler and Robertson 1991; Hutton 1989; Carlson 1987).[3] In *Ties That Bind: The Interdependence of Generations,* a report sponsored by the Gerontological Society of America, aging advocates have launched a rhetorical counter-offensive against these repeated attacks on the viability of Social Security. The declared purpose of the report is to "assist with the reformulation of the generational equity debate . . . and with the search for an appropriate framework for the aging society." Its authors argue for a quite different conception of what would constitute a socially "equitable" distribution of resources among generations in American society. In their view, maintaining a continued (or even expanded) federal commitment to guarantees of security in old age—which successive generations of Americans have struggled for the better part of this century to achieve—is both fair and possible. In an "equitable" policy solution, the higher social costs associated with responding to the needs of a rapidly aging society ought to be distributed "based on the principle that those most able to contribute to societal progress, regardless of age, bear the greatest burden," with the "higher-income and able elderly people contributing their fair share." They suggest that instead of seeking to incite intergenerational warfare between young and old, responsible public officials should adopt a "multigenerational agenda" that emphasizes the "common stake" that exists between generations that are, in reality, highly "interdependent" (Kingson, Hirshorn, and Cornman 1986).

In response, conservative critics have insisted that such arguments on behalf of preserving current Social Security and Medicare arrangements—however well-intentioned—are naive and unrealistic, ignoring "the facts." The "hard demographic realities" of an unfavorable old-age dependency ratio (ratio of retirees to workers), sluggish economic growth, and massive budget deficits, they argue, dictate that programs and benefit levels for the aged will "inevitably" have to be "scaled back" in coming decades in order to "save" the Social Security system from fiscal "collapse" (Schobel 1992; Peterson and Howe 1988; Torrey 1982). With the lower fertility rates that have prevailed among the current adult generation, these aging baby-boomers regrettably will find that they simply have not produced enough children to support them comfortably in retirement (Wattenberg 1987). Moreover, it would be "inequitable," they argue, to expect future generations to bear the financial burden of doing so, thereby constricting their own opportunities in life (Longman 1985; Hewitt 1986; Lamm 1985, 1987). Furthermore, they warn, it would be the height of irresponsibility for policymakers to continue making "gratuitous" promises of support in old age to the present generation of working adults when government will "obviously" be unable to deliver on those promises down the line (Boskin 1986, 1988). It "inevitably follows," they advise, that responsible policymakers should encourage both the present and future generations of workers to begin seeking "independent" retirement and health care alternatives to public support in their golden years (Ferrara 1985; Goodman 1985; Ricardo-Campbell and Lazear 1988; Chakravarty and Weisman 1988).

Lessons from the Past: A Retrospective History of the Social Construction of Old-Age Justice

Few Americans would disagree that considerations of cost and fairness between generations should be taken into account in devising solutions to the problems of supporting citizens in old age. In this book we suggest that there are a number of prior questions that need to be carefully examined, however, before policy analysts and the media rush to accept these "inevitable facts" and their "inevitable policy consequences" as gospel. Among these questions are the following:

1.   What social forces, sectors, or groups stand to gain the most from declaring that a "crisis" exists? What policy "solutions" are being implied by these crisis definitions of the situation? What *other* possible policy solutions are thereby systematically being ignored, and hence kept *out* of the public debate? Given the widely divergent fates of rich and poor elderly in the United States, for example, wouldn't it be equally plausible to declare an impending "crisis of class inequity" or perhaps a "crisis of need satisfaction among the aged poor"?

2.   Have similar crisis definitions and counter-definitions arisen *before* in the history of American old-age policy struggles? If so, who stood to gain and who to lose from promoting those earlier definitions of the realities of old age? What lessons can be drawn for dealing with current policy dilemmas?

3.   How might a "social construction of reality" theorist view these recent attempts to redefine the legitimacy of Social Security as a social institution and the aged as deserving recipients? What kinds of symbolic imagery are being employed to portray the old, the young, and the relationship between the two? Is the social construction of political enemies involved here? If so, how does this negative imagery come into play? Who is "good" and who is "evil" according to these revised definitions of sociopolitical reality? Are there scapegoats? Are there implied victims, heroes, and so forth? Perhaps most important, in what ways might this distorted symbolism constrain the range of choices available to policymakers in formulating old-age policies over the next several decades?

4.   Have twentieth-century old-age policies constituted legitimate social reforms of the circumstances of elderly Americans, or are they better understood as token legislation and symbolic reassurance measures, undertaken by anxious elites in order to deflect threats of potential restructuring of the socioeconomic order posed by radical reform movements?

In addressing fundamental questions like these, a look at the history of old-age policy reform struggles is instructive. In this volume we suggest that the dynamics of these present issues, and their implications for future aging policies, cannot be understood apart from what has gone before. One cannot devise prudent designs for the future without comprehending the past. To intelligently evaluate these current rhetorical claims and their validity requires that one consider them within the broader context of the history of aging policy struggles as they have evolved over centuries. We argue, further, that it is important to understand the symbolic politics of how similar public debates over issues of old-age justice have been "framed" by senior rights advocates and their opponents in the past in order to justify resource claims in society. Have similar rhetorical devices been used in the past by conservative societal forces in order to head off aging program expansion? What rationales were used by advocates of progressive reform to promote better economic and social conditions for the aged?

Such questions are best addressed by critically examining the processes by which American old-age problems, social change organizations, policy solutions, and their accompanying rationales have been socially constructed over time. In this volume we have therefore made it our purpose to provide a historical description and analysis of the ongoing phenomenon that has been variously called "senior power," the "senior movement," and the "gray lobby"—to which we shall refer subsequently as the "senior rights movement." It is our hope that this book, by helping to illuminate the past, will contribute to a more sophisticated understanding of the political challenges posed by a rapidly aging population leading into the early decades of the twenty-first century. Accordingly, in the chapters that follow we examine the origins of, societal resources available to, and power of the ongoing old-age policy reform movement as it has developed in the American context.

A major feature that distinguishes this study from other histories of American old-age politics is its emphasis on the role played by *symbolic politics* in the evolution of twentieth-century struggles to achieve social justice for the elderly. Our historical account underscores the importance of symbolic gestures and counter-gestures that have been used by both senior rights advocates and their opponents to influence the direction of events and to sway public opinion on aging issues. We argue that emergent problems of old age, the policies designed to address them, and the movements to extend or repeal those policies have in large part been *socially constructed*. Throughout this century, conflicting definitions of the realities of aging have reflected the pre-

dominance of competing societal values, conceptions of social problems, and their appropriate solutions. These, in turn, represent
attempts to justify and protect the vested interests of different sectors
in American society.

In tracing the dialectical interplay between these progressive
reform mobilizations and reactionary counter-mobilizations over time,
the analysis that follows focuses on critical points in the history of old-
age struggles—arguing that such "crises" have often been arbitrary
social constructs, conveniently declared to achieve political or economic ends rather than necessarily reflecting objective social realities.
We find, moreover, that these socially defined crisis points in the history of aging politics have typically involved a struggle between senior
rights movement advocates and the opponents of reform to *frame the
debate* over what is, or is not, *equitable*—that is, to define the terms of
public discourse about old-age problems and to dictate which values
and interests will subsequently be given priority in a "fair" public policy response. As we shall see in subsequent chapters, the pivotal struggles for Social Security in the 1930s, for Medicare in the 1960s, and
the neoconservative backlash against both in the 1980s and 1990s provide instructive examples. Efforts to control the direction of the public
debate have, in each instance, centered on competing definitions of
what would constitute an equitable relationship between classes, age
groups, and generations in American society.

We suggest that the present preoccupation with the "coming crisis
of Social Security" and "generational inequity" in government and
academic circles is best understood against the backdrop of these
historical trends. *Viewed from this broader temporal perspective, the
present public debate over what to do about the "crisis of the Social
Security system" can be seen to be only the most recent manifestation of
a recurrent struggle to define the context of American public discourse
about social justice in old age.* Extrapolating from historical patterns,
we project that the future of Social Security, Medicare, and related
federal policies will depend heavily on whose definition of "fairness"
with respect to aging issues ultimately prevails in the rhetorical battle
for the hearts and minds of Americans, and not just on demographic
and economic trends alone. In an era of political consultants, ideological think tanks, and increasingly sophisticated manipulation of mass
media images for political purposes, the ability to "frame the
debate"—to define popular priorities, mobilize opinion, and thereby

set the nation's issue agenda—is likely to be the pivotal factor that determines the direction of American old-age polices over the next several decades.

The Social Construction of Political Realities: A Framework for Analyzing Aging Reform Politics

In order to intelligently distinguish the realities of aging in America from the rhetoric that surrounds aging policy, we need to first step back and understand the ways in which political "realities" are socially defined, as that process applies to crises, policy solutions, reform movements, and social problems in general. As will become increasingly evident in the historical chapters that follow, political symbolism and the skillful manipulation of public perceptions have often been as formative in shaping American old-age politics as the more tangible realities of economic conditions, group resources, and demographic change. We do not mean to imply by this that the structure of society and the material resources of competing interests have been unimportant. Quite the contrary. What we do suggest, however, is that changes in aging policies over time have often occurred in conjunction with concerted efforts at mass persuasion through use of political language and political gestures—which in turn represent attempts to justify, or protect, the resource claims of different sectors in American society. In short, we suggest that politics is not merely, as Harold Lasswell was fond of pointing out, a matter of "who gets what, when, and how," but also a matter of who *defines* what, when, and how.

The most commonly used approaches to political analysis—rational-choice theory, interest-group pluralism, functionalism—tend to be less than adequate for explaining this "who defines" aspect of reform politics. There are both material *and* symbolic dimensions to most aging policy reform conflicts, and those traditional approaches have little to say about the latter—namely, the purely persuasive, dramatic, rhetorical, propagandistic, legitimizing, and consent-manufacturing aspects of the political process (Gamson and Lasch 1983; Gamson 1988).

The work of "social construction of reality" theorists within sociology, and "symbolic politics" theorists within political science, is therefore immensely helpful in overcoming this shortcoming of the standard analytic paradigms. The social-construction-of-reality approach builds on insights into the nature of human social action derived from the "symbolic interactionist" tradition of George Herbert Mead (1934) and other early American sociologists of the Chicago School. Whereas functionalists hold that established social structures and shared social standards shape human action, essentially implying that there is a "right" way to interact socially in any given context, analysts like Mead (1934), Blumer (1969), Goffman (1959, 1974), Burke (1969), Gamson (1988, 1992) and others have instead stressed the creative, less circumscribed aspects of human interaction. This approach is particularly appropriate for describing the dynamics of sociopolitical movements for change, since unusual situations such as civil disobedience campaigns, marches, and riots typically lie outside the conventionally defined parameters for behavior. Social behavior in such instances cannot be fully understood in terms of the normal cultural prescriptions, because a struggle to legitimize new definitions and delegitimize old definitions of social reality is taking place.

Another distinct advantage of the symbolic interactionist perspective is that it pays special attention to the ways in which participants in the construction of historical events attach *meaning* to those events, to their own actions, and to the actions of other participants. According to Mead, Goffman, and others, it is impossible to describe human interaction—political or otherwise—without addressing this symbolic nature of the human animal. Although many other species interact socially, humans are unique creatures in the degree to which they employ complex symbols in defining and redefining the meaning of features of their social environment. Humans attach symbolic definitions to virtually every aspect of their lives. As anthropologist Clifford Geertz observed, "Man is an animal suspended in webs of significance he himself has spun" (1973, 5).

The symbolic interactionists, then, imply that what individual social actors take for granted as being social "reality" is in fact a social product, composed of myriad shared meanings that are communicated and interpersonally validated through language and gesture. This assumption provides the point of departure for social-construction-of-reality theory (Berger and Luckmann 1966). The epistemological premise on which social-construction-of-reality theory is based is the observation that within any given social context there is no such thing as a single, correct, "objective" definition of reality. What constitutes social truth—with respect to the condition of the elderly or any other group—is therefore culturally and morally relative. The same set of "facts" may take on different meanings for different groups or individuals at different times, and thus would be experienced as constituting different realities. What is experienced as being "reality" in any given context is built up in complex layers of meaning out of words, symbols, and definitions of events. Everyday "common-sense" reality reflects what Berger and Luckmann call the "common social stock of knowledge," which "everybody knows." This consensual reality, which most citizens in any sociopolitical order uncritically experience as being "the truth" or "the facts," is therefore actually one that has been arbitrarily constructed and has come to be accepted as the basis for collective interpretations of the world—which, as interpretations, can also potentially be *re*interpreted. Social problems, reform movements that arise to seek solutions to problems, the development of new social laws, administrative plans for carrying them out, and evaluations of their success or failure—all ultimately represent arbitrary social constructs.

The question of who defines, who interprets, and who is in a position to frame debates over social issues and determine which issues will be considered important enough to place on the national agenda is therefore a key source of power in any society. Within political science, the study of these definitional processes is usually referred to as "symbolic politics." Murray Edelman—the chief exemplar of this approach—disputes the conventional model of politics that takes for granted that citizens in modern democracies live in a world of facts and that voters respond rationally to objective information they receive through mass media. He argues that the "political spectacle," to which citizens are daily exposed through media news accounts, represents not a set of concrete facts but rather an artifically contrived *interpretation* of reality. Political enemies, threats, crises, problems, movements for change, compromises, laws, and leaders are all socially constructed, and as such take on meanings that perpetuate interests and statuses in society (Edelman 1964, 1971, 1977, 1985, 1988).

Edelman observes that the adept use of techniques of "mystification" by established elites plays a central role in arousing popular support for desired policies, in immobilizing opposition, and in achieving "quiescence" among subject populations. Inspired by the symbolic interactionists, twentieth-century language theorists, the poststructuralists, and the postmodernists,[4] he portrays this ongoing "political spectacle" in any society as consisting of arbitrarily defined symbols and gestures whose function is to construct, deconstruct, and reconstruct the meanings of past events, relationships between social groups, and public expectations. Language forms and mass media, in particular, play a seminal role in this social construction of political problems, movements, leaders, and the declaration of crises.

One useful insight afforded by this approach is a sort of Copernican view of the public policy formation process. Policymaking elites and academic policy analysts typically proceed on the basis of an unexamined temporal premise as to the relationship between social problems and their remedies—namely, that problems first appear, and responsive government agencies thereafter search rationally for the appropriate ways to solve them. In actual practice, however, "the solution typically comes first, chronologically, and psychologically" (Edelman 1988, 22). That is, "problems" are typically created to justify desired solutions. Because the desired solution actually comes first, and then a definition of the problem, Edelman argues that definitions of social "problems" and their proposed "solutions" are actually arbitrary, and that both are social constructs (which can therefore also potentially be *de*constructed). Applied to the so-called Social Security crisis, for example, this model would suggest that the New Right already had retrenchment in aging programs firmly in mind *before* it seized on the "problems" of a "financial crisis of Social Security" and "generational inequity."

The fact that definitions of social problems and their solutions are arbitrary social constructs means that situations that at one point in time are regarded as unproblematic may subsequently be redefined by policy elites as being serious problems requiring public solutions. Conversely, socially damaging conditions such as slavery, discrimination, or poverty may not be defined by elites as being significant political issues at all. The latter become what Peter Bachrach (1967) has referred to as "nondecisions" or "nonissues." Edelman observes that "perhaps the most powerful influence of news, talk, and writing about problems is the immunity from notice and criticism they grant to damaging conditions that are not on the list" (1988, 14). In recent years damaging conditions "not on the list" of those promoting the idea of a Social Security "crisis" might, for instance, be said to have included the living standards of the elderly poor, inadequate health care coverage, and class-based inequities in the distribution of social rewards and employment opportunities among the elderly. During the Reagan and Bush administrations, in particular, these need-oriented aging program priorities were overshadowed by a preferred emphasis among policy elites on issues of "cost containment," the "threat of financial insolvency," and "intergenerational (rather than interclass) equity."

This selective agenda-setting plays a major role in legitimizing and maintaining inequalities. By virtue of their disproportionate access to the means of communication and public persuasion, political elites and the dominant societal groups they disproportionately represent are easily able to avoid attracting public attention to the social conventions from which they benefit, particularly maldistribution of wealth and privilege (Ginsberg 1986; Schiller 1989; Kellner 1990). The "nonissue" status of such problems is often held in place in the long run by "ideological premises that are so widespread in some people's everyday language that they are not recognized as ideological at all, but accepted as the way the world is constituted" (Edelman 1988, 15).

A consistent motif of the symbolic politics approach, then, is the variety of potential meanings inherent in any emergent social "problem," which stems from different interests seeking to promote their preferred courses of action as "solutions." The "problem" is a signifier that focuses on a label for a purported threat to society: "generational inequity," "the bankruptcy of the Social Security fund." The defined problem is particularly likely to be accepted by the public as constituting a credible threat if it can somehow be plausibly related to a dominant cultural theme. Hence the popularity of Reagan's anti-tax, anti–welfare-state rhetoric as governor of California in the 1970s and as president in the 1980s, during a period of nostalgic neo-individualism.

What makes citizens so eager to accept official explanations of events remote from their daily experience without questioning those explanations? Part of the answer lies in their need for "symbolic reassurance." Edelman notes that "for a public anxious to understand them, or only marginally interested, an official cue readily becomes the key influence" (1988, 25). When public anxiety is aroused in response to a defined state of "crisis," government action that would ordinarily meet with popular defiance is more readily accepted. The perception that a "crisis" exists brings with it the expectation that, until conditions improve, people must endure certain unpleasant forms of deprivation that they would not otherwise tolerate. Often an officially declared crisis is in reality little more than one rather unspectacular episode in a long sequence of related problems. What makes that particular episode a "crisis" is not so much the problem's potential severity for ordinary citizens as it is the problem's utility for governmental or corporate elites who want to mobilize action in pursuit of some end without encountering popular resistance. The crisis designation creates a malleable public climate in which previously unacceptable practices and ideas are suddenly legitimized and long-accepted ideas are rejected. This in turn leaves leaders with much-expanded authority to adopt previously unthinkable policy remedies. Announcement by authorities of the existence of a crisis prepares the public for the idea that sacrifices must first be made before things can improve. Although they may appear on the surface to be shared equally, these required "sacrifices" are usually borne disproportionately by the least privileged sectors of society (Estes 1983, 446–47).

If the conceptual framework outlined above is applied to the late-twentieth-century public debates over the future of Social Security and Medicare, what does one find? A consistent pattern has emerged over the past several decades in which well-financed think tanks, anti–welfare-state politicians, newspaper columnists, and radio talk show hosts have thus far experienced considerable success in redefining Social Security—probably the most successful and popular federal program of this century—as a "failed" system facing "crisis." The rationale for proposed cutbacks in federal expenditures on aging programs has been consistently framed as being due to strictly objective, nonpolitical "facts" of changing demography and "overgenerous" benefit payments to the elderly. This constricted definition of the situation has thus far eclipsed a number of plausible alternative explanations of the current problems in financing Social Security—including, in particular, their being attributable to unsuccessful monetary and fiscal policies pursued by elite decisionmakers in recent years (Quadagno 1989, 1992; Myles 1991, 300–304).

Causes and facts surrounding the so-called impending crisis have been distorted in the public's mind and in the media's representation of the issues. As sociologist Carroll Estes points out, the key to understanding what has been happening in recent decades to the Social Security system is to recognize that the "crisis" really has two dimensions: a symbolic and a material one. The "symbolic" dimension lies in the recent redefinition of old people as constituting a "problem to society," whose cost is too great, thereby diverting national attention from deeper and potentially more compelling policy problems and failures (Binstock 1983a). Attempts have been made by insurance industry spokesmen, economists, journalists, and public officials to delegitimize and scapegoat the elderly by linking them in the public mind with emerging problems in the American economy. In the process of selling this crisis designation to the American public to rationalize social program retrenchments, the cost of taking care of the needs of older Americans has often been portrayed by "economic experts" as "busting the budget" and as "robbing younger generations" of their fair share of America's resources and opportunities (Estes 1983, 1993; Minkler 1991; Binney and Estes 1988; Minkler and Robertson 1991).

The "material" dimension of this arbitrarily declared crisis lies in the resulting redistribution of societal resources. As Estes astutely observes, the various definitions of the Social Security crisis and proposed solutions to it "would institutionalize the advantage of different groups and social classes through policies that ultimately are legislated and implemented to deal with it" (1983, 451). To incumbent decisionmaking elites, the utility of declaring an "impending crisis" in Social Security lies in the fact that emerging problems in the system may be conveniently depicted to the public not as a product of failed fiscal policies devised at the top but of impersonal forces of "demographic change" and "inadequate planning for retirement" by individuals—thereby relieving public officials of the responsibility. This preference for projecting a crisis version of the problems with Social Security has been given additional credence by sensationalistic media accounts. Uncritical media acquiescence to the crisis definition (it makes for an interesting story), and the infrequency with which the public has been exposed to any contrary interpretation (why complicate a good story?), have contributed to an erosion of the American public's confidence in the future of the Social Security system.

As we shall see in subsequent chapters, this sort of wholesale manipulation of public sentiments via mass media is nothing new. In past aging-policy reform struggles as in the present one, "who gets what" has depended heavily on who holds the power to define social reality and to persuade others of the validity of those definitions.

Tracing the "Natural History" of American Senior Rights Struggles: The Approach of This Book

The bulk of this volume is devoted, retrospectively, to a historical analysis of the dynamics of aging-policy reform struggles as they have developed over the past two centuries. Since the protracted political battles to extend elderly social rights have often displayed many of the characteristics of an ongoing movement, we have found it useful to organize the historical account that follows around Armand Mauss's "life cycle" theory of the "natural history" of a social movement (1971, 1975). Mauss has argued that all movements for social change pass through more or less predictable stages of development: *incipiency, coalescence, institutionalization, fragmentation,* and *demise.* A growth curve representing this five-stage life cycle would have a shape approximating the normal curve, with the third stage at the apex (see Figure 1.1). In the chapters that follow, we make it our purpose to trace—within each of these successive stages of the senior rights movement—the dialectic struggle that has taken place between progressive senior rights advocates and conservative opponents of reform to "frame the debate" over societal definitions of fairness and social justice in old age.

Having here introduced the theoretical framework that informs our analysis, we turn our attention in chapter 2 to a description of some of the early historical trends that acted as preconditions for the eventual emergence of a senior rights movement in twentieth-century America. We discuss social forces in the 1800s and early 1900s that began to create a perceived need for active government involvement in solving some of the economic and social problems of aging in modern industrial societies, paying particular attention to changing definitions of the elderly, their societal role, and their social rights.

Chapters 3 and 4 describe the dynamics of the *incipiency* stage, marking the beginning of a senior rights movement in twentieth-

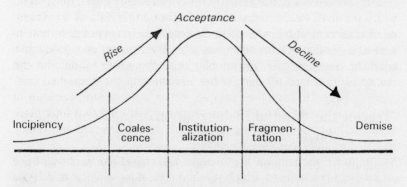

Figure 1.1. Successive stages in the natural history of a social movement. Adapted from Armand Mauss, *Social Problems as Social Movements* (Philadelphia: J. B. Lippincott), 66.

century American politics. In chapter 3 the origins of the movement are traced to several organizations and prominent individuals who began lobbying for the idea of old-age pensions during the 1920s and 1930s, including the Fraternal Order of the Eagles, the American Association for Labor Legislation, supporters of Upton Sinclair's EPIC program, the Ham and Eggs group, Abraham Epstein's American Association for Social Security, and the Townsend Movement. The analysis in this chapter focuses on some of the political symbols and rhetorical devices that were used by pension-reform advocates to frame the public debate over social justice in old age, as well as those employed by conservative opponents of pension reform.

Chapter 4 continues this description of the incipiency stage, analyzing the impact of the Great Depression on the emerging old-age pension movement and the impact of the pension movement on the passage of the Social Security Act of 1935. It is argued that the Social Security Act constituted a classic historical instance of co-optation of a social movement's demands for social change by the established social order. The adept use of gestures of "symbolic reassurance" by Roosevelt and policy elites to mollify supporters of more comprehensive pension schemes is analyzed in considerable depth. The decline of the Townsend organization and other prominent pension-reform groups in the aftermath of passage of the act is attributed to the divisive effects of the success of Roosevelt's Social Security legislation as an act of co-optation of the old-age pension movement's demands for more radical change.

The "coalescence" stage of the American senior rights movement, which occurred between the early 1950s and mid 1960s, is documented in chapter 5. It includes a discussion of the emergence of nationwide senior advocacy organizations, the development of a productive coalition between this "gray lobby" and organized labor, and the impact of organized old-age politics in achieving the legislative landmarks of the 1960s. The example of the struggle for passage of Medicare is used to illustrate the symbolic posturing that took place between proponents and opponents of progressive old-age policy reform during the coalescence phase.

Chapter 6 focuses on the process of *institutionalization* of the senior rights movement, which reached critical mass in the mid 1960s and early 1970s. The institutionalization process is described as it took place in four sociopolitical domains: (1) the development of a coordinated national network of senior advocacy associations with large memberships (the AARP, the National Council of Senior Citizens, etc.), which enabled the movement and its sympathizers to apply continuous electoral and lobbying pressures on lawmakers; (2) the initiation of regular White House Conferences on Aging, to sound out grievances and consider reform proposals; (3) the creation of a permanent bureaucratic structure within the executive branch—the Administration on Aging—to represent elderly interests; and (4) the emergence of a nationwide cadre of professionals in aging-related fields, with a vested interest in promoting services for older Americans.

In chapter 7 we discuss social forces that might conceivably lead to the "fragmentation" and "demise" of the movement in coming decades, although such a development is by no means inevitable. We consider the possibility that one source of the demise of the senior rights movement could be the power of another emerging social movement—the New Right—which has fundamentally different objectives and defines "equity" in fundamentally different terms. We discuss the ideological basis and political strength of the New Right, assessing the late-1970s tax revolts, the election of Ronald Reagan, the impact of Reagan-era policies on the quality of life for elderly Americans, the power of senior advocacy organizations to resist social program retrenchments relative to other constituencies, and the partial success of the Reagan and Bush administrations in shifting the context of the old-age equity debate from issues of adequacy, need, and equity between classes to issues of cost-containment, merit, and "generational inequity."

In the concluding chapter, "Framing the Equity Debate in an Era of Mass-Mediated Political Realities," we consider the possible impact of precedents set during the Reagan and Bush years on the potential for future activism on behalf of older Americans leading into the twenty-first century. As the population of the United States continues to age, projected demographic trends clearly indicate that the near future will bring large numbers of older people who live to experience political struggles over issues of equity and social justice. Moreover, as the ongoing revolution in telecommunications moves us further into a postmodern era of mass-mediated political realities, the power to symbolically "frame debates" in the public mind can be expected to become even more central to political outcomes than it has been in the past. We consider alternative future scenarios for old-age politics in the United States, projecting that, as has frequently been the case in the past, future efforts to control the direction of the public debate will continue to center around competing definitions of what would constitute an equitable relationship between generations and classes in American society. Extrapolating from past trends, we predict that, whatever scenario ultimately unfolds, it will be the success of the politically influential in "selling" one or the other of these interpretive packages to the American public, rather than any "objective" demographic or economic trends per se, that will primarily determine the direction of American old-age policies over the next several decades.

Chapter Two

Defining Justice for the Old in a Young Nation

Historical Antecedents of Twentieth-Century Struggles

> *It is painful to see old age working itself to death, in what are called civilised countries, for daily bread. . . . To provide for all those accidents, and whatever else may befal, I take the number of persons who . . . after fifty years of age, may feel it necessary or comfortable to be better supported than they can support themselves, and that not as a matter of grace and favour, but of right.*
>
> *Thomas Paine, 1792[1]*

> *I fear the giving mankind a dependence on anything for support in age or sickness besides industry and frugality during youth and health tends to flatter our national indolence to encourage idleness and prodigality.*
>
> *Benjamin Franklin, 1768[2]*

The first rumblings of what we today call "senior power" surfaced on the American political scene in the early decades of the twentieth century, when disgruntled citizens mobilized in support of old-age pensions. In fact, however, some of the social forces that gave rise to those struggles reflect earlier developments in the nation's history. This chapter examines processes of social definition and change in a young American nation that began to produce the impetus for construction of public solutions to problems associated with old age. We discuss the social forces in seventeenth- through early twentieth-century America that created a perceived need for some form of government involvement in assisting dependent and indigent elders. Throughout, we pay particular attention to changing definitions of the rightful place of elderly citizens in the social order, their obligations, and their social rights.

Definitions of the Status and Social Worth of Elders in Early America

In colonial America the population was relatively young. Although age composition varied somewhat from one locality to the next, in most settlements about half of the inhabitants were typically below the age of 16 (Wells 1975). Only a select few survived beyond "three-score winters." Those who did were generally "venerated" by the community. In the sermons of religious authorities and speeches of civic leaders, normative guidelines defining the proper place of aged citizens usually dictated that those who had "attained to threescore" deserved to be accorded respect and deference by younger members of society. Given the high incidence of illness, injury, and death in colonial America, longevity was widely revered as a commendable personal achievement. To survive to old age was seen as a sign of wise and virtuous living, favored by Providence (Fischer 1980). The Reverend Cotton Mather of Boston—articulating common definitions of the inherent dignity of old age in late seventeenth-century New England—wrote in a dedication to an elderly friend that "Were there nothing else to commend my regards for you, besides Old Age, which your out-living of threescore winters has brought you to the border of, that were enough to give you a room in my esteem, and reverence, and veneration" (1690, dedication page).

The Puritans assumed it to be self-evident that "the law written in their hearts by nature has directed them to give a peculiar respect and deference to aged men. In most civilized nations they have done so" (I. Mather 1716, 63, 120). While these prescriptions were apparently not always heeded in practice, it is nonetheless clear that for youth to do otherwise was regarded as a breach of prevalent standards of moral decency and fairness between generations. The Reverend Increase Mather of Boston, chastising young people who would ridicule the elderly for their frailty, warned that "to deride aged persons because of those natural infirmities which age has brought upon them is a great sin" (1716, 132). Similarly, the Reverend Samuel Willard inveighed against ungrateful children who might consider defaulting on their financial obligations to parents in old age, admonishing that "children that have been the Charge of their Parents to bring them up to be capable of doing something, should not presently, in hope of doing better for themselves, desert their helpless Parents . . . and let them shift for themselves" (1726, 608). In colonial New England the "elders" of a community—particularly males of substantial means— were commonly ascribed roles of authority, power, and prestige in local affairs. This practice was regarded as being at once socially useful and equitable to the elderly, given their hard-earned life accomplishments, accumulated wisdom, and presumed moral expertise. The prevailing assumption was that "old men know more than other ones," and were therefore unquestionably "fittest to give counsel . . . fittest to be trusted with the greatest and most honorable offices" (I. Mather 1716, 133). Even after their competence had clearly begun to wane in advanced old age, elected officials and the clergy were rarely forced to resign or retire, and they often served until they died. Indeed, as contemporary historian W. Andrew Achenbaum points out, early Americans "would have been surprised to learn that the elderly as a group would be described one day as roleless and unproductive persons who inevitably and willingly disengage from active life" (1978, 9).

One symbolic manifestation of the respect commanded by elder citizens in early American communities can be seen in their seating arrangments during public gatherings. In preindustrial New England the meetinghouse functioned as a central place of worship and public business. The order of seating was a symbolic representation of the stratification system of the community, with the most desirable seats going to those held in highest honor. In Hingham, Massachusetts, in 1682, for example, the most honored seat—directly beside the pulpit—was occupied by the elderly widow of the minister's predecessor. On the bench below the pulpit sat the Elders, whose ages in 1682 were 73, 86, and 92. Successive rows seated the "old guard" of the town, the widows and wives of Elders and Deacons, middle-aged men and their wives, young bachelors and maids, young married couples, children, and, in the least-honored seats, servants, Indians, and blacks (Coolidge 1961, 435–61).[3]

Equally symbolic of the esteem accorded the elderly was the colloquial language of the times. Terms with honorific connotations—*pro-*

genitor, eldern, grandsire, grandame, forefather, venerable—were commonly used to describe elderly persons during the colonial and post-Revolutionary years. Other expressions, such as *greybeard, gaffer, fogy, superannuated,* and *old guard* (which were later to take on more pejorative connotations), constituted terms of respect and affection toward the aged during this early period (Fischer 1980, 90–94).

Of course the actual treatment received by the aged did not always live up to these exalted normative ideals. Disillusioned older persons would sometimes discover to their dismay that their status had derived more from their property or the nature of their profession than from their age per se. And the frailty and dependency of the aged was sometimes resented by those charged with managing their infirmities. Persons of humble origins, in particular, were likely to be despised rather than esteemed in their advanced years (Haber 1983, 16–25; Demos 1978, 222–24; Achenbaum 1978, 11, 62, 64–66). Still, the overall trend in early America was one of affirmation of the basic social worth of those who had "attained to threescore years."

As we shall see later in this chapter, that sense of secure social worth—and many of the opportunities that accompanied it—began noticeably to erode during the nineteenth century. The subsequent loss of status and opportunity was to become a chronic source of insecurity to many older Americans, which in turn became an incentive for seeking public solutions to problems of aging through the political process during the twentieth century.

Early Patterns of Social Provision for Dependent Elders

When adventuresome Europeans began constructing colonies in the New World, they brought with them Old World customs of social protection for the "lame, impotent, old, blinde, and such other among them being poore" that had been evolving in Europe since medieval times.[4] Some settlers also brought emerging Lockean liberalist notions of limited government, private property, and individualism (Hartz 1955). Early American patterns of public care for dependent elders therefore reflected a congeries of the old preindustrial protectionist ideas associated with the mercantilist era, mixed with new liberal-individualist concepts of limited state sovereignty, the importance of self-reliance, and voluntarism (Rimlinger 1971; Coll 1972). Owing in part to the timely influence of the latter set of ideas, this new American social order was from the outset a society with a stubborn preference for responding to the needs of its citizens through private, voluntary arrangements that would mediate between the individual and society without necessarily invoking the "coercive" powers of centralized governmental authority (Lubove 1968, 1–24).

Within this new cultural context, the burden of providing for aged persons who could no longer actively contribute was borne by a combination of the family, religious organizations, and the local community. Social provisions for dependent elders took a number of forms, varying considerably from one locality to the next and often depending on the social standing, gender, and ethnic background of the aged recipient. Typically an attempt was made to administer relief in a manner that would minimally disrupt the lifestyle and dignity of the recipient. When personal and family resources proved insufficient, local communities would sometimes pay a neighbor or a friend to provide the necessary care. Relief in an institution (the almshouse, "indoor" relief) was considered to be the alternative of last resort, usually applied only in cases involving severe physical or mental incapacity (Quadagno 1984a, 422–28, 441; Haber 1983, 25, 35–36). The following examples are characteristic of the types of arrangements commonly employed in early New England towns to provide for dependent elders during this period:

The towne are willing to give Thomas Bennet Thirteen pounds provided he mayntayn old patchin with meat drink clothing washing and Lodging for the Term of a Twelve month: and render him in clothing at the years end. (Fairfield, Connecticut, town records, 30 November 1682)[5]

There is an Aged Woman in my Neighborhood, poor, and lame, and sick, and in miserable Circumstances. I must not only releeve her myself but also summon together her several Relatives, that they agree to have her well-provided for. (C. Mather, 1713)[6]

On reading a petition from James Maxwell praying for relief in his old age— alledging he was a Contributor while he was in a capacity—The Society voted that he . . . be allowed out of the box Twenty Shillings, and time to come during life Ten shillings each quarter after this and the Treasurer is ordered to pay the same. (Records of the Scots' Charitable Society of Boston, November 1718)[7]

From the Revolutionary period through the early years of the nineteenth century, public provisions to assist the elderly and other dependent groups generally reflected a "divine stewardship" principle. The practice of benevolence to the needy was viewed as a "connecting link between divinity and humanity." Civic leaders, preachers, newspaper editors, and charity representatives during this period defined public obligations to help aged dependents in terms of the "duty of the rich and those who are in comfortable circumstances, to provide for the relief of the suffering poor" (*New York Evening Post,* 5 January 1810).

The prevalent philosophy of social provision during this period held that assistance was to be offered to those in need on terms that were as charitable and unconditional as possible, such that "even those whose vices have occasioned their distress, should not be suffered to die in despair" (*New York Daily Gazette,* 4 January 1791). Post-Revolution humanitarians promoted the idea that the practice of helping persons who were unable to support themselves in old age was spiritually uplifting, and hence was beneficial to the well-being of the community at large. De Witt Clinton eloquently expressed this tolerant attitude toward assistance to the needy in a 1793 address on "Benevolence," delivered before the Holland Lodge, in which he reminded his audience how "glorious" and "God-like" it was to "step forth to the relief of . . . distress; to arrest the tear of sorrow; to disarm affliction of its darts; to smooth the pillow of declining age" (Clinton 1793, 15).

Changing Definitions of Equity and Deservingness in the Jacksonian Era

By the second decade of the nineteenth century, however, a noticeable shift toward greater austerity and restrictiveness in the administration of public relief had begun to take place in the major New England cities, with negative implications for the quality of care received by elderly persons who depended on the public dole for their subsistence. This shift was apparently precipitated by reactions among the nonpoor strata to emerging pressures of a weak economy and increasing tax rates. At a more fundamental level, the policy shift appears to have been related to the accelerating transition from an agriculture-based economy to a more urban, capitalistic economy, which required a strengthening of work norms among the laboring classes and a more "rugged individualist," less community-oriented societal ethos (Powell and Williamson 1985; Kutzik 1979, 38–50).

Between 1790 and 1840 a series of economic and demographic changes helped set the stage for a redefinition of prevailing assumptions about public relief. While these redefinitions were not specifically aimed at the dependent elderly per se, they had profound effects on the quality of public care they were thereafter to receive as a category of the poor. Owing largely to escalating immigration pressures, the population of the United States quadrupled between 1790 and 1840 (U.S. Department of Commerce 1960). East Coast cities suddenly found themselves swamped by successive waves of immigrants, many of whom ended up living on the public dole, which in turn strained city budgets. In addition to the immigration pressures, cities also had to cope with a steady influx of rural migrants to urban areas, further contributing to the rapid growth of relief rolls. Also swelling the ranks of the poor was a series of depressions, the worst of which occurred between 1815 and 1821 as a result of the Napoleonic Wars (Coll 1969, 21). These steady increases in the number of persons dependent on relief inevitably led to corresponding increases in government expenditures, and hence also in the tax burden on nonpoor strata. According to a report by Mr. Josiah Quincy, chairman of the Committee on the Pauper Laws of the Commonwealth of Massachusetts, the financial burden of supporting the poor in that state increased fivefold between 1791 and 1820 (Cummings 1895, 34–37). In the city of New York annual appropriations for poor relief exceeded all other items in the budget during this period (*Minutes of the Common Council of the City of New York 1784–1831,* 1917, 476–77). In Philadelphia public expenditures on poor relief grew from about $47,000 in 1800 to $95,000 in 1820, producing an unrelenting escalation in poor taxes from $50,000 to $140,000 over this same period (Clement 1985, 49).

In turn, these increases in the tax burden on the more fortunate classes prompted public officials to initiate a series of studies on "the growing evils of pauperism" (Quincy 1821; Yates 1824; Board of Guardians 1827). The impetus for launching these poor law "investigations" apparently came from a growing impatience among political representatives of the nonpoor echelons of society to discover ways to "economize on" relief expenditures, thereby reducing the associated tax burdens. The Yates investigation of pauperism in New York worried that "the poor laws tend to encourage the sturdy beggar and profligate vagrant to become pensioners on the public funds" (1824, 952). Philadelphia's Board of Guardians likewise harrangued indignantly in their 1827 study that "It is neither reasonable nor just, nor politic, that we should incur so heavy an expense in the support of people, who never have, nor ever will, contribute one cent to the benefit of this community" (1827, 28). Similarly, the Quincy report in Massachusetts seemed obsessed with "the evils resulting from a public, or compulsory, provision for the poor" (1821, 5). Although the surface rhetoric of these official inquiries continued to express token sympathy for the plight of the poor, the benevolent preoccupation with meeting the needs of the indigent, the aged, and the sick that had characterized post-Revolutionary relief efforts had largely disappeared (Bodo 1954). In its place, the revised agenda of welfare reform was now clearly to reduce public expenditures and thereby reduce taxes to the non-poor—by finding ways to consolidate the services rendered and to eliminate as many "shirkers" as possible from the public dole.

In the 1820s problems within the relief system that had been tolerated for decades as little more than chronic annoyances were suddenly elevated in official rhetoric to the status of a major public crisis—which, it was said, would require immediate study and fundamental reevaluation of existing practices. With the "solution" of reduced relief expenditures already firmly in mind prior to the outset of the investigations, political elites in the major East Coast cities diligently set about searching for ways to redefine the issue of "the evils of pauperism" to the public in such a way that "the facts and reasons" would convincingly warrant a reduction in services to the poor. Careful perusal of Josiah Quincy's "Report of the Committee on the Pauper Laws of this Commonwealth" in Massachusetts, for example, reveals that the sponsors of the inquiry considered it "of the highest consequence" that the "facts and reasons" contained in the study should "draw the attention of their fellow citizens to . . . prepare their minds to adopt and to cooperate in the establishment of such a system" as would be "sanctioned and supported" by the investigation (1821, 1–2). The 1827 "Report of the Board of Guardians of the Poor of the City and Districts of Philadelphia" likewise indicated that the purpose for making "such observations, as may be suggested by a review" was to "accomplish a radical reform" in existing Pennsylvania relief practices and emphasized the necessity of "the public mind" being "prepared for a change" so that citizens would be "cordially disposed to unite in effecting it" (Board of Guardians 1827, 1, 24).

One rhetorical device repeatedly used by these "official inquiries" in reframing the context of the poverty issue was to shift the blame—

and hence also the responsibility—for inability to support oneself away from society at large and to place it solely on the poor individual. The poor were now being portrayed not as neighbors who had fallen on bad times through no fault of their own (as had been the dominant view during the post-Revolutionary years) but rather as an underclass of quasi-criminal "beggars" and "vagrants" who shunned work because they preferred to live at public expense.

By implication, this new causal interpretation extended to older paupers as well as younger ones. Official accounts of the sources of indigence shifted from social conditions and misfortune to what today would be called "culture of poverty" explanations—emphasizing instead the poor's deficient morality, lack of motivation to work, and inability to defer gratification. Quincy's study of pauperism in Massachusetts, for instance, asserted, "It may be confidently stated that the chief sources of pauperism in this country are idleness, improvidence, and intemperance. If any laws can be devised to lessen the operation of those causes, pauperism will be lessened nearly in the same proportion" (1821, 31). Similarly, in Philadelphia's 1827 report, the Board of Guardians of the Poor observed that "indolence, intemperance, and sensuality are the great causes of pauperism in this country. Notwithstanding the imbecility induced in their habits and vices . . . the course of the practice of this class, is to be brought to the Alms House, in a state of disease or intoxication . . . and after being cured, restored, and supported . . . they are permitted to depart, to enter upon the same career of vice and indulgence, until they are again brought back . . . and pursue the same circle" (1827, 26–27).

Another component of this new official rhetoric of cost containment involved a moralistic search by reactionary elites for evidence of corruption and mismangement in relief administration. Exaggerated accounts of the extent of waste and fraud in the administration of public assistance were used to justify the need for restrictive revisions in existing poor laws.[8] The Quincy report contended that public poor relief "has been the source of abuse, mismanagement and waste; that supplies if given in money are mischievous and misapplied, when given for necessities, as expended by the men, in ale . . . when given the articles of food and clothing, they were often sold to obtain luxuries" (1821, 7–8). The Board of Guardians of the Poor, chastising the Philadelphia relief apparatus, declared that the "most grievous error of our unwieldy system, is the abuse of the administration of relief" (1827, 23). Similarly, the Yates report in New York made frequent mention of the "gross abuses which have grown out of these laws," adding that there was "an evident want of economy in the disbursement of the public funds, appropriated for the support of the poor in several towns and counties" (1824, 952–53).

Among those who sponsored and conducted these protracted investigations (which were, incidentally, themselves quite costly to taxpayers) a consensus emerged that the crux of the problem was to be found in the "enormously expensive" system of "outdoor relief." The Quincy, Yates, and Board of Guardians reports agreed that of the various methods of poor relief "the most wasteful, the most expensive, and the most injurious to their morals and destructive of their industrious habits is that of supply in their own families" (Quincy 1821, 9). The solution recommended by all of these investigations was therefore that relief be administered in poorhouses, since "wherever that plan has been fairly tried, the expense of supporting paupers has decreased 33 percent, and in many cases 50 percent" (Yates 1824, 958).

The Poorhouse "Solution" and the Deterioration of Public Assistance for the Aged Poor

Having succeeded in reframing both the problem and the appropriate public solution, policy elites in New York, Massachusetts, and Pennsylvania enthusiastically began implementing the recommendations of their respective "investigations" by constructing county almshouses. Following their lead, most other states initiated construction of poorhouses between 1820 and 1840. Indeed, as social historian Blanche Coll points out, "So very impressive were the arguments of men like Quincy and Yates . . . that by 1860, few localities of any size lacked almshouses" (1969, 22). In Massachusetts alone 144 poorhouses were erected between 1820 and 1840, and by the close of the Civil War 80 percent of long-term relief recipients in that state were residing in almshouses. In New York the Yates investigation led to passage of the County Poorhouse Act (1824), requiring construction of at least one poorhouse per county (Quadagno 1984a, 429–30; Rothman 1971, 183; Schneider 1938, 235–46).

An unfortunate byproduct of this officially "sanctioned and supported" redefinition of the causes and cures for poverty was that relief in institutions increasingly supplanted "supply in their own families" as the major source of public support to the elderly poor during the remainder of the nineteenth century. Their crime was guilt by association with the "undeserving" poor. The anticipated success of the new almshouse strategy was premised on the assumption of actual ability to work among the majority of the inmates, who were presumed to be merely lazy and deficient in character. Jacksonian era reformers defined "paupers" as being not so much in need of help as of moral redemption. The Philadelphia Board of Guardians' reform recommendations, for instance, asserted that "the poor in consequence of vice, constitute here and everywhere by far the greater part of the poor" (1827, 26).

Those who advocated the almshouse alternative as a method of relief claimed that most persons dependent on the public dole were able-bodied, nonaged adults. In so doing they substantially underrepresented the proportion who were actually old, physically disabled, insane, or children (Coll 1969, 21). The Philadelphia Guardians' report confidently explained that "it is found by experience, that generally speaking, all this class can do something . . . and often not at all short, of the ability to perform daily, the complete task of a day-labourer" (1827, 26–27). In their zeal to reinforce work norms, the authors apparently did not notice (or did not wish to acknowledge) their own discrepant data—which elsewhere in the same report indicated, for example, that in the Baltimore Almshouse, "there is an average of one-fourth sick, one-fourth children, and nearly a fourth aged and infirm, or lame, or maimed, and incapable of labour" (1827, 5). For public officials anxious to appease a restive populace, this convenient misunderstanding of the extent of the poor's incapacity to work provided a plausible rationalization for minimizing public expenditures in support of society's least productive members—a rationalization that had the rhetorical advantage of being entirely consistent with basic American cultural premises like self-reliance, limited government, and the Protestant work ethic.[9]

According to the surviving historical evidence from almshouses erected during this period, the realities of poverty apparently did not match their overseers' optimistic rhetoric as to the high proportion of "able-bodied" paupers. The records of the Blockley Almshouse of Philadelphia for the year 1848, for example, indicate that the combined elderly and infirm inmates comprised approximately 77 percent of all persons in residence there. Only 192 men and women (approximately 12 percent) out of a total of 1,509 inmates were actually capable of performing work (Klebaner 1952, 211). In fact, "able-bodied" inmates were often so scarce that poorhouse supervisors found it necessary during the summer months to hire farm laborers from the general population (Coll 1969, 24–25).

This moralistic tendency to exaggerate the number of "able-bodied" paupers (who were characterized as undeserving of public help) had the unfortunate consequence of further eroding already tenuous levels of public sympathy and support for all categories of the poor, including the elderly. The resultant decline in relief funding over the next several decades led to deteriorating conditions for aged inmates in city and county poorhouses, which became increasingly plagued by overcrowding, meager provisions, and abuse of inmates by staff. With widespread adoption of the "more economical" poorhouse approach, many elderly Americans whose personal and familial resources had been depleted found themselves with no alternative but to cohabitate with some of the most unsavory characters in the community—the diseased, the insane, and alcoholics (Powell and Williamson 1985).[10]

Over the next several decades (in the pre–Civil War years) those who had opposed the poorhouse alternative as inhumane and unworkable were quick to expose the deficiencies of this new system. Opponents of "indoor" relief argued that the rhetorical claims for its ability to deter "vicious and idle" paupers had been greatly overblown. The morally upright, truly needy poor would avoid almshouses out of a sense of shame, they admonished, while the shiftless would not hesitate to take advantage of them. Others pointed out that care in institutions was actually more expensive to administer than "outdoor" relief had been, noting that it would ultimately be cheaper to place dependent elderly, poor, sick, mentally ill, and orphaned persons with relatives or friends, who could supervise their care without uprooting them from their accustomed surroundings.

The most trenchant criticisms, however, came from those who were incensed at the deplorable conditions that had resulted from the almshouse "solution." In New York, where adoption of Yates Report recommendations had led to the construction of almshouses in 51 of 55 counties, an 1838 report of the State Assembly revealed evidence of deteriorating conditions and gross overcrowding in county almshouses (Coll 1969, 25–26). Again in 1857 another committee studying poorhouse conditions returned with a grim picture of inhumane treatment of inmates in New York's poorhouses, where "may be found the lunatic suffering for years in a dark and suffocating cell, in summer, and almost freezing in winter . . . where the aged mother is lying in perhaps her last sickness, unattended by a physician, and with no one to minister to her wants" (New York State Senate 1857, 157).

During the course of their inquiry, the 1857 Select Senate Committee to Visit Charitable and Penal Institutions witnessed conditions so squalid that "common domestic animals are usually more humanely treated than the paupers in some of these institutions." The almshouses they visited were "badly constructed, ill-arranged, ill-warmed, and ill-ventilated." The stench was typically "very noxious, and to casual visitors, almost insufferable." The facilities were severely overcrowded, with up to 45 inmates per dormitory, and "sleeping boxes arranged in three tiers one above another." Medical care was poor to nonexistent. The committee observed that "the inmates sicken and die without any medical attendance whatever." In one county poorhouse, which had an average population of 137 inmates, the committee reported that there had been 36 deaths in a single year, "and yet none of them from epidemic or contagious disease." They concluded that such a high mortality rate constituted "inexcusable negligence," adding that "want of suitable hospital accommodations is severely felt in most of the poor houses."

The cells and sheds to which paupers were confined were "wretched abodes, often wholly unprovided with bedding." In some poorhouses, inmates were observed to be residing "in a state of nudity" in cells that were "intolerably offensive, littered with long accumulated filth of the occupants, and with straw reduced to chaff by long use as bedding, portions of which, mingled with the filth, adhered to the inmates and formed the only covering they had." As for the food, it was often "not only insufficient in quantity, but consisted partly of tainted meat and fish. The inmates were consequently almost starved." Summarizing the cumulative effects of poorhouse conditions on inmate health, the committee concluded that "good health is incompatible with such arrangements. They make it an impossibility."

With such powerful concrete evidence at their disposal, the committee jumped at the opportunity to discredit the assumptions of the more conservative 1820s investigations that had deemed indoor relief the most efficient, economical, and humane solution to the problem of pauperism. They suggested instead that the poor could best be maintained through "the proper and systematic distribution of outdoor relief." This alternative, they contended, was "more efficient and economical." It would also be, they asserted further, more humane to "worthy indigent persons" such as the aged, since they could be "kept from the degradation of the poor house, by reasonable supplies of provisions, bedding, and other absolute necessities, at their own homes" (New York State Senate 1857, 150–54).

The committee went on to call into question the validity of a major underlying assumption of the 1820s studies—namely, that poverty was necessarily caused by individual deficiencies—observing that among the almshouse inmates they had encountered many "persons of great worth and respectable character, reduced to extreme poverty, not by any vice or fault of their own, but by some inevitable loss of property, or of friends and relations, who, if living would have supported them in their age and infirmities." The committee argued that it was unfair and cruel to force those whose poverty was "the result of disease, infirmity, or age producing positive inability to earn a livelihood" to leave their familiar surroundings and involuntarily cohabitate with the "unworthy" poor (New York State Senate 1857, 153).

Unfortunately, despite these and other graphic descriptions of squalid conditions prevalent in most poorhouses of the day, the attempt to reframe the issue of pauperism—in more sympathetic terms that would suggest the need for a return to outdoor relief—largely failed to produce any major change in conditions. These institutions, after all, performed an important social control function for more prosperous citizens by keeping the "dangerous classes" in check and by reinforcing work norms in a rapidly industrializing capitalist economy (Quadagno 1984a, 432; Scull 1977; Piven and Cloward 1971). "Indoor relief" continued to be the dominant form of public provision for the aged poor and other dependent groups for the remainder of the nineteenth century and on into the early years of the twentieth (Coll 1969).

Early Pension Prototypes

The Social Security Act of 1935 is commonly assumed to have been the first nationally funded pension system proposed and enacted in the United States. In fact, both the idea and the practice of old-age pensions can be traced back much further. In the early years of the new republic, Thomas Paine had advocated pensions as an equitable way to prevent impoverishment in old age. In *Rights of Man* Paine outlined the social arrangements necessary to ensure that the common man in "civilized countries" would be treated fairly in old age:

At fifty, though the mental facilities of man are in full vigor, and his judgment better than at any preceding date, the bodily powers for laborious life are on the decline. . . . At sixty his labour ought to be over, at least from direct necessity. . . . To provide for all those accidents, and whatever else may befal, I take the number of persons who . . . after fifty years of age, may feel it necessary or comfortable to be better supported, than they can support themselves, and that not as a matter of grace and favour, but of *right*. (1792, 487–88)

Paine proposed that a relief plan be established that would abolish the existing Poor Laws and substitute instead a combination of an old-age pension, guaranteed employment, and family allowances. According to Paine's progressive scheme, all citizens over 50 years of age would receive a modest annual pension, to be funded through a land tax. He anticipated that if his plan were to be implemented, "the hearts of the humane will not be shocked by . . . persons of seventy or eighty years of age, begging for bread. The dying poor will not be dragged from place to place to breathe their last, as a reprisal of parish upon parish. Widows will have a maintenance for their children, and not be carted away, on the death of their husbands, like culprits or criminals" (1792, 493). Despite its innovative qualities, however, Paine's proposal unfortunately received little attention in his day.

The first national pension scheme to actually have an impact on the lives of at least some elderly Americans was the Revolutionary War military pension, which provided half-pay for life to disabled veterans of the war, with benefits funded by the states (Glasson 1918, 20–23). A considerably more substantial military pension scheme was enacted by Congress in 1862. While the Civil War pension constituted a major improvement over the terms of the Revolutionary War pension, numerous restrictions remained. Only Union soldiers injured in combat and their dependents were eligible to collect benefits. Pension benefits were also contingent on rank and degree of disability. In the decades following the Civil War, however, the terms of the military pension were gradually expanded. The expansion occurred in response to the expressed needs of aging veterans, in response to lobbying pressures, and also because extension of pension benefits became an effective method for political parties to attract electoral support during the period of intense electoral competition that took place between 1870 and 1896. In 1879 the Arrears of Pension Act was passed, which extended coverage retroactively to veterans with disabilities who had failed to sign up earlier for pensions. These veterans were thereafter eligible for a pension in addition to a lump-sum payment of all accumulated arears. Not surprisingly, the new law led to thousands of new claims.

It was also during this period that the first American pension reform organization, the Grand Army of the Republic, became active in American politics. Composed primarily of war veterans who sought further liberalization of the Civil War pension laws, the organization rapidly gained membership, and became politically active in lobbying Congress for reforms and in persuading additional veterans to sign up for pensions (Dearing 1951). Additional reforms were forthcoming. The Dependency Pension Act was passed in 1890, extending coverage to Union Army soldiers who had never been injured or seen combat. In effect, this liberalization of the law created a de facto old-age pension system for three quarters of a million veterans (Skocpol and Ikenberry 1983, 79, 95). In 1912 the system was further extended, specifying that "the age of sixty-two years and over shall be considered a permanent specific disability within the meaning of the pension laws" (Williamson and Pampel 1993, 89).

Predictably, this series of reforms in the Civil War pension laws led to higher government expenditures. Veterans' pensions rapidly became the single most costly item in the federal budget (excluding debt service), accounting for between 21 percent and 40 percent of federal expenditures from the 1880s through the 1910s. By the turn of the century the Civil War pension system had evolved into a massive national system of old-age support, which at least temporarily masked the growing need among elderly Americans for a more permanent old-age insurance system similar to those which were being created in Europe to cover the entire population (Orloff and Skocpol 1984, 728; Glasson 1918, 273; Fischer 1977, 169–70).[11]

Rugged Individualism, Social Darwinism, and the "Unfit" Aged

Another development in nineteenth century America—which had less favorable implications for the social treatment of old Americans—was the ascendance of a societal ethos of "rugged individualism." Territorial expansion into the frontier regions, coupled with the rapid growth of industrial capitalism, produced a new social climate in which Lockean individualism flourished as a belief formula justifying unrestrained free enterprise practices, while simultaneously discouraging public expenditures on disadvantaged groups such as the elderly. In particular, two underlying premises of this ideological package had implications for social care of dependent elders: (1) the belief that each individual was solely responsible for his own welfare (and hence ought to rely on his own resources); and (2) the belief that society's benefits ought to be distributed strictly on the basis of individual performance or productivity, rather than according to need. Both premises tended to work against humanitarian attempts to sustain adequate levels of public assistance to the needy aged, and provided convenient rationales for keeping their plight off the public conscience.

The post–Civil War period saw a new class of industrial capitalists emerge as a powerful force in American society, searching for novel ideas to further rationalize their economic imperatives. War-related profits had fueled the fires of industrial expansion, and after the war this placed the new industrialists in a position to effectively dominate the economic life of the country. The introduction of machinery in factories, enabling production on a mass scale, began to transform the conditions of common laborers, making them increasingly dependent on industrial capitalists for their livelihood. With economic competition from southern planters now eliminated from the scene, and growing numbers of industrial laborers depending on them for their subsistence, wealthy industrial elites in the Northeast seized on the philosophy of "social Darwinism" as a convenient intellectual formula to legitimize their growing dominance of American society during this period.[12] Based on an analogy from Darwinian biology, social philosopher Herbert Spencer claimed that just as, over time, evolution selected an elite in nature, so also did social evolution require the inevitable emergence of an elite within human societies, which was selected through the process of free competition.

This idea had a marvelous resonance with existing cultural principles of individualism and laissez-faire capitalism. Spencer, along with his foremost American disciple William Graham Sumner, hailed the emergence of the new powerful industrial elite in postwar America as a quintessential example of "survival of the fittest." This revised social definition of what constitutes progress—namely, that unrestricted competition naturally selects the best, to the long-run betterment of all—provided a plausible defense for great accumulations of wealth and the development of an increasingly ruthless economic elite in the latter half of the nineteenth century.

Whereas the rapid dissemination of this idea was good news for the well-to-do, the young, and the healthy, it stigmatized and marginalized those who were poor, aged, and dependent. They were defined as inferior and worthless to society. Spencer's social Darwinist doctrine was adamantly opposed to the idea of societal responsibility for the "less fit" and to any form of public intervention whatsoever on their behalf. To intervene on behalf of "the weak," social Darwinists argued, would be contrary to human evolutionary progress through natural selection. Within this ideological frame, public generosity to the aged, indigent, and infirm—whether provided through the state or charitable advocates of the poor—was defined as being not only unproductive but actually counterproductive, due to its interference with the "beneficent" processes of natural selection. Spencer wrote that "it seems hard that widows . . . should be left to struggle for life or death. Nevertheless, when regarded not separately, but in connection with the interests of universal humanity, these harsh fatalities are seen to be full of the highest beneficence—the same beneficence that brings to early graves the children of diseased parents, and singles out the low-spirited, the intemperate, and the debilitated as the victims of an epidemic." Spencer considered strict abstention from giving any form of public aid to "the unfit" to be a "rigorous necessity" which, he worried, "these paupers' friends would repeal, because of the wailings it here and there produces" (1868, 353–54).

Social Insecurity: Declines in Elderly Status and Economic Opportunity

In an era of ruthless industrial expansion, justified by individualist and social Darwinist rationales, the untamed energy of youth was gradually being redefined as more important to societal well-being than the mature wisdom of age.[13] Reflecting the changing spirit of the times, the January 1872 *New England Almanack* characteristically explained to its readers that "years do not make sages, they make only old men" (1872, 22). As the shift from an agriculture-based to an industrial-capitalist economy accelerated during the nineteenth century, the status of the elderly began to lose some of its economic basis. The power and status of the old in early American communities had derived largely from their ownership of property and the accumulation of a lifetime of expertise in a valued craft. The revolution in property relations that occurred with the accumulation of industrial capital, stock markets, corporations, and factories, however, contributed to a depreciation of the overall social usefulness of elderly citizens, particularly those residing in cities. When laborers in urban industrial settings became too old to perform factory tasks to the satisfaction of their employers, they were often perfunctorily discarded, to be replaced with younger, more energetic workers. Unable to find another job, and without property of their own, more and more discarded workers found themselves with no means of financial support in their declining years.

In a brave new industrial world of mass production using unskilled labor, the nation's economy had become less dependent on the acquired wisdom and experience of seasoned workers. One observer described this new social climate as one in which "the search for increased efficiency" and the "practically universal worship of the dollar" created conditions for aging workers where "gray hair has come to be recognized as an unforgivable witness of industrial imbecility, and experience . . . instead of being valued . . . has become a handicap so great as to make the employment of its possessor . . . practically impossible" (*Independent,* August 1913, 504).

Adding to these mounting social pressures, by the early decades of the twentieth century a number of demographic changes were taking place as well. The American population was aging. The percentage of elderly Americans, which had risen gradually during the nineteenth century, was now beginning to grow at an unprecedented rate. In 1860 only 2.7 percent of the American population had consisted of persons 65 years of age or over. By 1900 this figure had risen to 4.1 percent and continued to increase—to 4.7 percent in 1920 and 5.4 percent in 1930. In absolute numbers, there were more than twice as many aged adults living in the United States by 1930 than there had been in 1900. In just three decades the elderly population rose from 3,089,000 to 6,634,000 (Committee on Economic Security 1937, 141).

These demographic trends took place concurrently with an increase in unemployment and dependency among the nation's elderly. During the rapid expansion of industrial capitalism that took place in the post–Civil War decades through the early twentieth century, employers became increasingly reluctant to hire and retain older workers (Seager 1930, 68). Available statistics show a steady increase in unemployment rates among the elderly. The percentage of males over 65 who were in the labor force fell from 70 percent in 1890, to 64 percent in 1910, to 58 percent by 1930. Concomitantly, the percentage who were forced to depend on public assistance rose dramatically, from 23 percent in 1910, to 33 percent in 1920, to 40 percent by 1930 (Fischer 1979, 55; Achenbaum 1978). These deteriorating conditions among the nation's older citizens were particularly acute in densely populated urban areas.

Whereas elderly unemployment and poverty had clearly become major social problems by the latter decades of the nineteenth century, the massive Civil War pension system acted to temporarily camouflage the severity of these problems. After peaking in the 1910s, however, the number of elderly veterans eligible for war pensions then began to drop, leaving more and more elderly Americans without pension protection against the vicissitudes of old age.

Moreover, private-sector pension plans had been slow to develop in the American context, and very few Americans were actually covered by them. Although some unions developed their own pension plans, only 7 percent of the American workforce had become unionized by 1904. Overall, by 1914 only 1 percent of American employees could count on any form of pension coverage to provide them with some measure of security in old age. In this context, the only alternatives available to the vast majority of older Americans were reliance on accumulated personal savings, support by their children, or, if these failed, commitment to a poorhouse (Fischer 1979, 52–55).

It was this confluence of changing definitions of aging, economic trends, and demographic changes that was finally to propel age-related concerns to the forefront of American politics in the early decades of the twentieth century. The existence of these deteriorating social conditions for the aged was to provide a receptive audience for humanitarian reformers' appeals for social justice and the construction of a senior rights movement.

Conclusion: Six Preconditions to the Emergence of a Senior Rights Movement

The historical account in this chapter highlights six major trends that, together, helped create the context within which twentieth-century senior rights struggles were later to unfold:

1.   While elder citizens were generally held in high esteem in early America, the shift from an agriculture-based economy in colonial times to a more urban, capitalistic economy by the end of the nineteenth century was accompanied by a gradual decline in the status, social worth, and social opportunities accorded to the elderly.

2.   The establishment early in the nation's history of a societal ideology based on widely accepted premises of Lockean individualism and social Darwinism set up a "limited government" cultural context that would later make comprehensive, European-style governmental solutions to aging problems appear less appealing to policymakers and the public than more restrictive, "contributory" approaches.

3.   Prior to the twentieth century the issue of dependency in old age was defined as a residual component of the more general public debate over appropriate policies for dealing with the poor. The aged were not treated as a separate welfare constituency in their own right, as is the case today. In practice, this often meant getting herded together indiscriminately with other categories of dependent and impoverished persons in public "poorhouses." Their particular needs were rarely addressed as such—with unfortunate consequences for the quality of care received by the aged poor.

4.   There was an early development—particularly during the Jacksonian era—of a style of public rhetoric by means of which spokesmen for the more affluent, privileged segments of American society began to frame debates over policies for the aged and other dependent groups in such a way as to rationalize keeping public expenditures low and program commitments minimal. As we shall see in subsequent chapters, very similar rationales for "keeping the poor off our conscience" were later to be used in justifying twentieth-century retrenchments.

5.   Early pension prototypes—such as Thomas Paine's 1792 proposal and the Revolutionary War and Civil War pensions—played an important role as forerunners of modern Social Security policies. These early proposals helped establish the concept of pensions in the public mind, constructing new societal norms and expectations of society's obligation to support citizens in old age.

6.   From the post–Civil War years through the early decades of the twentieth century the combined pressures of unprecedented growth in the elderly population and rising unemployment among older Americans began to expose the inadequacies of existing

American policies for care of dependent elders, creating mounting pressures for some type of progressive reform.

Together, these trends constitute the historical backdrop against which twentieth-century reformers' appeals for social justice for the elderly were later to be played out, and out of which a senior rights movement was to arise.

Chapter Three

The Incipient Senior Rights Movement

Legitimizing Pensions in the Public Mind

We are beginning to emerge from the darkness of a once understandable but no longer tolerable indifference in regard to the fate of old people, whose sin is, whose only sin may be, that they are inevitably the victims of an economic order which makes provision for old age all but impossible.

Rabbi Stephen Wise, pension reformer and vice president of the American Association for Social Security, 1930[1]

What a self-respecting people really needs is not a system of old-age pensions but a population made sufficiently skilled by education and sufficently self-controlled and well-disposed by the hold of religion so that old-age pensions would be superfluity. Unless real reform comes from within, the problem will never be solved.

Calvin Coolidge, 1931[2]

It was not until the first quarter of the twentieth century that issues related to aging began to be taken seriously in the American context as social problems in their own right, requiring separate political solutions. As we observed in Chapter 2, changing definitions of aging and social conditions accompanying industrialization in nineteenth-century America had increasingly isolated older citizens from the mainstream of American social life, leaving them abandoned in old age to a plight that included their devalued status, high unemployment, inability to afford medical care, poor housing conditions, and inadequate or nonexistent pension coverage.

In the early decades of the twentieth century these chronically unsatisfied needs and accumulated grievances began to surface with a vengeance on the American political scene, providing the impetus for political action and the construction of a senior rights movement around the catalyzing issue of old-age pensions. This chapter describes the incipient movement for old-age justice that emerged during this period, and examines the major pension reform organizations of which it was comprised—the Fraternal Order of the Eagles, the American Association for Labor Legislation, Upton Sinclair's EPIC program, the Ham and Eggs group, the American Association for Social Security, and the Townsend Movement. We trace the development of these emerging pension advocacy groups, and analyze the rhetorical themes that they and their conservative political adversaries used in seeking to frame the public debate over the need for old-age pensions during the 1920s and 1930s.

Emergent Pension Reform Groups during the Incipiency Phase

According to Armand Mauss (1971, 1975), every sociopolitical movement for change can be characterized as having a "natural history" or "life cycle" that consists of a sequence of five successive stages through which it passes in the course of its development (see Figure 1.1). Mauss observes that the typical sequence through which all movements pass consists of stages of incipiency, coalescence, institutionalization, fragmentation, and demise. According to this conceptualization, social movements originate with a period of "incipiency." In this formative stage of a new movement, a "concerned public" (in this case, elderly Americans and their advocates) seeks to construct a shared identity based on the perception of a common threat to their interests. In the case of the incipient senior rights movement, the impulse to political action by representatives of the elderly arose out of the series of mounting frustrations accompanying rapid industrialization (as described in Chapter 1). These processes of change in nineteenth- and early twentieth-century American society increasingly marginalized older persons, leaving many of their needs unmet and producing shared feelings of "social insecurity."

In the incipiency stage, activities by the concerned public usually include the expression of grievances and demands via the mass media by holding ad hoc meetings, and by writing letters to political representatives. The most difficult task to accomplish at this stage if the movement is to progress further is to forge a common identity and coherently delineate the political goals of the budding protest group. At some point the conceptual boundaries that symbolically differentiate the interests and views of the concerned public from those of the societal mainstream must be defined. This process inevitably involves redefining the meaning of aspects of consensual reality related to the problems with which the new movement is concerned, and then convincing prospective recruits, the media, influential public officials, and the public of the legitimacy of the alternative definitions. Accomplishing this task, in turn, requires the development of an effective rhetoric of persuasion (Gamson 1988, 1992).

The Fraternal Order of the Eagles and the American Association for Labor Legislation

The incipiency phase of the American senior rights movement can be said to have occurred roughly between the early 1920s and the late 1930s. The origins of the movement are traceable to several loosely organized voluntary associations that began campaigning on behalf of old-age pensions during this period, promoting their various proposed solutions to the worsening social problems of aging in American society and vying for the allegiance of older Americans, the public, and public officials.

Perhaps the most influential of these early reform groups was a national brotherhood called the Fraternal Order of the Eagles. The Eagles were organized into an "Aerie" in every state and each year held a national Grand Aerie, which provided a forum for the expression of common grievances and new ideas for reform. In the period immediately after the end of World War I, the political climate in the United States had become ripe for the emergence of old-age activism. At a time when the American economy was in a deep postwar recession, national Eagles leader Frank Hering was able to convince the organization's rank and file that they should devote a substantial portion of their resources to promoting the idea of old-age pensions.[3] A model pension measure was initiated in the Eagles' Indiana state Aerie in 1921 and was endorsed by the national Grand Aerie in that same year (Lubove 1968, 137).

Already equipped with the organizational advantage of a preexisting framework on both local and national levels, the Eagles enthusiastically began to draft state pension bills, organize community pension clubs, and conduct lobbying campaigns in state legislatures to secure passage of pensions. They also developed an ad hoc coalition with local branches of the United Mine Workers and the American Federation of Labor in several states. The relationship with politically experienced labor groups provided the Eagles with a source of organizational skills and know-how, as well as access to an additional pool of potential recruits to the Fraternal Order (Quadagno 1988b, 68–70).

In their publicity campaigns and lobbying efforts for state old-age pensions, the Fraternal Order consistently maintained that the responsibility for old-age dependency rested not with the individual but with society. Modern industry, they argued, tended to prematurely age the common worker, whose efficiency and speed on the job typically began to decline by age 40 or 50, at which point he lost his job security and was often thrown out in favor of more vital, younger men. An early pamphlet of the Eagles maintained that if societal conditions had hastened the obsolescence of the average worker, then it was the responsibility of society to provide a regular governmental allowance to all aging workers "in consideration of past services." The pamphlet elsewhere explained that it would be equitable for the common worker to receive a regular government subsidy in old age because "those who through years of humble toil have helped to create the wealth by which taxation is borne" ought to be "entitled to honor and independence in their old-age through pensions."[4] Other "civilized democracies" had forged ahead and established old age pensions. Why then, they asked rhetorically, should such an industrially progressive nation as the United States lag behind in the area of social progress by denying its elderly adequate pensions?

The Eagles' pension-reform efforts almost immediately began to produce tangible results. Three states—Pennsylvania, Montana, and Nevada—adopted old-age pension plans in 1923. Over the next decade a majority of the remaining states were to follow suit with similar pension plans (Achenbaum 1978, 122–23). Despite these encouraging symbolic legislative victories, however, pension amounts remained skimpy, eligibility requirements were very strict, and the plans were

mostly voluntary rather than compulsory. Moreover, several of the
original state pension plans were subsequently declared unconstitutional by state supreme courts (Pratt 1976, 16). Thus even with new
state pensions in place in a number of states, by as late as 1930 over 95
percent of aged Americans remained without pension assistance of
any kind, and not a single southern state had adopted an old-age pension plan (Quadagno 1988b; Fischer 1979, 56).

On the positive side, the Fraternal Order of the Eagles had managed to set important precedents for the burgeoning senior rights
movement—by establishing the principle of governmental responsibility for old-age security and by initiating model legislation in the majority of American states. Perhaps most important, the inspiration
provided by the Eagles proved contagious, stimulating similar
attempts by other pension advocacy groups in the 1930s, when the
Great Crash and the deepening depression that followed drove home
the vital need for federal-level solutions to the economic problems of
elderly Americans and the need for political action to secure more
favorable public policies.

Another association that did much to further the cause of state old-
age pensions during the 1920s was the American Association for
Labor Legislation (AALL), which had been founded in the early 1900s
by University of Chicago professor John Commons. Under the enlight-
ened leadership of Commons's protégé, John Andrews, the organization collaborated with the Fraternal Order of the Eagles in drafting the
"model pension bill" that was introduced in state legislatures throughout the country in the 1920s. The AALL's journalistic vehicle, the
American Labor Legislation Review, helped to promulgate arguments
in favor of the adoption of old-age pensions, carrying numerous articles, editorials, and political cartoons devoted to pension-related issues
and continuously monitoring the progress of new bills as they were
introduced in various states. The substantial cumulative impact of the
AALL on the development of old-age pension schemes in the 1920s
and 1930s can perhaps best be gauged by its members' disproportionate representation among the staff of the Committee for Economic
Security—which Roosevelt entrusted in the early 1930s with the task
of formulating a national social security proposal for consideration by
Congress. Edwin Witte, the executive director of the CES; Arthur
Altmeyer, Roosevelt's assistant secretary of labor; and staff assistants
Murray Latimer and J. Douglas Brown were all AALL members (Pratt
1976, 13–14).

Upton Sinclair's EPIC Program

During the 1930s Southern California rapidly emerged as a nexus of old-age activism. In many urban areas there the percentage of the population over the age of 65 was twice the national average. Moreover, elderly unemployment rates there were substantially higher than for the nation as a whole. In this fecund milieu, a variety of old-age pension schemes were introduced by social reformers. One prominent example was a reform program proposed by muckraking novelist Upton Sinclair in 1933. Sinclair had established himself as a popular author of novels urging humanitarian reforms—the most famous of which, *The Jungle*, had exposed the unsanitary and inhumane conditions prevalent in meat-packing plants in the Chicago stockyards and inspired passage of the Meat Inspection Act and the Pure Food and Drug Act (Mitchell 1992; Fischer 1979, 56).

In 1933 Sinclair captured the California Democratic party's nomination for governor and proceeded to draw up a party platform to address problems of the deepening depression. The platform featured an innovative 12-point program that he confidently proclaimed would "End Poverty in California." Drawing on his literary flair, Sinclair cleverly reduced his reform package to the progressive-sounding acronym EPIC and used it thereafter as the symbolic slogan for his gubernatorial campaign. The proposed comprehensive program of economic reform—which featured a generous old-age pension scheme—was so sweeping that it caused entrenched California businessmen and conservative politicians to "go into a sweat that hasn't completely dried up yet" (Townsend 1943, 170). The old-age provision of the EPIC plan proposed a $50 per month pension to all Californians over the age of 60 who had resided in the state for at least three years (Fischer 1979, 57).

Unfortunately for Sinclair and his EPIC program, the 1934 gubernatorial campaign that ensued proved to be, according to one observer, "probably the bitterest, most frenzied, most vituperative, and most unethical struggle" in the history of California politics (Putnam 1970, 34). Sinclair's opponents—a coalition of threatened business interests, Republicans, and conservative Democrats—launched a hysterical campaign of dirty tricks and mudslinging via the media, in which they claimed that Sinclair's EPIC really stood for "End Poverty, Introduce Communism." The red-baiting by California conservatives cost Sinclair the election, and his political fortunes declined precipitously thereafter, undermining further attempts to implement his pension plan in California (Sinclair 1934; Putnam 1970, 32–48; Mitchell 1992). (See Figures 3.11, 3.13, 3.14, and 3.18.)

The Ham and Eggs Group

Another influential pension-reform association to emerge in Southern California during the 1930s was the "Ham and Eggs" group. Based in Hollywood, the movement was initiated by Robert Noble, an unemployed radio announcer who had lost his job for endorsing Sinclair's EPIC plan. His newly created "California State Pension Movement" advocated a plan that called for unemployed elderly persons (over age 50) to receive a weekly scrip payment, which would be stamped with an expiration date to insure prompt spending. The scheme was a variant on the "dated money" idea, proposed by Yale economist Irving Fisher as a Keynesian "pump-priming" measure to "reflate" the depression economy by increasing circulation of money (1932, 1933). Noble promptly adopted the slogan "Twenty-Five Dollars Every Tuesday" for his plan. Shortly thereafter the movement fell into the hands of Willis and Lawrence Allen, who changed the slogan to "Thirty dollars every Thursday" (Fischer 1979, 57). As it obviously would have been difficult to mount a successful pension-reform campaign under this awkward slogan, its proponents sought a more common catchphrase. The answer came when a speaker, addressing a group of campaign workers, promised that before the ensuing election their group would become as familiar to California voters as ham and eggs (Moore 1939, Canterbury 1938).

The leaders of the Ham and Eggs movement were highly proficient at advertising techniques and the use of mass media (radio and newspapers), and did not hesitate to make generous use of those skills in promoting the virtues of their proposed old-age pension scheme. Their "Thirty Thursday" concept gained widespread popularity in California, with the movement soon boasting a formidable following of 362,000 enthusiastic dues-paying supporters. Ham and Eggs rallies often attracted thousands of adherents. An October 1938 article in the *Santa Rosa Press-Democrat* described the quasi-revivalist atmosphere at a typical mass rally as follows: "They open each meeting with a choir-like verse of Halleluiah. En masse they stand with outstretched arms and pledge allegiance to the giant American flag on the platform, and business is never taken up before the party cheer—'5-10-15-20-25-30-Thursday'—is yelled by 2,500 or more voices."[5]

Ham and Eggs leaders were masters at the manipulation of political symbolism, with a penchant for seizing on ripe opportunities to dramatize their cause. When a 62-year-old pauper named Archie Price killed himself in a public park in San Diego, leaving behind a suicide note that read, "Too young to receive an old age pension and too old to find work," Ham and Eggs seized on the incident to generate publicity for the movement and its political goals. Ham and Eggs members melodramatically exhumed Price's corpse, then staged an elaborate funeral in an upper-class cemetery—complete with 7,000 mourners and a long-winded funeral oration by Sheridan Downey, the Democratic party candidate for U.S Senator, in which Archie Price was passionately praised as a marytr who had died for the "right of senior citizens to dignity, to security, to life."[6]

A prime example of the hyperbolic rhetoric that often accompanied the movement's publicity forays appeared in the 24 December 1938 issue of *National Ham and Eggs*. That issue unveiled a new initiative, which it pompously advertised as a "surprise Christmas package . . . offering the greatest challenge ever faced by the present financial dynasty." Elsewhere this new program was described as "the trail blazing precedent smashing Retirement Life Payments Act to bring $30 a Week For Life to California Senior Citizens," which was "the Nation's No. 1 economic campaign" and "unprecedented in the annals of American economic life." In an editorial in the same issue entitled "Christmas Beacon of 1938," the Ham and Eggs program likened itself to "the rays of that star of 1938 years ago," which had "also announced the Christ-man of that time, whose only exhibit of wrath . . . expressed itself by whipping the money demagogues from the steps leading up to that temple which enshrines the welfare, happiness, and tranquility, which God ordained for humanity at large." The editorial went on to inveigh against the equally iniquitous "money demagogues of today, led by the international bankers," who, the article warned, "ruthlessly endeavor to crucify" the Ham and Eggs movement. The editorial concluded with the messianic prophecy that "the principles involved in 'Ham and Eggs' will eradicate their practices and bring peace and tranquility to humanity," in addition to "shearing the international bankers of their God-forsaken methods" of keeping the elderly "in methodical economic slavery" (*National Ham and Eggs*, 24 December 1938, 14 January 1939).

Such inflated rhetoric was surprisingly effective in marshalling support for Ham and Eggs political actions and in bringing money into the organization's coffers. Ham and Eggs leaders, filled with righteous indignation about injustices suffered by the nation's aged, moralistically divided the social world around them into good and evil, light and darkness, heroes and villains, generosity and greed. A particularly intense target of negative Ham and Eggs rhetoric was the California Bankers Association, which had made no secret of its opposition to the pension organization's generous proposals. Avaricious "international bankers" became a potent symbol of evil in Ham and Eggs publications and speeches, where they were variously described as "public enemy number one," "loan rangers," "money demagogues," and "greed mongers." Ham and Egg members portrayed themselves as heroic soldiers in a "God ordained" battle against "our iniquitous money system and the legalized racketeers who operate it." The object of this holy quest was to "dethrone the dollar dynasty" and to "make all the people understand its hellish character" (*National Ham and Eggs,* 3 December 1938, 24 December 1938, 3 June 1939, 5 August 1939, 23 September 1939).

Indeed, the public speeches of Ham and Eggs leaders often took on the unmistakable, repetitive quality of a "fire and brimstone" sermon. In a 1939 speech Roy Owens harangued—with a cadence that one might easily mistake for a modern televangelist—that:

They say that we've never been the head of a bank. . . . And we haven't!
They say we've never been the head of any big corporation. . . . And we haven't!
. . . They say we've never handled large sums of money. . . . And we haven't!
But we're going to handle them and you can tell that to your bankers!
. . . They say it will shake the financial structure of the world. . . . And it will!
They call us crackpots. . . . And we are! We're going to crack their pots wide open![7]

Unfortunately for devotees of the movement, the leaders of Ham and Eggs turned out to be "pension panacea peddlers." The "pots" they proved most successful in "cracking wide open" were the pocketbooks of their elderly followers. A typical appeal for funds in *National Ham and Eggs* implored: "What we must have is money to get these petitions printed. . . . All that remains is for you to stop for a minute and think about what thirty dollars a week for life means to you. Then get in and do your part" (*National Ham and Eggs,* 21 January 1939). As one might expect under such circumstances, the movement eventually disintegrated amid a cloud of scandal (Fischer 1977, 179; Putnam 1970, 89–114).

Abraham Epstein and the American Association for Social Security

In sharp contrast to the populist, sensationalistic style of the Ham and Eggs movement, the American Association for Social Security (AASS) adopted a highbrow approach to advocating old-age pensions. The organization—originally called the American Association for Old Age Security—was founded by a social insurance expert named Abraham Epstein, who went on to serve as its executive secretary for the remainder of his career. It was Epstein who coined the term *social security,* which he added to his organization's name in 1933. A graduate of the University of Pittsburgh, Epstein became research director of the Pennsylvania Old Age Pension Commission in 1918. In *Facing Old Age,* published in 1922, he argued that the time had come for the United States to face the need for a government-administered pension system that would meet the problems of poverty in old age. He pointed out that all other "civilized" nations had enacted some form of old-age insurance, described the major types of systems then in existence, and urged that the United States emulate the British prototype by establishing a noncontributory pension system (as opposed to the German and French systems of social insurance).

As research director of the Pennsylvania Old Age Pension Commission, Epstein was active in securing passage in 1923 of the Pennsylvania act. When the state Supreme Court declared a number of its provisions unconstitutional, Epstein decided that attempts to get it rewritten were futile, resigned his position as director, and formed the American Association for Old Age Security. Based in New York, the new pension-advocacy organization operated on a budget of under $5,000 in the first year. Already by 1928 Epstein had enlisted a dues-paying membership of 400 in the cause, which expanded to more than 4,000 by 1931 (Chambers 1963, 164–65).

The organization's political strategies were in most respects similar to those of other reform groups of this era, such as the AALL and the Eagles—namely, generating publicity, building a membership base, formulating model pension bills, and lobbying for their passage.

Epstein was an able speaker and gave lectures on old-age pension issues to social service agencies, religious societies, labor unions, and on the campuses of major universities. In fact, after 1929 Epstein reached the point where he was receiving more speaking invitations than he could possibly honor. Epstein and the other social insurance experts who formed the core of AASS were impatient with the existing individualistic "voluntary charity" approaches to relief for the aged poor. Epstein, whose outlook was more socialistic than most of the other pension reformers, viewed the concept of social insurance as more than just a scheme for protecting individuals in old age. Because the capitalistic system in the United States could not be trusted to be responsive to the needs of older workers and the unemployed, the financial intervention of the federal government was required. He argued that if a pension plan was to genuinely alleviate the financial distress of older workers it would have to be redistributive in nature and regard the benefits received as a social right, not merely as a public dole (Pratt 1976, 14; Lubove 1968, 143). At a 1931 conference Rabbi Stephen Wise, another prime mover in the AASS, expressed similar sentiments when he explained that he advocated "security for the aged, not charity. Let's have an end of the notion that we are seeking just some miserable little dole of pittance with which to make life livable for the aged."[8]

The organization's monthly organ, the *Old Age Security Herald*, monitored the progress of pension legislation at state and national levels, and contained polemical articles by Abraham Epstein, Isaac Rubinow, Stephen Wise and other prominent social insurance experts. In addition, the journal devoted considerably more space to news about foreign pension developments than was to be found in the publications of any of the other American pension reform groups—as illustrated by the following headlines occurring in the *Herald* between 1930 and 1934: "Europe Happy with Social Insurance," "English Experience: All British Parties Back Pensions," "Progress in Germany," "The New French Insurance Law," "Labor Legislation and Social Provision in Italy," "New Zealand Protects Old Age of 28,995," "No Poorhouses in Holland," "Old Age Security in Australia," "'Jump in, the Water Is Fine,' Beckon Canadians," "Ontario Pensions 37,000," "Pensions in the Five-Year Plan," "Uruguay Cares for Its Aged" (*OASH* 1930–34, vols. 4–7). These and other articles appearing in the *Herald* shared a common rhetorical implication that America was still backward and uncivilized in the area of social justice for its elderly citizens. What, then, could concerned Americans do about this blatant discrepancy? The AASS's answer was perhaps best expressed in a May 1930 membership appeal:

> AMERICA IS BEHIND THE TIMES!
> Its neglect of the aged is unparalleled
> in the annals of the great nations.
> Help wipe out this blot
> on our country's record.
> JOIN THE AMERICAN ASSOCIATION
> FOR OLD AGE SECURITY
> and promote the fight to obtain social justice for
> the unfortunates who are old, feeble, and poor.
> (*OASH* 4, no. 5 [1930]: 3)

Although this highbrow organization never quite managed to amass the huge popular following enjoyed by groups like the Townsend Movement or the Eagles, Epstein's AASS did succeed in creating a great deal of interest and serious public discussion about old-age pensions among prominent intellectuals, opinion influentials, and public officials during the 1930s. In that sense at least, it was influential in framing the national debate over old-age pensions. Roosevelt's legislation did, after all, borrow Epstein's new term *social security* as the title for the act (Pratt 1976, 15).

When it came to specific provisions, however, few of Epstein's informed suggestions were incorporated into the 1935 Social Security Act in anything even remotely resembling their intended form. As one of America's foremost experts on European social insurance, this was a source of deep frustration to Epstein. He was intentionally excluded from the deliberations of the Committee on Economic Security in formulating the act because Roosevelt considered his ideas for reform to be too extreme. Epstein was particularly embittered by the fact that the new Social Security law completely ignored his suggestion that old-age and unemployment insurance be subsidized from general revenues in a manner that would redistribute wealth. He considered Roosevelt's decision to base the legislation on the more conservative, pro-business "Wisconsin plan" to be a betrayal of his organization's efforts to secure comprehensive, noncontributory old-age insurance based on the European model. In testimony before Congress, Epstein criticized the Social Security bill as grossly inadequate. Lashing out resentfully at the "very slow and piecemeal achievements of our legislation," and complaining of the "emasculation of measures between their introduction and their passage," he appended a lengthy chapter detailing his objections (appropriately entitled "The Failure of the Social Security Act to Meet the Problem of Insecurity") to the revised edition of his *Insecurity: A Challenge to America* (1938, 677).

The Townsend Movement

While the Eagles, AALL, Ham and Eggs, and AASS all helped bring pressure to bear on lawmakers to enact old-age pensions during the incipiency phase, by far the largest mass-membership organization to emerge during this period was the Townsend Movement. Named after its founder, Dr. Francis Townsend of Long Beach, California, the organization was committed to legislative enactment of the "Townsend Plan." The plan proposed that all American citizens over 65 receive $200 per month ($150 in the initial version), under the conditions that elderly recipients spend the pension amount within 30 days (another Keynesian "pump-priming" measure) and that they refrain from participation in the labor force (to reduce unemployment among younger workers) (Holtzman 1963; Putnam 1970, 49–71). The revenues to support the pension plan were to come from a universal 2 percent sales tax on all business transactions. Townsend and his followers argued that if implemented the plan would hasten economic recovery from the depression, as well as provide some degree of relief from suffering for the elderly poor.

The charismatic "Father Townsend" was a skillful orator and writer who knew how to use symbolism to great political advantage (Cantril 1948, 169–209). The Townsend Plan idea was said to have been conceived when Townsend gazed out his window one day and beheld, in a dirty alley cluttered with garbage cans, "three haggard, very old women, stooped with great age, bending over the barrels, clawing into the contents." Townsend, incensed at an unjust social order that would allow such suffering to take place unabated, then began yelling uncontrollably with "wild hatred" at the inhumanity of such a spectacle, whereupon his wife warned that the neighbors might hear him. To this he replied, "I want all the neighbors to hear me! I want God Almighty to hear me! I'm going to shout till the whole country hears!" Inspired by the incident, he then promptly sat down and wrote up a blueprint for his pension plan, to see to it that such a disgusting spectacle should never again occur in America (Milne 1935, 2; Holtzman 1952, 63–66; Schlesinger 1960, 29–30).

There was only one thing wrong with this widely accepted account of the birth of the Townsend Plan idea. It wasn't true. Apparently the tale of the old women and the garbage cans was pure political myth, albeit a highly effective one in marshalling popular support for the movement. Abraham Holtzman (1952, 63–66; 1963, 32–35), an expert on the Townsend Movement whose Harvard dissertation was devoted to that subject and who subsequently authored a respected history of the movement, maintains that the garbage can incident was invented as a convenient political fiction for popular consumption. Similarly, political historian Jackson Putnam concludes that the incident "though dramatic, is probably apocryphal." Townsend was also quite adept at creating political slogans. The idea of "Youth for Work and Age for Leisure" did much to help him attract a national following. Putnam observes that while Townsend genuinely believed in the viability of his pension plan on its own merits, he was nevertheless "willing to use whatever verbal trickery he needed to promote it. His greatest skill lay not in the field of social and economic theory . . . but in the field of pro-paganda" (1970, 50, 52).

The process of attracting a following for his ideas began on 30 September 1933, when Townsend, who had lost his job at the age of 67 and "had little else to do," wrote a letter that was published in the "Vox-Pop" column of the *Long Beach Press Telegram*. In that letter he sketched the main features of what would later become known as the Townsend Plan. The letter contained Townsend's diagnosis of the "cause" (overproduction) of the Great Depression and a prescription for its "cure" (revitalized consumption). Townsend estimated that the total public cost of his proposed pension for the elderly would be between $2 and $3 million per month. He argued that the time had come for popular attitudes toward the proper role of government to change, and that it would be necessary for government intervention in the economy to be substantially increased in order to carry out the plan. In a modern industrial society such as the United States the mass public ought to "expect and demand that the central government assume the duty of regulating business activity" (Holtzman 1963, 34–40; Townsend 1943; Putnam 1970, 51). Shortly thereafter Townsend placed a one-inch advertisement in the *Long Beach Press Telegram* to appeal for help in promoting his new pension idea. To his surprise, a dozen enthusiastic supporters showed up the following day, ready to work on the campaign. In October of the same year Townsend and his supporters began circulating petitions calling for enactment of his plan, and within two weeks they were able to collect over 4,000 signatures (Fischer 1977, 181). By the end of 1933 Townsend was already well on his way to becoming a prominent national personality.

Townsend joined forces with an old business associate, Robert Earl Clements, who thereafter managed the financial affairs of the organization. Over the next year Townsend and Clements began the laborious process of constructing a national organization to promote the pension plan. Their promotional strategy for winning popular support consisted of carefully staged mass meetings and the development of a network of "Townsend Clubs." In the mass meetings, adherents and potential supporters were exposed to inspirational speeches by Townsend and others hired to speak in favor of the plan. The Townsendites published a newspaper, the *Modern Crusader*, which first appeared on 7 July 1934 and was replaced in 1935 by the *National Townsend Weekly,* which quickly achieved a circulation of over 30,000 (Neuberger and Loe 1936, 67; O'Byrne 1953, 50–52). It was the Townsend Clubs, however, that formed the backbone of the burgeoning organization. The creation of the clubs was an organizational masterstroke, which facilitated the rapid proliferation of the movement throughout the country. Over the next several years Townsend Clubs were founded in every state, with approximately 1,200 created in California alone. The clubs coordinated political action at the national and local levels and provided an ongoing forum for communication between the leadership and the general membership. They also helped to maintain morale among the mass membership through the vicissitudes of political victories and defeats.

The style of political rhetoric employed by the Townsend organization made use of four major symbolic devices, which when combined proved to be highly persuasive. The first involved an appeal to older adults' unsatisfied need to feel psychologically and socially secure in the face of advancing age. The Townsend organization, of course, shared with other pension-reform groups the usual emphasis on relieving economic insecurity among the aged and was adept at "generating honest anger at basic injustices" (O'Byrne 1953, 93). Beyond this, however, it was unique in the extent to which it also sought to address their social and psychological insecurities. The Townsend

Plan and the Townsend Clubs—attempting to symbolically restore some of the elderly's lost dignity and social status—defiantly challenged the prevalent negative stereotypes of older adults that held that they were unproductive, useless, and undignified. In Townsend meetings and publications the nation's senior citizens were celebrated not as has-beens but as the proud architects of the social order, the people who had "built America." Those who were to receive pensions would not be on the public dole but would be honored as "distributor custodians" of the country's economic resources, helping to make their country strong by spending their pension allotments. Feelings of impotence and worthlessness in old age were countered by direct participation of Townsend members in the political process. They actively circulated petitions, attended rallies, and distributed campaign literature. Involvement with others in the Townsend Clubs encouraged aged persons to make new friends, and hence helped counteract feelings of social isolation (Putnam 1970, 51–52). Inspirational songs sung at the meetings, such as the following, illustrate the defiant sense of renewed dignity and empowerment that the Townsend organization sought to engender in its elderly members:

> We're going to town with the Townsend Plan;
> We'll put new life in Uncle Sam.
> We'll wipe the depression from the earth;
> Our nation is due for another birth.
> We draw no lines of color or creed;
> Of political parties we have no need.
> We're on our way and we know where;
> And we'll stir things up when we get there . . .
> We're coming Fifty Million Strong;
> The fight'll be hot and it won't be long.
> If Congress bucks and won't behave,
> We'll ride over them like a tidal wave.
> When the battle smoke has blown away,
> And our Country awakes to a better day,
> The world will grasp us by the hand,
> And thank the Lord for Townsend's Plan.[9]

Besides this therapeutic aspect of participating in the organization's activities, there was a religious appeal as well. Here one finds some similarities to the symbolism used by the Ham and Eggs group. Townsend frequently hired Christian ministers as his spokesmen to lend legitimacy to the movement and its controversial message. As was the case with the Ham and Eggs movement, Townsend rallies sometimes took on the quasi-religious character of revival meetings. Townsend rapidly developed a messiahlike image. The 12 August 1934 issue of *National Townsend Weekly,* for instance, proclaimed that hundreds of thousands of Townsend's followers had come to "firmly believe that God planted the seed of a divine thought in the soul" of "Father" Townsend. As had been true of the Ham and Eggs movement, the symbolic deification of the leaders of the Townsend Movement tended to become more pervasive and hyperbolic as the movement progressed, and the leaders-as-saviors rhetoric became increasingly intense. An article written by Townsend in an issue of *Modern Crusader* constructed a direct analogy between his mission and that of Jesus Christ. Townsend wrote that "As on the eastern shores of the Sea of Galilee, two thousand years ago, a mighty upheaval of spiritual forces began to break the bonds of humanity, which had held the race in slavery to the doctrine, might was right . . . may it not be that . . . two thousand years later, a movement is being born of the common people's suffering, that will have as profound an effect upon the race in its upward climb toward its star of destiny?" (17 October 1934). The resemblance to Ham and Eggs political rhetoric is striking—particularly in the motif of salvation from suffering and in the use of the "beacon of light" metaphor to represent the intrinsic goodness of the movement and its sanctified leaders as a path out of the darkness of economic slavery.

A third rhetorical device used by the Townsendites to frame the pension debate was the idea that the Townsend Plan represented a miraculous economic nostrum for all of the nation's ills (as opposed to being merely a program to put more aged Americans on the public dole). Townsend's background as a physician in Long Beach made it seem plausible for him to play the role of a social healer who was attempting to cure the ills of a sick socioeconomic system. Given the vulnerability of most of his followers to illness, and their inability to afford adequate health care, this was indeed a powerful metaphor. Townsend argued that his social prescription would stimulate employment for younger people, increase consumption (by requiring aged recipients to spend their pension allotments), increase production, and generally restore a healthy balance to the country's economic system (Putnam 1970, 52–53).

A final theme that pervaded the rhetoric of the Townsend Movement was its pseudo-conservatism. Although the proposed features of the Townsend Plan were in many respects quite radical for the time, movement leaders were faced with the problem that its membership base consisted disproportionately of white, middle-class, Anglo-Saxon, Protestant Americans, a good many of whom were Republicans. (A similar organizational dilemma was to face American Association of Retired Persons leaders later in the century.) Townsend Movement rhetoric was therefore ingeniously designed to downplay the inherent radicalism of the movement and its reform proposals and to underscore its mainstream and conservative aspects. Townsendites emphasized the idea that the plan was more moderate than other contemporary pension proposals, and that it sought to achieve its objectives within the established order rather than in opposition to it. This tactic gave an appearance of conventionality and legitimacy to the venture. Townsend publicly emphasized his opposition to socialistic "soak the rich" proposals and made much fanfare of his refusal to ally with Upton Sinclair and EPIC in California politics. Another technique used to make the plan and its leader appear more conservative was to portray Townsend not as a radical reformer, but as a traditional American patriot. In the pages of the *National Townsend Weekly*, a commonly used ploy involved placing Townsend's photograph among pictures of traditional American heroes like Washington, Jefferson, and Lincoln. Because of his tall, gaunt, Lincolnesque appearance, juxtaposition of Townsend's photograph with the latter was particularly effective.

At its peak, the Townsend Movement attracted more than a million supporters nationally. The potential political clout of the organization became abundantly clear when Townsendites in Long Beach, California, attempted to oust an incumbent congressman they considered too insensitive to senior rights issues. Townsendites instead backed their own candidate, 72-year-old John S. McGroarty, who went on to win the 1934 election. The victory sent an unmistakable signal to elected officials in the state and across the nation that disgruntled older Americans were a political force to be reckoned with. During a legislative battle with the Townsend forces in the following year, for instance, one besieged senator complained that "people called up and threatened me with everything from recall to lynching." Another remarked that "they're putting the heat on from every angle" (Putnam 1970, 54–55, 66).

Congressman McGroarty, who owed his victory to the Townsend forces, promptly went to Washington and proceeded to introduce a

House bill to enact the Townsend Plan. Unfortunately for the Townsendites, President Roosevelt and backers of the more conservative "Wisconsin plan" had their own ideas on how best to provide security for older Americans, and McGroarty's measure was eventually defeated by a four-to-one margin. Although Townsend and his supporters were ultimately unable to prevail in securing congressional enactment of their preferred plan, public officials across the nation—including the president—had nevertheless been forced to sit up and take notice of the increasing political salience of the flourishing senior rights movement. The spectacle of the Long Beach election had demonstrated to incumbent politicians that they ignored the expanding clout of the organized elderly at their own peril. Moreover, there can be little doubt that psychological pressure brought to bear on lawmakers by the menacing presence of an alternative plan with a massive national following helped hasten passage of the 1935 Social Security Act and the 1939 amendments.

Rhetorical Themes Used by Pension Rights Advocates

These, then, were the major pension-advocacy groups that comprised the incipient senior rights movement from the early 1920s through the late 1930s, and some of the strategies they devised for pursuing their political objectives. These groups knew all too well that the prospects for achieving those objectives were contingent on being able to legitimize the idea of old-age pensions in the public mind. Senior rights activists knew that unsatisfied needs among the nation's elderly and the presence of new reform organizations would not in themselves be sufficient to bring about lasting social change. Perhaps the objective realities of elderly need-deprivation would make some political messages sound more plausible to the American public than others. But pension advocates understood that ultimately, as Murray Edelman writes, "[I]t is not reality in any . . . objective sense that matters in shaping political consciousness and behavior, but rather the *beliefs* that language helps evoke about the causes of discontents and satisfactions, about policies that will bring about a future closer to the heart's desire" (1985, 11).

In this section we pause to look more closely at the major rhetorical themes and condensed symbols that progressive reformers used in attempting to frame the public debate over the need for old-age pensions. We will then turn to a consideration of the themes employed by their conservative political adversaries in opposing public pensions. Where possible, representative illustrations of the language and images that were used in popular media to frame the debate have been provided for the reader (Geertz 1973; Gamson and Lasch 1983).

During the 1920s and 1930s the major pension-advocacy groups and their sympathizers wisely chose to frame the debate over old-age justice around a central motif of "social security." The eventual adoption of this phrase by national political leaders to signify the legislation that was ultimately to pass Congress demonstrates just how effective this frame was in arousing and channeling public sentiment toward their goal. The success of this frame in legitimizing pensions to the American public was also evident in national opinion polls, which by 1935 showed 89 percent of Americans favoring federally administered old age pensions (Gallup 1972, 1: 9, 76).

The core concept around which the "social security" interpretive package revolved was the notion that public pensions constituted the only just and civilized solution to the mounting problems of insecurity in old age. Inherent in this overall frame was the assumption that the origins of the problem were external to, and hence beyond the control of, individual aged persons. That is, social insecurity among the elderly was caused not by personal failings but instead by societal dysfunctions and the vicissitudes of fate. Individuals were therefore not at fault for their inability to support themselves in old age. Rather, it was society, natural aging processes, and abstract contingency that were the source of the problem. The elderly were innocent victims, not culprits. The implied solution, therefore, was also external to the individual. If individuals could not legitimately be considered responsible for causing the problems they encountered in their later years, then it was cruel and unfair to hold individual aged persons responsible for solving them.

According to this broad rhetorical frame, then, if "the problem" was social insecurity, it followed that "the solution" was for society to actively assume its rightful responsibility for restoring that security via public pensions. During the 1920s and 1930s this core message—of public pensions as the only just alternative to the specter of social insecurity among the aged—was articulated by reform-minded progressives through a variety of images and rhetorical arguments presented in public media. The chief exponents of this progressive frame included the pension-reform groups, social welfare experts, and sympathetic intellectuals, journalists, and politicians.

California Rescuing Her Aged

There's No Place Like Home

Figure 3.1. Drawing from a 1928 issue of the American Association for Labor Legislation's *American Labor Legislation Review*. This silhouette earlier appeared on the title page of the California Department of Social Welfare's "Old Age Dependency."

One of the most persuasive elements within this overall "social security" rhetorical package was an appeal to the American ideal of preserving the integrity of "home and family." In public speeches by movement leaders, in liberal newspaper editorials, and in pro-pension political cartoons the nation's aged were depicted as fragile, endearing homebodies, who deserved to receive "aid in their own homes" in their declining years so that older couples and their families would not become unnecessarily separated by a trip to the poorfarm. Pension reformer Rabbi Stephen Wise perhaps best summarized this "home and family" theme in an emotional 1930 speech to the National Conference on Old Age Security, in which he argued that

we have no right to take old men and old women out of their homes and doom them in the poorhouses and almshouses solely because of curable economic insufficiency. The one thing to which the aged should have a right is to remain under their own roofs, and to remain by their own hearths, to preserve inviolate, with the aid of the State, their homes—simple, humble, insufficiently equipped they may be—but still their homes, their last human anchorage. (Wise 1930, 12)

The theme was also prevalent in visual portrayals of the aged during this period. For example, the title page of a California Department of Social Welfare report on "Old Age Dependency" features a striking silhouette of a good-natured elderly couple having tea and pleasant conversation together at the family dining table (see Figure 3.1). Beneath the silhouette is the caption "There's No Place Like Home." The American Association for Labor Legislation later used the same silhouette in a 1928 issue of its *American Labor Legislation Review*, adding the header "California Rescuing Her Aged." A less cheerful "family" portrayal from this era—a political cartoon featured in *Eagle Magazine* in January of 1925—shows a distraught elderly worker clutching a family member for comfort as he reads a termination notice from his employer (see Figure 3.2). A plaque, prominently displayed on the wall behind, proclaims "Bless Our Home." Again, the event is depicted as taking place around the family dining table.

Affected by pension movement images such as these, sympathetic politicians who took up the cause made judicious use of the family-preservation theme in their arguments on behalf of pension legislation. Senator David Walsh of Massachusetts complained that in the absence of a system of public pensions "many married sons and daughters, in order to spare their aged parents the disgrace and bitterness of pauperism, assume burdens which cannot be borne except at the cost of depriving their own children of . . . the opportunities of success, and of dooming themselves in turn to an old age of helpless dependence" (Walsh 1927, 224). Promoting his proposed federal old-age pension bill in 1930, Senator C. C. Dill of Washington advised Senate colleagues that public pensions would be a preferable way to meet the needs of the elderly because the results were "incomparably more satisfactory both to those who receive old age assistance and to their relatives and friends" (*ALLR* 20, no. 1 [1930]: 67).

A closely related rhetorical theme, often invoked in conjunction with the appeal to preservation of home and family, was the negative image of the poorhouse as an inhumane institution. Poorhouse symbolism was used extensively in the pages of AASS's monthly, *Old Age Security Herald,* where the theme was hammered home with such articles as "He Prefers Death to Poorhouse," "'Abolish Poorhouses,'

Figure 3.2. Cartoon from the *Eagle Magazine,* January 1925.

Urges N.C. Board," "Poorhouses like Prisons," "Pull Down the Poorhouse!," "Poorhouse Derogatory of Dignity," "Let's Padlock the Poorhouse," "Washington Aroused over Poorhouse Costs," "The Poorhouse in Retreat!," "Delaware First State to Banish Poorhouses." This recurrent image of productive, dignified elderly citizens forced to live out their last days in run-down poorhouses was one of the AASS's most effective media appeals (Pratt 1976, 21).

The "inhumane poorhouse" theme proved especially effective in overcoming popular resistance to public pensions as being "socialistic" or "un-American." It involved a forced choice between two cleverly circumscribed policy alternatives. The scenario presented to the American public was one in which they must choose between either banishing elderly dependents to live out their last days in wretched poorhouses or the "only alternative"—adopting European-style, comprehensive, noncontributory pensions. However apprehensive Americans might feel about embracing public pensions, the idea seemed mysteriously attractive when considered alongside the inhumanity of existing poorhouses. This rhetorical simplification of policy alternatives had the ingenious effect of making opponents' arguments against comprehensive public pensions appear to be callous, inhumane, and uncivilized. For example, when Calvin Coolidge attacked the concept of old-age pensions in his syndicated column in 1931, the (pro-pension) Lowell, Massachusetts, *Currier-Citizen* promptly responded by labeling the former president a "friend of the poorhouse" (*OASH* 5, no. 4 [1931]: 2).

As in the rhetoric of nineteenth-century progressive reformers, vivid descriptions of degenerate conditions were used to shock the public out of its complacency and overcome ideological resistance to the idea of providing increased public support. For instance, one nationwide investigation of poorhouse conditions, undertaken in the mid-1920s by a coalition of pro-pension fraternal organizations, presented findings on the "shameful waste and inhumanity of American poorhouses" in several articles appearing in *American Labor Legislation Review*. In a tone reminiscent of the 1857 Select Senate Committee's report (see chapter 2), architects of the study melodramatically observed that the poorhouse "is our human dumping ground into which go our derelicts of every description. Living in this mess of insanity and depravity, this prison place for criminals and the insane, are . . . respectable, intelligent old folk, whose only offense is that they are poor." Seeking to incite public outrage, the report characterized the American poor farm as "the most inhumane institution that exists on the face of the earth. It is unclean, vicious, wicked. It is the shame of the states and communities." The *Review* went on to editorialize that the only alternative to these institutions was "the present movement in America to replace the 'costly, antiquated and inhumane' poorhouses with . . . old age pensions" (15, no. 4 [1925]: 360–62; 17, no. 3 [1927]: 244–45). Not surprisingly, the national press found such scandalous descriptions hard to resist, and eagerly joined the fray, as did opportunistic politicians. A

THE RESCUE SHIP

Courtesy of New York Evening Journal.

Figure 3.3. Cartoon by Nelson Harding, drawn for the *New York Evening Journal* and reprinted in the February 1930 *Old Age Security Herald*.

pro-pension *New York Times* editorial moralized incredulously, "How can there be comfort for them when the buildings are in most cases unfit for habitation, filthy, vermonous, foully unsanitary? How can there be protection when they have to mingle in narrow quarters with other inmates who are criminals or suffer from loathsome diseases?"[10]

Visual metaphors proved even more effective in conveying this theme to the public. A political cartoon entitled "The Rescue Ship," featured in the February 1930 *Old Age Security Herald*, likened the "bleak existence" experienced by "aged dependents" in the nation's poorhouses to being trapped on an island (isolated from the rest of

Figure 3.4. Cartoon by John Miller Baer, *American Labor Legislation Review,* June 1930.

Reprinted courtesy of the United Transportation Union.

society), without hope of further contact with civilization (see Figure 3.3). Emblazoned on the side of an approaching ship, which had at long last come to rescue them, were the words "old age pensions bill." Another revealing cartoon, published in the *American Labor Legislation Review* in 1930, depicted an endearing old couple approaching a fork in the road of life, at which they must choose between two alternative paths for the remainder of their journey (see Figure 3.4).

To their political "left" was the old-age pension office. "Over the hill" to their political "right" was the poorhouse. The potential effects of passage of national pension legislation were symbolized by the friendly figure of Uncle Sam, who had just closed the road to the poorhouse, inviting them instead to follow the leftward path, where a bright sun was rising, rather than the rightward path, over which hovered ominous clouds. The caption read, "It would be a welcome detour!" As in verbal expressions of this rhetorical theme, only two policy alternatives (paths, roads) were portrayed as possible: inhumane poorhouses and public pensions.

The poorhouse theme was, in turn, closely intertwined in propension rhetoric with an appeal to sympathy for the "abandoned" elderly. This portrayal conjured up images of frail, helpless aged persons, mercilessly discarded by an uncaring society to face sickness and death alone. The appeal was to a sense of guilt, to Christian compassion, and to the fear of one's own eventual abandonment. Rhetorical messages containing this theme implicitly asked "Will *you* too someday be abandoned in old age, sickness, and poverty?" The theme is evident in the "Rescue Ship" cartoon (see Figure 3.3), for example, where the "aged dependents" are shown as having been deserted by society and are therefore in need of rescue by federal pension legislation. Drawing on the same analogy, a *Washington D.C. Times* editorial characterized the nation's neglected elders as "derelicts on the sea of life" (*OASH* 5, no. 12 [1931]: 6). Another "abandonment" cartoon (not shown), appearing in *American Labor Legislation Review*, depicts an aged couple huddled alone in the darkness on a park bench on a cold winter night, with the caption "Not Wanted" (20, no. 1 [1930]: 72).

Verbal expressions of this theme were also quite common. A 1930 *New York Telegram* editorial admonished, "It is almost as cruel for a state to put off caring for its helpless old people, as for children of aged parents to neglect to provide for them."[11] In its 1931 Christmas season issue, the *Old Age Security Herald* seized the occasion to feature front-page headlines declaring "Americas Forgotten Aged in Deep Distress" and "Disgraceful Neglect Emphasized by Holiday Season Appeals." The issues's lead story lamented that even at Christmas the "despairing cry of disinherited, starving and forgotten aged was heard throughout our broad land. . . . In municipal lodging houses, hallways and alleys, tottering old men and women recalled former days of affluence and bygone Christmas cheer in the agony of slow starvation. Such was the Christmas of the indigent aged in a land which is proud of its abundant riches" (*OASH* 5, no. 12 [1931]: 1).

To whom or to what, then, was this miserable plight of America's abandoned aged ultimately to be attributed? Who was to blame? Pro-pension rhetoric of the 1920s and 1930s invariably pointed an accusing finger at the greedy, ruthless practices of "big business" in the "modern industrial age." This explanatory chain contained two distinct causal links. The *general* cause of the elderly's insecurity was symbolized in a broad theme of "fat cats vs. the frail elderly." And deriving from this broader issue of business insensitivity to elderly needs was the *immediate* cause of their misfortune, "the spectre of unemployment," for which modern industry was seen as being entirely to blame.

With the advent of the depression of the 1930s, the economic interests of industrial employers and their older employees had increasingly come to be viewed as divergent, taking on a class-conflict character rarely experienced in the American context. During this period the modern capitalistic system of industrial production was portrayed by many pension advocates not as a wondrous source of economic abundance but rather as the primary cause of economic want among the nation's older citizens. Frank Hering, leader of the Fraternal Order of the Eagles, placed the blame squarely on the shoulders of "modern industry," arguing in 1923 that "modern machinery with its remorse-less force and merciless precision, not only shuts out from gainful vocation the failing eyesight, the enfeebled nerve, and unsteady hand of old age, but its intense strain during the years of vigor brings these disabilities prematurely upon the honest toiler" (Hering, 1923). Similarly, pension reformer Abraham Epstein, in his *Insecurity: A Challenge to America*, defined the elderly's problems as stemming from "economic insecurity, which weighs down our lives, subverts our liberty, and frustrates our pursuit of happiness. The establishment of industrial production has rendered our lives insecure to the point of despair." Epstein went on to portray the prevailing industrial system as "the outstanding obstacle to national well-being and prosperity. It is both the cause and effect of depression" (1938, 3, 18).

This class-conflict–oriented "fat cats vs. the frail elderly" theme found its most poignant expression in a *Pittsburgh Press* cartoon enti-tled "Strutting His Stuff," which was later reprinted in the *Old Age Security Herald* (see Figure 3.5). As was typical of depression-era car-toons, the concentrated wealth of large business interests was symbol-

Figure 3.5. Cartoon drawn for the *Pittsburgh Press* and reprinted in the June 1933 *Old Age Security Herald.*

ized in the form of a corpulent figure in a pin-striped suit. The image was of the stereotypical "fat cat" of ruthless big-business greed that had unjustly monopolized the wealth and resources of the nation. Placed in stark contrast with this corpulent figure in the cartoon (note the light and dark imagery) were tired, downtrodden, emaciated work-ers—the common man, the little guy. In contrast with the petty greed of the former, the latter were depicted as having unselfishly sacrificed a lifetime of labor for the good of family and society, for which they therefore presumably deserved to receive a pension from society in their old age as a just reward.

In "fat cats" rhetoric of this sort—the overstuffed, greedy forces of modern industrial monopoly—were typically portrayed as being involved in a sinister conspiracy to prevent the elderly from getting their pensions. In the "Strutting His Stuff" cartoon, for example, "old age pensions defeated" was (rather unrealistically) depicted as being the number-one priority of American business. A similarly paranoid lead article in the February 1933 *Old Age Security Herald*, entitled "Economy or Greed—Which Is It?," charged that "greed and narrow-mindedness, under the guise of economy, stalk over the land determined to crush further the poorest of the poor and the weakest of the weak . . . wiping out every trace of social justice and every spark of humanity in the United States. . . . The blind and greedy forces who are responsible for the unprecedented and shameful destitution prevailing throughout the U.S. are determined to surrender not a penny of their iniquitous wealth nor an ounce of their power" (*OASH* 7, no. 2 [1933]: 1). This tactic of scapegoating big business for all of the elderly's misfortunes was also used by Upton Sinclair in promoting his EPIC Plan, by Huey Long in promoting his "share the wealth" proposal, and by the Ham and Eggs group in promoting their "Thirty Thursday" plan. As noted previously, the public rhetoric of the latter group, in particular, sermonized incessantly against the "hellish character" of "the present financial dynasty" and the "legalized racketeers who operate it," whose unchecked greed was said to be responsible for keeping the nation's elders in "methodical economic slavery" (Putnam 1970, 89–114).

Despite its heavy anti-establishment overtones, this image of corporate avarice as the source of old-age insecurity found its way into the popular press and the public pronouncements of pro-pension politicians. In a hearing on old-age pensions, Congressman F. H. La Guardia of New York reminded his colleagues that "the prosperity of the country cannot be measured by the stock-ticker. It can be measured only in terms of human beings and the reduction of poverty." During the same hearing, Congressman Hamilton Fish, Jr., of New York urged that "It is time to establish parity between property and human rights. We have been swinging too much toward property rights."[12] And Representative C. G. Selvig of Minnesota, in a press statement calling on Congress to look into the "constructive remedy"

Drawn by I. M. Slocum

Figure 3.6. Cartoon from the January 1930 *Old Age Security Herald.*

of an old-age pension system, suggested that it was only fair that the government "should tax the great accumulations of wealth enough to permit all of our people to look forward to a respectable and comfortable old age."[13]

But how, exactly, had these "blind and greedy forces" of modern industrial monopoly managed to produce the "unprecedented and shameful destitution" prevailing among the nation's elderly? Pension reformers argued that the *immediate* cause of old-age insecurity was to be found in the "spectre of unemployment" and the discriminatory industrial hiring and firing practices that were responsible for it. In a 1930 sermon delivered in New York, pension advocate Rabbi J. X.

—Newark News

Figure 3.7. "Drawn Blindly." Cartoon drawn for the *Newark News* and reprinted in a 1930 issue of the *American Labor Legislation Review.*

Cohen described the nation's elderly as "the sorry victims of a lust for mechanical efficiency." Noting that "the 'dead-line' of employment in many plants is 40 years and in some it has been placed at 35 years," he suggested that the true cause of the elderly's insecurity was the "morally and ethically disastrous" policies of American industrial concerns, which beyond that age perfunctorily flung older workers, like "less effective machines, onto the scrap heap" (*OASH* 4, no. 3 [1930]: 9).

This theme of elderly unemployment owing to industrial deadlines was quite common in pension-advocacy cartoons of the day, and is evident, for example, in the "Bless Our Home" cartoon discussed earlier (see Figure 3.2). Another classic political cartoon of this genre, which appeared in the January 1930 issue of *Old Age Security Herald*, clearly illustrates the inferred causal link between industrial practices and elderly insecurity. In "Walking the Industrial Plank" (Figure 3.6), wealthy industrialists are represented as pirates, one of whom is labeled "greed" and the other "pension opponent." An aging employee is shown being forced by these industrial pirates to walk the plank of their pirate ship into a "sea of despair." In the background, an "indifferent public" looks on apathetically. Another cartoon entitled "Drawn Blindly," featured in the *American Labor Legislation Review* in 1930, depicted the powerful hand of American industry drawing an "employment deadline at forty years" on the ground in front of six elderly workers. The wasted talents of the six arbitrarily discharged workers were labeled, respectively, "trained strength," "skill," "reliability," "experience," "settled character," and "caution" (see Figure 3.7). The industrial unemployment theme even showed up in a panel of the well-known comic cartoon "The Gumps," which initially appeared in the *Chicago Tribune* and was later reprinted in the *American Labor Legislation Review* (see Figure 3.8). As in other contemporary media depictions of this theme, the Gumps cartoon stressed the arbitrariness and cruelty of discarding experienced older workers in the prime of their skill, and ruthless industrial employers were portrayed as being the cause of old-age insecurity.

For pension reformers, journalists, and politicians who found that all of this anti-industry rhetoric smacked too much of socialism for their taste, the theme of "pensions as progress" offered a more palatable, but no less effective, alternative. One did not necessarily have to be critical of the underpinnings of the existing economic order to argue that adoption of old-age pensions would represent social progress. The "progress" appeal was particularly effective when combined in advocacy rhetoric with the "inhumane poorhouse" theme. In a November 1924 address to the Pennsylvania State Conference on Old Age Assistance, pension proponent Janet Workman related the "well known fact" that the "entire system of poor relief and almshouse care are antiquated institutions, relics of a civilization long past, totally unsuited to modern conditions." Pension advocates were fond of pointing out that with existing poor laws dating back to the Elizabethan statute of 1601, and with elderly needs in modern industrial society having long since outgrown the institution of the almshouse, it was "difficult to conceive that we could have gone on until this day with the instruments provided three hundred year ago, practically unchanged" (Workman 1925, 302–3).

Remarkable progress had been made in other domains of American life; why then, pension proponents asked rhetorically, should

Figure 3.8. Panel from the comic strip "The Gumps," by Sidney Smith, reprinted in a 1926–27 issue of the *American Labor Legislation Review*.

Americans resist social progress in dealing with the problem of old-age dependency? As reformer Isaac Rubinow put it, "If we can carry the cost of automobile expansion and of expensive road building and even the cost of municipal corruption, I think we may safely assume that America is rich enough to carry the burden of a decent provision for the aged" (*ALLR* 20, no. 1 [1930]: 65). New York Congressman

Beginning to Catch Up

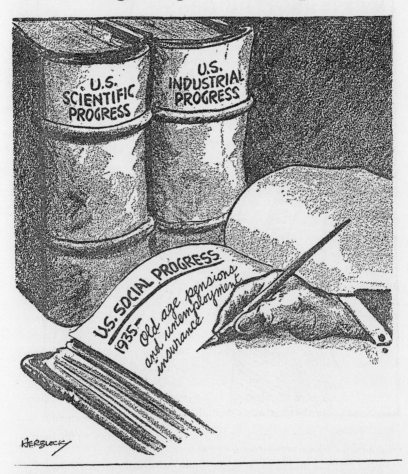

Figure 3.9. "Make 1935 the Social Insurance Year!" Cartoon, by Herblock, from a 1935 issue of the *American Labor Legislation Review.* Reprinted by permission.

Hamilton Fish, Jr., in a 1930 House Labor Committee hearing, remarked that the country "should cease doing the ostrich act. We are the only nation which has so far failed to face the issue of the dependent aged" (*OASH* 4, no. 3 [1930]: 8). A political cartoon in the

American Labor Legislation Review, entitled "Beginning to Catch Up," made essentially the same point in visual form (see Figure 3.9). According to pension-rights rhetoric, then, anyone who resisted legislative enactment of old-age pensions was ipso facto guilty of obstructing the onward march of human civilization. In classic pro-pension rhetorical form, John O'Toole of the Pennsylvania State Old Age Pension Commission inveighed in 1927 against "Chamber of Commerce propagandists" whose sentiments and political tactics in opposition to pensions he characterized as "typical of but a very inconsiderable number of narrow-minded and bigoted persons who throughout the centuries have stood in the path of progress" (*ALLR* 17, no. 3 [1927]: 286–87).

Newpapers and magazines found this "progress" theme irresistible, and eagerly conveyed the message to the public. A 1930 syndicated column, carried in 26 Scripps-Howard newspapers throughout the country, faithfully echoed the logic underlying the pension movement's "progress" argument, reasoning with syllogistic precision that "as the richest nation we should be the most generous. Assuming that we are the most generous, it must be confessed that much of our giving is still of the old personal charity type and too little of the organized social relief type. . . . [T]he United States, despite its boasted humanitarianism, is the only industrial nation which has done nothing to make old age more secure. Nations which some of us consider backward have gone quietly about the business of caring for the aged, while we have been busy in the more spectacular pursuit of great fortunes for the few."[14]

As this excerpt illustrates, the tactic of pointing to successful advances in other modern countries (hoping thereby to create a "bandwagon effect" in the United States) was a highly persuasive variant on the progress theme. The pages of the AALL's *American Labor Legislation Review* were replete with articles celebrating foreign pension law developments and urging America to follow suit. Canadian advances, in particular, were exploited as a ripe source of pro-pension propaganda. Conservatives' arguments that "European" social insurance was not applicable to the American context were rendered ineffective by the Canadian counterexample. Canadian pension experience was therefore seized on by advocates as an opportunity to debunk critics' objections. And they did so in *Review* articles like "Old Age Pensions Don't Discourage Thrift, Says Canadian Official" and "Old Age Pensions in Canada Prevent Waste."[15]

Epstein's American Association for Social Security developed this "comparative progress" rhetoric into a fine art, devoting numerous articles in its *Old Age Security Herald* to coverage of pension progress "around the globe." The January 1931 "Around the Globe" section, for instance, featured international updates on "Old Age Security in Australia," "32 Years of New Zealand Pensions," "New French Law Launched Smoothly," "No Poorhouses in Holland," "Canada Pensions about 50,000 Aged," "Italian Social Insurance Promotes Stabilization," "For Columbia's Farmers," and "Uruguay Cares for Its Aged" (*OASH* 5, no. 1 [1931]: 4–5). As in the pages of the *Review*, the most fertile rhetorical comparisons in the *Herald* were usually with Canada, and supportive statements from Canadian public officials and newspaper editorials were invoked whenever possible to lend legitimacy to the idea of public pensions. An exemplary article in the April 1930 *Herald*, entitled "'Jump in, the Water Is Fine,' Beckon Canadians" chided Americans for their tardiness in adopting progressive legislation, observing that "the Dominion old-age security plan works out satisfactorily, and many Canadians find it hard to understand why it should take their more powerful and richer southern neighbor so long to fall in line and do for its aged what every other civilized nation has already done" (*OASH* 4, no. 4 [1930]: 4–5).

Thus far we have seen that the overall "social security" frame used by senior rights advocates to legitimize pensions was comprised of component themes of home preservation, the inhumane poorhouse, the abandoned elderly, "fat cats vs. the frail elderly," the specter of unemployment, and pensions as progress, and that these variations on the main theme tended to be mutually reinforcing in pro-pension rhetoric. But what was the conception of fairness that lay at the heart of this symbolic package? Popular judgments about what is considered "fair" or "equitable" for a group such as the elderly typically involve a mental comparison of that group's contributions to society with the rewards it derives from society. If the public perceives that the rewards received by the elderly (e.g., support in old age) are proportionate to the contributions they have made (e.g., work, taxes), then the situation will be seen as "equitable," "fair," or "just." If, however, contributions are perceived as greatly exceeding rewards, or if rewards greatly exceed contributions, the situation will usually be seen by the public as "unfair," "inequitable," "unjust" (Adams 1965; Lerner 1977; Austin and Hatfield 1980). The final pro-pension appeal that we shall consider, the "pensions as just reward" theme, made abundant use of this basic psychological principle, playing on widespread popular impressions that a discrepancy existed between what elderly citizens had contributed to American society during their productive years and the meager rewards they were receiving for those efforts in old age. Pension reformers of the 1920s and 1930s defined the existing relationship between contributions and rewards in American society as being grossly unfair to the aged, arguing that old-age pensions ought to be offered as a "deserved reward" or an "earned right" that would restore a sense of social justice to the nation's elderly in their declining years.

The essence of this definition of old-age justice was captured in an address given by William Green, president of the American Federation of Labor, to the 1931 National Conference on Old Age Security, in which he argued that

all their lives they have toiled and served but now, in the evening of life, they find their income was inadequate to meet their material and social needs. . . . At such a period society must step in, protect them, feed them and care for them. This is a social duty which must be met and the Nation's obligation, which must be discharged. It can only be done in a humane, just, and practical way through the enactment of uniform, practical, wise and just old age pension legislation. (Green 1931, 3)

A pro-pension Utica, New York *Times* article (later reprinted in the February 1931 *Old Age Security Herald*) characterized pensions as "the delayed payment of a social debt," reasoning that "every person who earns his living, and pays taxes, whether he knows it or not, makes a contribution to the general welfare. . . . Old age pensions are the return which society makes for these services" (5, no. 2 [1931]: 9). A *Minneapolis Star* editorial (reprinted in the *Old Age Security Herald*) likewise reasoned that the nation's elderly deserved public pensions because "they have helped build up this great and prosperous country, and should be rewarded in their old age for the sacrifices and hardships they have endured" (5, no. 12 [1931]: 5). Some reformers even referred to the nation's aged as "veterans of industry," implying that the precedent of rewarding war veterans with pensions should be extended as well to those who had faithfully served their country in peacetime industrial pursuits (Walsh 1927, 224). Others preferred to describe the equitability of pensions using a language of basic citizen rights. Wendell Johnson, head of the Toledo Social Service Federation, told a church group in September 1930 that every

American was "entitled as a matter of right" to a pension allowance in old age because "security in one's job, and security for old age are fundamental necessities" (*OASH* 4, no. 10 [1930]: 8).

The focus of pro-pension conceptions of fairness in the 1920s and 1930s was almost exclusively on what society owed its elder citizens. Other fairness issues of potential importance—such as personal obligation to save for one's own retirement, and issues of the fairness of the intergenerational and interclass transfers that would be required in order to fund the proposed retirement benefit schemes—were usually downplayed, or ignored altogether. As we shall see, this pension movement strategy of intentionally narrowing the definition of old-age equity and excluding related fairness issues from consideration was, paradoxically, to have negative ramifications for the climate of support for aging programs in subsequent decades, when unresolved equity issues would resurface and threaten to undermine the very programs senior movement advocates had fought so hard to legitimize.

Rhetorical Themes Used by Pension Opponents

Throughout the 1920s and 1930s, this expanding chorus of political voices endorsing the idea of "social security" grew steadily louder in lawmakers' ears. There were, however, powerful vested interests within American society that stood to lose a great deal if pensions were ever to become legitimized in the public mind and adopted as the law of the land. That the United States had thus far been slow to consider national pension legislation was, after all, no accident. The surface reluctance of policymaking elites to address elderly problems reflected the much deeper reality that, as Murray Edelman reminds us, "a problem to some is a benefit to others; it augments the latter group's influence. . . The term 'problem' only thinly veils the sense in which deplored conditions create opportunities" (1988, 14). Entrenched groups that saw themselves as benefitting from the status quo—the National Association of Manufacturers, the National Metal Trades Association, state and national Chambers of Commerce, the American Medical Association, southern Democrats, and conservative politicians, intellectuals, and journalists—vowed not to take this challenge to their prerogatives lying down. Spokesmen for these established interests promptly went to work developing an aggressive counter-rhetoric that they hoped would successfully discredit the "radical" ideas being promulgated by the new pension rights movement.

Whereas pension supporters had woven their public rhetoric around a motif of "social security," the central theme sounded by their conservative adversaries was the notion of "self-reliance as the American Way"—a value that pension opponents warned would be irreversibly compromised were the "European" precedent of publicly financed old-age pensions ever to be adopted. In their view, the pension question was not just an isolated political issue—it was a matter of national identity. Opponents portrayed public pensions as representing a basic symbolic threat to the entire American way of life and the laissez-faire individualist premises on which the social order had thus far been constructed. Conservative economist Samuel Crowther admonished in a 1930 *Forbes* article that the "prime difficulty with the present old-age pension agitation" lay in the fact that the movement's philosophy was "not an American theory. . . . We can abandon all that we have learned or we can build a self-reliant citizenry" (Crowther 1930a, 34).

Movement supporters had defined the elderly's misfortunes as being due to external circumstances beyond their control, arguing that it was therefore necessary for society to step in and assume responsibility for provision in old age. In response, their political opponents appealed instead to the deep-seated American belief in individualism—that every individual is the architect of his own fate, and hence must rely on his own private resources in preparing for the ravages of old age. Attacking the concept of "public" pensions in a syndicated column in 1931, former president Calvin Coolidge sermonized that "real reform" must come "from within." What "self-respecting" Americans really needed, then, was "not a system of old age pensions but a population made sufficiently skilled by education and sufficiently self-controlled and well-disposed by the hold of religion so that old-age pensions would be superfluity" (*OASH* 5, no. 4 [1931]: 2). In a legislative debate over old age pensions in Massachusetts, one Senator rather indelicately carried this ethos of "personal responsibility" to its logical conclusion when he moralized that "if any man has lived to the age of sixty or seventy with no children to support him and without sufficient savings to care for him, he ought to die" (4, no. 7 [1930]: 2).

Since this sort of attack on the character and deservingness of the aged themselves was likely to be perceived as insensitive, most anti-pension rhetoric concentrated instead on undermining the credibility of the reform plans and those who had proposed them. Critics charged that adopting the proposed pension legislation would result in

Figure 3.10. "Chock-full of Genii." Cartoon by Dorman H. Smith for the
27 March 1935 *San Francisco Examiner.*

Reprinted by permission of the *San Francisco Examiner.*

an "unworkable bureaucratic nightmare." This theme took advantage
of the habitual American anxiety about governmental solutions to
human problems, and was by far one of the most effective rhetorical
ploys within the overall "preserving American self-reliance" frame.
The various old-age pension schemes were portrayed as ill-conceived,
wasteful, and impractical, and their creators as hopelessly idealistic
dreamers. Testifying before a House subcommittee in 1930, National
Association of Manufacturers spokesman Noel Sargeant attacked the
proposed reform plans as being "impractical economically" and as
"involving an enormous amount of administrative detail." He warned
that, if adopted, these plans would inevitably lead to an unmanageable
quagmire of endless bureaucratic red tape and inefficiency—stifling
business, economic growth, and private initiative. Citizen hopes that
the problems of old age would somehow magically be solved by such

Figure 3.11. Upton Sinclair's EPIC campaign as seen in a mid-1930s cartoon from the *San Francisco Examiner.*

public plans could only end in disillusionment (U.S. House of Representatives 1930, 194).

An anti-pension political cartoon in the *San Francisco Examiner* entitled "Chock-full of Genii" condensed this "unworkable bureaucratic nightmare" scenario into a powerful visual metaphor (see Figure 3.10). The cartoon shows a wishful American citizen (labeled "the hopeful") wielding a magic lamp (the Townsend Plan), out of which suddenly springs four frightening apparitions—"shattered dreams," "disappointment," "disillusionment," and "political hokum." A similar visual critique in the *San Francisco News* lampooned Upton Sinclair's EPIC plan, representing it as a poorly constructed, makeshift flying contraption—with Sinclair as the inexperienced would-be pilot. A skeptical California voter, who had "done plenty of crashing already" was shown declining Sinclair's invitation to take a ride in the strange "EPIC" contraption and hurriedly fleeing the scene (see Figure 3.11). The "nightmare" theme also appealed to Americans' anxieties that creating new public bureaucracies to serve the aged might lead to tyrannical "big government" domination over the citizenry. A clever

'Napoleons'

Figure 3.12. Cartoon by Edmund W. Gale from the 4 November 1938 *San Francisco Examiner*.

Reprinted by permission of the *San Francisco Examiner*.

election-year cartoon appearing in the *San Francisco Examiner*, for example, personified the Ham and Eggs plan as "Napolean," then wondered rhetorically what would happen if voters were ever to turn the plan loose on the state of California by endorsing it at the polls (see Figure 3.12).

A closely related theme, implied by the bureaucratic nightmare image, was the idea that adoption of public pensions would "encourage idle dependency." This theme played on citizens' fears that the proposed plans would destroy work incentives among older adults and foster a new class of lazy elderly dependents who would live out their remaining years unproductively on the public dole. Cautioning readers not to be taken in by "the emotional approach" of pension rights advocates, *Forbes* columnist Samuel Crowther observed in 1930 that "there are young bums as well as old bums, and neither has any claim whatsoever upon society" (1930a, 34; 1930b, 18). National Metal Trades Association spokesman W. E. Odom informed a congressional committee that old-age pensions would be "contrary to fundamental American principles of individualism" because they would "subsidize improvidence and remove the incentive for economy and thrift" (U.S. Senate 1931, 39). Noel Sargeant of the National Association of Manufacturers made a similar plea before Congress, lamenting that he could find "in the current agitation for public old age pensions . . . very little consideration of the effect their establishment might have upon such distinctly worthwhile individual and social values as thrift, forethought, frugality, and individual initiative" (U.S. Senate 1931, 78). More effective still were visual expressions of the "idle dependency" theme, the most devastating of which came in a series of carefully orchestrated attacks on Upton Sinclair's EPIC plan and its proposed $50-a-month pension. In a barrage of political cartoons published in major newspapers, threatened business interests and conservatives cast Sinclair as a lightheaded dreamer whose EPIC plan would attract millions of elderly bums across the California border to plague the state's already overburdened economy (see Figures 3.13 and 3.14).

Opponents of the pension idea also played on anxieties about escalating taxes, arguing that the steep tax rates necessary to finance public pensions would prove far too expensive for the American public ever to afford. In a habitually anti-statist society, the libertarian theme of "keeping Big Government off the taxpayer's back" could be counted on to strike a responsive chord. National Metal Trades Association spokesman W. E. Odom brought the unfairness of the "greatly

'On to California!'

Figure 3.13. Upton Sinclair's EPIC campaign as seen in a mid-1930s cartoon from the *San Francisco Examiner.*

increased taxes to be paid" to the attention of a congressional committee in 1931, pointing out indignantly that "the proposed plan will not only place an excessive additional burden upon taxpayers but . . . (the aged and those who serve them) would receive a large additional income at the direct expense of the taxpayers" (U.S. Senate 1931, 40). This unfair taxation theme was vividly captured in a *New York Times* cartoon (later reprinted in *Literary Digest*) entitled "Oh Grandma, What Big Teeth You Have!" An early forerunner of what would later become the "Greedy Geezer" stereotype, the "Grandma" cartoon depicted a huge, overweight elderly woman feasting greedily on the nation's hard-

Bids For The Winter Tourist Trade

Figure 3.14. Upton Sinclair's EPIC campaign as seen in a mid-1930s cartoon from the *Chicago Daily News*.

earned revenue. In the background, a lean taxpayer looked on in a mixture of envy and bewilderment. Grandma's gigantic teeth spelled "taxes," symbolizing the unfairness of the "tax bite" necessary to finance old-age pensions (see Figure 3.15). Another typical cartoon

'Oh, Grandma, What Big Teeth You Have!'

Figure 3.15. Cartoon by Edwin Marcus from the 23 June 1935 *New York Times*.

emphasizing the unfairness of pension-related income transfers appeared in the *Boston Evening Transcript*. Old-age pension architects Francis Townsend, Upton Sinclair, Franklin Roosevelt, Huey Long, and "the lunatic fringe" were shown "in bed" together, unified by their common redistributive desire to "spread the wealth" that had been so laboriously earned by honest American taxpayers (see Figure 3.16).

Politics makes strange bedfellows

Figure 3.16. Depression-era cartoon from the *Boston Evening Transcript.*

A rather more ruthless attempt to delegitimize the pension idea involved using the media to stigmatize the plans, their creators, and their sympathizers as "socialistic" or "extremist" (and hence un-American). Pension critics argued that not only did these plans blatantly violate the time-worn American principles of individualism, laissez-faire economics, limited government, self-reliance, and private thrift, but they were also inspired by communists! Evident in the "spread the wealth" cartoon, this theme portrayed the various plans as

Figure 3.17. "Look out!" Cartoon by Fred O. Beibel for a late-1935/early-1936 issue of the *Richmond Times-Dispatch*.
Reprinted by permission of the *Richmond Times-Dispatch*.

extremist "embarrassments" to their sympathizers within the two mainstream parties (particularly the Democrats), implying that the political fortunes of sympathetic politicians would decline precipitously if they were foolish enough to persist in supporting these outrageous schemes invented by the "lunatic fringe." Appealing to Americans' fear of communism, pension opponents aggressively portrayed the new reform schemes as the "entering wedge of socialism." This rhetorical device depended for its effectiveness on getting the public to believe in a domestic version of domino theory. If provision for old age were "socialized," other domains of American social life would inevitably follow, and where would it all end? W. E. Odom of the National Metal Trades Association warned a congressional committee that "state operated pensions are essentially socialistic. . . . It may be inferred, too, that passage of an initial old age pension bill will be followed by demands for legislation on all sorts of other social measures" (U.S. Senate 1931, 39–40).

The extremism theme lent itself to attacks on the character and intentions of the pension scheme architects. A *Richmond Times-Dispatch* cartoon, with the alarmist "Look Out!" caption, depicted Townsend and his pension plan as a radical "third party threat" to the stability of the American two-party system (see Figure 3.17). A more ruthless red-baiting blitz was carried out by entrenched California business interests attempting to undermine the popularity of Sinclair's EPIC plan. During his gubernatorial campaign, major California newspapers were saturated with cartoons depicting Sinclair as a would-be communist dictator (Mitchell 1992). One typical cartoon, published in the *Los Angeles Examiner*, likened Sinclair's political aspirations to those of Stalin, Hitler, and Mussolini, warning voters that "Here comes another man on horseback, another dictator! . . . Sinclair ought to be able to follow Stalin—in fact he has been following him all through his campaign for Governor." Another cartoon asked rhetorically, "Shall the Stamp of Sinclairism Crush California?" and cautioned citizens that "Sinclairism plans to confiscate your investments in property by excessive taxation" (Sinclair 1934, 93, 133). In still another tactic, a bogus "Red Currency" was printed by his opponents and distributed to potential California voters to dramatize the devastating economic effects the "socialistic" EPIC plan would have on the state's economy were Sinclair to be elected. Prominently displayed on these "sincLIAR" dollars, which were "not very good anywhere," was an early generational inequity slogan: "redeemable, if ever, at the cost of future generations." The original intended meaning of Sinclair's "EPIC"—End Poverty in California—was altered by his opponents to mean "Endure Poverty in California" and "Easy Pickings in California," and the mock currency was supposedly endorsed by "UTOPIAN Sinclair, Governor of California" (see Figure 3.18).[16]

Yet another device for portraying the pension idea as un-American was to imply that it would violate the U.S. Constitution. However appealing these plans might appear to be in the short run as panaceas for elderly woes, opponents suggested, the problem remained that they were ultimately illegal. National Association of Manufacturers

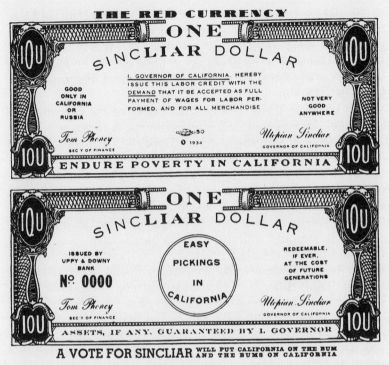

Figure 3.18. Illustration from Upton Sinclair's *I, Candidate for Governor, and How I Got Licked* (Pasadena, Calif.: Sinclair, 1934), 149.

president J. E. Edgerton released a widely publicized statement in 1930 that attacked the "multiplying proposals for public old age pensions" as anti-American "sea waves of emotionalism . . . beating furiously against our constitutional barriers" (*OASH* 4, no. 7 [1930]: 3). Fortunately for pension foes, a series of timely anti–welfare-state, anti-labor Supreme Court decisions during the 1930s gave this position credibility. Court decisions declaring the National Recovery Administration unconstitutional and invalidating the Railroad Pension Act cast a shadow of doubt on the likely constitutionality of any publicly administered old-age pension program.

When the Railroad Pension Act was struck down by a five-to-four Supreme Court decision, pension opponents seized the moment to depress popular expectations that the constitutionality of public pensions could ever be defended. A conservative column in the *New York Herald Tribune* hailed the decision as "a wholesome lesson in Constitutional law for the advocates of hasty change." The *Boston Evening Transcript* concurred that it was "obviously a warning to Congress." The *Denver Post* celebrated the decision as "the worst setback the New Dealers have received. . . . [I]t not only junks their scheme for pensioning railroad employees, but it knocks the props out from under President Roosevelt's fantastic social security program." The *Richmond Times-Dispatch* likewise concluded that the prospects for national old-age pension legislation had "struck a judicial snag against which it will be impossible to proceed further." The *Butte, Montana, Standard* smugly concluded that the larger constitutional lesson would henceforth be that "Congress cannot arbitrarily take money from one group of citizens to give it to another." Visual metaphors were also used to drive home the point. A *Philadelphia Evening Public Ledger* cartoon entitled "Not According to Schedule" represented the Social Security bill as one of several boxcars on a train of legislation headed for Congress. The engine of the train (labeled "Railroad Pension Act") had just struck a huge rock (labeled "Supreme Court") on the legislative track, thereby derailing the train. A similar cartoon in the *Louisville Courier-Journal*, entitled "Proceed with Caution," again portrayed the pending old-age pension legislation as a train hopelessly stalled on a legislative track. This time it was a railroad crossing warning signal (labeled "Railway Pensions Court Decision") that prevented the train's forward movement (*Literary Digest* 1935 [May 18]:12).

All of these various rhetorical ploys within the "American self-reliance" frame proved useful as anti-pension scare tactics, planting doubts in the public mind about the feasibility of proposed old-age insurance schemes. But negative propaganda tactics were unlikely to quell the mounting national pension fever for long. Conservative defenders of the status quo therefore found it necessary to devise plausible "non-public" solutions to the problem of elderly insecurity, and they began aggressively selling them to the citizenry as "practical" alternatives to government support. Pension foes promoted the idea that rather than create an expensive, unmanageable public bureaucracy to serve aged dependents, the nation should instead take greater steps to encourage personal habits of private thrift in saving for old age. After all, they argued, this was the only conceivable solution to elderly woes that would remain consistent with the American cultural traditions of individualism and self-reliance. A widely read June 1930 *Forbes* article by conservative economist Samuel Crowther, for example, suggested that the "real" solution to problems of old-age insecurity was to be found in a disciplined program of voluntary thrift within families, aided by retirement insurance purchased through private companies. Entitled "Insure Your Child for Old Age," the *Forbes* piece took the position that "If . . . we are looking to old age insurance and the promotion of a self-respecting citizenry, then the state comes into the picture as an insuring corporation—and it has been our experience that the state cannot perform any purely business function as cheaply or with as large a public service as can a private corporation skilled in that business." The only realistic solution to old-age insecurity, therefore, was through private insurance. Crowther argued that $300, properly invested at age one, would provide "$50 a month life income," thereby solving the problem of economic insufficiency in old age (see Figure 3.19). Conservatives argued that the best model for "self-reliant" provision in old age was to be found in the successful precedent of life insurance provided through private companies. In this way, Americans could "have old age provided against as adequately as death is now provided against." Crowther's 1930 article in *Forbes* confidently concluded that "a solution is thus arrived at . . . a definite, concrete and actuarially sufficient accumulation can thus be made in such a manner that the independence and security of the employee will be assured without charity and on the basis of self-reliant initiative, thrift and foresight" (Crowther 1930b, 23, 40).

At least to the more privileged sectors of the population, such arguments sounded convincing enough, resonating easily with individualistic attitudes toward the meeting of social risks that prevailed in the United States through the end of the 1920s. Rugged individualism was still in vogue during that decade, supported by a booming stock market and a rise in real wages that had "lulled the majority . . . into a condition of more or less acquiescent satisfaction" (Douglas 1936, 4). But with the coming of the depression of the 1930s, the climate of public opinion began noticeably to shift. Americans became less and less receptive to such "self-reliance" arguments. As a result, while anti-pension scare tactics were at least able to defeat some specific pension schemes (EPIC, Ham and Eggs, and eventually the Townsend Plan), they failed miserably in their broader task of convincing the American citizenry to abandon the idea of publicly administered old-age pen-

Insure Your Child For Old Age

Figure 3.19. Illustration for the article "Insure Your Child for Old Age," *Forbes*, June 1930.

Reprinted by permission of *Forbes* magazine.

sions. Despite the best efforts of pension foes, the pension concept continued to gain momentum as the 1930s progressed.

A Tentative Victory for the Movement

All things considered, it is clear that senior rights activists of the 1920s and 1930s ultimately proved quite successful in their quest to legitimize the idea of old age pensions in the public mind. They were able to do so by deftly using the media to get a growing segment of the American public to resonate with the themes of their message of "social security" as the solution to the problem of "social insecurity." Pension reformers managed to frame the public debate in such a way as to orchestrate a great deal of popular pressure on otherwise reluctant political elites, which in turn resulted in pension legislation being placed higher and higher on the nation's agenda.

This successful persuasion process occurred in two phases. In the first, the movement's challenge was to get influential mass media to take its proposed reforms seriously and convey its pro-pension message to the public. This it accomplished admirably. A nationwide survey conducted in 1931 indicated that by that year the vast majority of American newpapers had come out in favor of pensions. Out of 3,244 editorials in prominent newspapers dealing with pensions, 2,086 were favorable as compared with only 587 against the pension idea. Pro-pension editorials outnumbered anti-pension editorials in 44 of the 49 states.[17] The extensive media coverage in turn focused popular attention on the potential advantages of old-age pensions, inspiring a groundswell of public support. By 1935 polls showed that fully 89 percent of the American public had been persuaded to support the idea of old-age pensions for needy persons (Gallup 1972, 1: 9, 76).

In the second stage of the political persuasion process, this mass opinion mobilized in favor of the pension idea provided political leverage. Elected officials were compelled to consider adopting new policies, consistent with their perception of the mounting pro-pension sentiment within the electorate. There were "votes in pensions." As Senator C. C. Dill put it, "The truth of the matter is that there isn't any legislation in this country that has quite such a deep appeal to the rank and file of the people as legislation designed to give comforts of life to those who are poor in their old age. . . . This sentiment, this demand that the aged poor shall be insured . . . is a growing influence, and a growing power" (Dill 1930, 2). President Franklin Roosevelt reportedly asked Frances Perkins, head of his Committee on Economic Security, to come up with a plan for an old-age security system as quickly as possible because "the Congress can't stand the pressure of the Townsend Plan unless we have a real old-age insurance system, nor can I face the people without having . . . a solid plan which will give some assurance to people of systematic assistance upon retirement" (Altmeyer 1966, 10).

At least for the time being, the new movement's conservative political adversaries seemed relatively inept in their attempts to frame the debate in a way that would undermine popular support for pensions. Unfortunately for the movement, however, there were in fact not one but *two* significant political battles that would have to be won if the burgeoning senior rights movement was actually to achieve its reform objectives. The first battle had been the rhetorical struggle to convince the American public of the urgent need for old-age pensions—which supporters had largely won. Beyond this, however, lay a further political battle to define the form and content of the resultant legislation. As we shall see, in the latter political contest the movement's optimistic agenda for reform was to be cleverly manipulated by established elites, leaving many of the movement's original reform goals unrealized, and its supporters seriously dissappointed and demoralized.

Chapter Four

The *Original* Social Security Crisis

*Economic Depression and Elite Responses to
Reform Pressures*

> *They do not have to worry about the Townsend Plan because it clearly
> would not work. . . .   The only practical alternative is a contributory
> system. . . . At this time the enlightenment of the people of this country
> upon the real issue . . . seems to me the major responsibility of all who
> believe that a contributory plan is vastly preferable to gratuitous pen-
> sions for everybody.*
> > Edwin Witte, executive director of the President's Committee on
> > Economic Security, 1936[1]

> *The work and recommendations of the Committee were cloaked in
> mystery. The public had no inkling of the specific types of legislation to
> be recommended. . . . In fact, the inauguration of the Act has been
> accompanied by such an unprecedented barrage of propaganda and
> ballyhoo as to further confound the issues and thus postpone the bridg-
> ing of the gap between the Social Security Act and genuine security. . . .
> [M]uch of the Social Security Act is more glitter than gold.*
> > Abraham Epstein, executive secretary of the American Association for
> > Social Security, 1938[2]

Although the core values and reform objectives of the incipient senior
rights movement were already in place by the 1920s, it took the
unprecedented economic hardship and social dislocation of the Great
Depression of the 1930s to finally force significant readjustments in

American policies toward the elderly. These harsh economic realities, together with pressures generated by the old-age reform organizations—the Townsend Movement, AALL, the Eagles, AASS, Sinclair's EPIC, the Ham and Eggs group—combined to create a volatile political climate in which elites had to take notice. Government officials were forced to recognize the growing political prominence of the elderly's interests and demands. This chapter examines how policy elites responded to these escalating movement demands for fundamental change, and addresses several key questions: Was the Social Security Act of 1935 genuine reform, or was it merely token legislation designed to symbolically reassure a restive populace? What effect did passage of this ameliorative legislation have on the movement? Having succeeded so brilliantly in legitimizing the idea of pensions in the public mind, how did movement leaders then manage to fumble at the legislative stage, losing control over the process of shaping the reform agenda?

The Social Security Act: Co-optation as a Response to Elderly Grievances

The impact of the depression on the lives of elderly Americans was severe. Unemployment was even higher among the elderly than among other age groups. Millions of older employees lost their jobs and, unlike younger workers, had little hope of successfully reentering the work force once conditions improved. By 1935 more than half of the 65-and-over population was jobless (Holtzman 1963, 22). Most older workers were not covered by pension schemes. Those who were often found to their dismay that their plan had been discontinued or was on the verge of bankruptcy. Between 1929 and 1932 alone, 45 plans—responsible for payments to 100,000 American employees—were discontinued. Personal savings of most aged workers, minimal even in prosperous times, proved woefully inadequate during the depression years. Nor could elderly Americans count on any substantial amount of family support, as most depression families experienced difficulty in providing for even their immediate members (Achenbaum 1978, 128–29).

A combination of pressures on political elites in the early 1930s led to old-age security being placed higher and higher on the legislative agenda. In addition to their concern about electoral consequences, policymakers were driven toward action by the need to deflect escalating demands for radical change (Olson 1982, 44), a desire to rejuvenate industry by increasing purchasing power (Piven and Cloward

1971, 89), and the hope of reducing unemployment by removing older workers from the labor force (Graebner 1980, 184). What these priorities had in common was an emphasis on preserving intact the existing institutional arrangements of society. As growing numbers of Americans experienced unemployment, depletion of family savings, foreclosures, and destitution, they began to resort to raiding relief agencies, violent protests, and rent riots. A central concern underlying the introduction of the Social Security Act was therefore that of *regime maintenance* in the midst of economic crisis and mounting popular discontent (Piven and Cloward 1971, 48–94).

According to Mauss, the initial response of the "host society" to an incipient social movement such as the senior movement typically involves "very little repression and a lot of co-optation" (1971, 62). "Co-optation" consists of "ameliorative gestures" designed to "neutralize the movement's criticisms of the established order," in conjunction with an extensive propaganda effort that stresses the values and interests the host society holds in common with the movement. Political psychologist Murray Edelman has characterized this latter tactic as "the politics of symbolic reassurance," in which the political establishment's aim is to delay, or to avoid altogether, making tangible policy concessions by fostering an atmosphere of quiescence (1964, 22–43). When a segment of the public is dissatisfied with existing policies and demands that they be reformed, the skillful orchestration of symbolic gestures—such as the appointment of a commission to study the problem, or passage of token legislation— serves to reassure the public that the situation is being dealt with. The purpose of this symbolic action by elites is to provide evidence that something is being done while in fact postponing (sometimes indefinitely) any genuine policy concessions.

This type of co-optation of a movement's goals and policy agenda by established institutions presents the movement with the dilemma of trying to maintain a distinct identity vis-à-vis an apparently permissive society. Accommodation and appeasement measures sap the vitality of the movement by making more difficult the essential tasks of maintaining intense commitment to principles and broadening the recruitment base. Mauss points out that if the host society's efforts at appeasement succeed in neutralizing the spirit and momentum of the movement, the demoralized movement may remain stalled in this incipient stage for years before it eventually regains its momentum (Mauss 1975, 190; 1971, 62).

By the summer of 1934, worsening conditions of mass impoverishment, the collapse of union pension and relief funds, and the growing popularity of "radical" pension proposals had produced a sense of urgency among American policy elites. Many of the nation's political and economic leaders felt that something needed to be done to assuage popular dissatisfactions and work toward restoration of economic stability (Olson 1982, 46). Reacting to mounting popular pressures, President Roosevelt advised Congress on 8 June that he planned to convene a group of experts to draft a new program that would protect Americans against some of the economic hardships that threatened their well-being. The task of the new cabinet-level Committee on Economic Security would be to search for "a sound means which I can recommend to provide at once security against several of the great disturbing factors of life—especially those which relate to unemployment and old age" (Roosevelt 1934, 4).

Roosevelt carefully selected members of his Committee on Economic Security so as to exclude persons who advocated more comprehensive or redistributive pension plans (Quadagno 1984, 640). Notably absent were some of the heavy hitters of the pension movement—Townsend, Epstein, and Rubinow, among others—whose proposals implied fundamental structural change. According to an account by then Assistant Secretary of Labor Arthur Altmeyer, Roosevelt and the committee felt compelled to come up with an alternative scheme that would accommodate the public clamor for an old-age pension plan while avoiding the redistributive implications of more radical schemes for the existing social structure. Altmeyer relates that "some writers have suggested that the popularity of the Townsend movement forced the President to develop some alternative plan. The President was, of course, concerned about the Townsend plan. But he was even more concerned about Senator Huey Long's 'share the wealth' movement. The Senator was never precise about how he would go about sharing the wealth . . . although the differing amounts he predicted were all large enough to appeal to the popular imagination, as was his slogan, 'Every man a King!'" [3]

There is little doubt that the president's public expressions of compassion for unemployed workers and the elderly poor were sincere. He clearly cared deeply about their plight. The Roosevelt administration's primary objective in introducing the legislation, however, was to stabilize and reinvigorate the economy. Promoting the welfare of workers and the elderly was of secondary importance in seeking passage of the act (Quadagno 1984b, 640). As Secretary of Labor Frances Perkins, head of the committee, explained in testimony before the Senate Finance Committee, the administration's economic logic in providing pension and unemployment benefits was that "by paying over monies to persons who would otherwise not have any income, you are creating purchasing power which will regularly . . . sustain the purchases which are to be made from the great manufacturing and mercantile systems of the country."[4] The president made clear to the committee and to Congress his desire to establish a public system of social insurance that would be based on the same equity principles as private insurance, insisting that the new plan be financed from worker contributions rather than from general government revenues.

Roosevelt's insistence that the pension insurance scheme be financed by payroll contributions (the FICA tax, Federal Insurance Contributions Act) was a masterful exercise in co-optation of the old-age pension movement's popular base of support. The inclusion of the FICA payroll tax provision gave American workers a direct, ongoing stake in Social Security and hence in the established governmental structure that dispensed the benefits. Roosevelt's gesture of symbolic reassurance succeeded in converting American workers' alienation from the established social order into a newfound sense of identification with it. The president wisely realized that payroll contributions would ensure that Social Security remained popular, and hence politically invulnerable in years to come. In response to criticism of the economic feasibility of his payroll tax, Roosevelt countered that "I guess you're right on the economics, but those taxes were never a problem of economics. . . . We put those payroll contributions there so as to give the contributors *a legal, moral, and political right* to collect their pensions. . . . With those taxes in there, no damn politician can ever scrap my social security program."[5] No "damn politician" ever has.

On 17 January 1935, six months after appointing the cabinet committee to develop a social insurance plan, Roosevelt submitted the report of the Committee on Economic Security to Congress. Extensive public hearings were then held by the Ways and Means Committee of the House of Representatives and the Finance Committee of the Senate, in which the pros and cons of the legislation became the subject of heated debates and lively press coverage. On 19 April the bill passed in the House; on 19 June it passed in the Senate. A joint Conference Committee then ironed out differences in the House and Senate versions, and the Social Security Act was signed into law by the president on 14 August.

As a response by policy elites to popular pressures that had been mounting for decades, the passage of the Social Security Act was in one respect a significant step toward realization of the goals of the pension movement. With the establishment of a nationally administered system of social insurance, the United States belatedly joined Western Europe in providing workers with some form of minimal public support to assure their subsistence in old age. While it may not have been evident at the time, the Social Security Act marked a pivotal shift in the administration of welfare functions from voluntary institutions to the public sector, and from local to federal levels of government. In so doing, it established ideological and legal precedents that paved the way for subsequent amendments to the Social Security Act that raised benefit levels, added survivors' and dependents' benefits (1939), added disability insurance (1956), introduced medical insurance for the aged (1965), incorporated automatic benefit adjustments for inflation (1972), and introduced indexing of earnings (1977).

In other respects, however, the legislation was a disappointment. It was considerably more modest in scope than Townsend, Epstein, Rubinow, and others had envisioned. In the development of the Social Security package, basic laissez-faire capitalist economic principles had merely been reformulated to the minimal extent necessary to reestablish normal societal functioning, carefully skirting more fundamental structural changes. The policy compromise between establishment and reformers involved few genuine concessions to the pension movement's value principles of societal (as opposed to individual) responsibility for elderly well-being, and distribution of benefits according to need (as opposed to contribution). The legislation was consciously designed to avoid redistribution of wealth. If anything, the net effect of its regressive tax system was to *increase* economic inequalities.[6] Eligibility and benefits were closely tied to the extent of worker contributions, and the legislation omitted government contributions. Whereas the rhetoric that accompanied the act promised sweeping reforms in the circumstances of elderly workers, an equally important objective was to get older employees out of the labor force in order to create employment for younger workers (Graebner 1980; Lubove 1968).

These and other shortcomings of the legislation immediately came under fire from prominent reformers and pension movement representatives, who had long advocated more comprehensive coverage with fewer restrictions. Townsend criticized the act as insufficient to meet the needs of elderly Americans. Ironically, he achieved his greatest popularity *after* Social Security was passed, as a leader of elderly discontent with deficiencies in the legislation. Recall (Chapter 3) that the Townsend Plan had proposed a pension of $200 per month, Sinclair's EPIC plan had advocated $50 per month, and the Ham and Eggs plan called for $30 per week. In contrast to these reform plans, the Social Security old-age pension, which would not even start until 1940, was to pay only $271 per year.

Pension reformer Isaac Rubinow was also disappointed with the narrow scope and provisions of the act. He protested that he had not "preached social insurance for thirty-five years in order now, at this late date, to abandon my ideal for the sake of a somewhat glorified system of public relief with a half a dozen means tests" (Lubove 1968, 176). Rubinow also complained that Labor Secretary Frances Perkins had treated Abraham Epstein "shabbily" by shutting him out of the decision-making process. Epstein, a highly qualified expert on European social insurance systems, had been angered by the conspicuous failure of Roosevelt's Committee on Economic Security to consult him in drafting the legislation. Epstein bitterly objected that instead of setting up an independent committee composed of the nation's most competent experts to study the problem, Roosevelt and the CES had instead employed a research staff "among whom most of the outstanding American authorities in social insurance were conspicuous by their absence" (Epstein 1938, 672).

Epstein and Rubinow were essentially in agreement in their assessments of the defects of the new law. Both reformers considered the Social Security Act incapable of providing Americans with genuine financial security in old age, because its provisions failed to include any significant measure of redistribution to the elderly. Only contributions from general government revenues, which Roosevelt and the Committee on Economic Security had consciously avoided in drafting the legislation, could make economic security a reality for the aged.

Both reformers also considered the exclusion of health insurance from the package to be a fundamental flaw. Without it true security in old age was not possible. Epstein charged that the American Social Security program was meager and ineffectual by comparison with the standards of old-age and welfare legislation in most other industrialized nations. Distinguishing between "social insurance" and "private insurance," he characterized the Social Security Act as a nationally administered example of the latter. True social insurance as practiced in Europe, Epstein argued, entailed "a socially adequate arrangement which will protect all workers as well as society from certain social hazards," not merely "individual protection according to ability to pay" (1938, 762). The most serious mistake made by the Committee on Economic Security, he concluded, had been to confuse governmental social insurance with private insurance, as a consequence of their myopic lack of familiarity with European social insurance practices (Epstein 1938, 669–82, 760–83).

Then, with remarkable prescience of events to come half a century hence, Epstein went on to complain, in a section of his *Insecurity: A Challenge to America* entitled "Younger Generation Bears Brunt of Burden," that "in transferring the accrued liability for old age dependency to the shoulders of the younger workers the Act places a back-breaking burden upon the younger people," adding that it would be "unjust to place this burden, which all society should bear, upon the younger workers alone," and "especially cruel and reprehensible to saddle such burdensome direct and indirect taxes upon these workers at a time when they are striving to raise families and need every dollar they earn." Epstein concluded his "Younger Generation" section with a stern admonition that "there is indeed no excuse whatsoever for singling out the working youth of the nation . . . to shoulder these enormous accrued costs" (1938, 789–90).

Not all criticisms of the new legislation came from the left side of the political spectrum, however. Although in 1935 many businessmen supported social security because of its potential for restoring national stability, some right-wing Republicans, southern Democrats, and states-rights advocates felt that the act had gone too far—setting dangerous precedents that would have to be reversed (Quadagno 1984a). Conservative critics worried that federal supervision of the program would lead to further encroachment of the federal government on the prerogatives of states, and that it was generally destructive of traditional American values of individual self-reliance, frugality, and laissez-faire economics (Fischer 1977, 185, 187). Congressman James Wadsworth complained that "this bill opens the door and invites the entrance into the political field of a power so vast, so powerful as to threaten the integrity of our institutions and to pull the pillars of the temple down upon the heads of our descendents." Others alleged that the act had established a public bureaucracy in the field of insurance in competition with private business, and that it would destroy the retirement systems set up by private industries (Altmeyer 1966, 37–38).

Shortly after President Roosevelt signed the measure into law, litigation was initiated questioning the constitutionality of its various provisions. Seven states objected to the federal legislation as an infringement on their rights, preferring to retain their own customs in deciding what constituted appropriate relief for the elderly and unemployed workers. The National Association of Manufacturers objected to the payroll tax on employers.

In May 1937, however, the Supreme Court verified the legitimacy of the Social Security program with two landmark decisions, defusing challenges to the act on constitutional grounds. In *Stewart Machine Company* v. *Davis* the court upheld the constitutionality of the unemployment excise tax on employers, and the federal-state funding apparatus. *Helvering* v. *Davis* approved the Social Security Act's old-age insurance tax provision and retirement benefit provision. In his opinion on the latter case, Justice Cardozo held that "Congress did not improvise a judgment when it found that the award of old age benefits would be conducive of the general welfare." These 1937 decisions established the constitutionality of the major provisions of the Social Security Act, reversing a string of more conservative previous decisions that had declared unconstitutional the Agricultural Adjustment Act, the Railroad Retirement Act, and the National Industrial Recovery Act (Altmeyer 1966, 56).

As a gesture of accommodation by the established political order, intended to assuage the growing restlessness of constituents, the success of the 1935 Social Security Act was primarily political rather than economic, as Roosevelt himself had acknowledged. It succeeded politically by breaking the momentum of the old-age protests of the day, upstaging a budding senior movement that had been organized almost exclusively around this one issue. Hurriedly conceived in response to a deepening national economic crisis, the legislation was as much an attempt to pacify the supporters of more comprehensive pension proposals as it was an effort to draft effective social reform aimed at satisfying elderly needs. Architects of the legislation had promised a sweeping alleviation of the economic hardships endured by older Americans. But the provisions of the legislation in fact proved to be much less spectacular than the accompanying rhetoric. Established political tradition ultimately prevailed—in the continued emphasis on the equity principles of private insurance; in the insistence on contributory, work-related criteria for eligibility and benefit distribution; and in the conscious downplaying of government contributions.

Aftermath of Co-optation: The Quiescent 1940s

When political elites successfully use ameliorative legislation to symbolically reassure a constituency that is clamoring for social change,
the effect is often one of "greatly increasing the co-optative element in
the mix" (Mauss 1975, 64). Smelser describes the impact of this co-
optive strategy on a movement as "the devisive effects of institutional
accommodation" (1962, 363). Apparent concessions to movement
objectives bestowed on the movement's sympathetic public by the
host society have the effect of "buying off" supporters. Many of the
movement's sympathizers begin to assume that things have really
improved—that the social problem that gave rise to the protest movement is in fact being solved. As a result, it becomes more difficult for
the movement to continue the essential tasks of broadening its
recruitment base and maintaining a firm commitment to principles
that have become increasingly difficult to differentiate from those
now professed by the host society. The movement is placed on the
defensive, in that it must redefine its boundaries vis-à-vis the establishment in order to maintain a distinct identity and purpose in the
minds of adherents. The process of redefinition, in turn, tends to
exacerbate doctrinal disagreements that exist between leaders of different strands within the movement. As Mauss (1975, 62) has
observed, this reactive response to the host society's apparent per-
missiveness may retard the growth of an incipient political movement
for some time before it manages to regain its momentum, or it may
even lead to the movement's demise.

In the aftermath of the passage of the Social Security Act of 1935,
the political effectiveness of the various component organizations of
the pension movement slowly began to wane. Leaders of different factions fell into fighting among themselves over policy nuances, dissipat-
ing the energies of groups within the movement and alienating in the
process some of its most influential members and financial contributors. In particular, Abraham Epstein became a vitriolic and uncompro-
mising critic of the Social Security legislation. He was deeply
disappointed that the new law failed to include any significant measure
of income redistribution, which according to Epstein was essential to
providing economic security for the elderly, and for workers in times
of unemployment. Bitter over his exclusion from the deliberations of
the Committee on Economic Security in the drafting of the legislation,
Epstein indignantly made public his hope that the courts would nullify

the old-age and employment titles of the Act, and urged states to refuse to participate in the tax-offset unemployment provision.

Epstein's public pronouncements exacerbated disagreements between his philosophy of old-age security and that of other leaders and organizations within the pension movement. Rubinow chastised Epstein for allowing his personal vendetta against members of the Committee on Economic Security and his disappointment with the limitations of the act to warp his judgment. Rubinow charged that if Epstein had waited as "long as I have and seen one disappointment after another, he wouldn't be quite so ready to advocate this theory of either everything or nothing" (quoted in Lubove 1968, 176). He further criticized Epstein for unwisely preferring a system of "public relief" to a system of "public insurance."

The effect of these doctrinal disputes on the morale and solidarity of the old-age pension reform movement was devastating. According to an account published in the official newsletter of the American Association for Social Security on the occasion of Epstein's death, Epstein's denunciation of the act as a regressive and dangerous measure produced a demoralized atmosphere in which "people reviled him, friends deserted him, half of the members of the association resigned. . . . Others went further and accused him of being in the pay of the Republican Party during the 1936 campaign" (*Social Security* 1942, 5).

The loss of organizational energies, membership, and financial support during this period was substantial. An appeal in the AASS newsletter in 1940 pleaded that the movement for old-age security in America "is passing through a most critical hour. . . . We are now threatened with a complete blackout! Our financial need is now more desperate than at any time in our history! Our activities may come to a complete halt" (*Social Security* 1940, 8). Similarly, the American Association for Labor Legislation lost the support of some of its most important contributors as a result of the bitter factional disagreements with Epstein and AASS (Pierce 1953, 416).

Dr. Francis Townsend, whose movement claimed three to five million followers by 1936, briefly reached the height of his popularity as a critic of the Social Security Act in the year following its passage. The Townsend organization began to decline precipitously thereafter, however. Movement activists and sympathizers became discouraged as it became apparent by the late 1930s that the Townsend Plan was unlikely to ever be adopted on Capitol Hill. The political mainstream had clearly opted for the "contributory social insurance" approach over more radical proposals. The beginning of the end came when Townsend became involved in an abortive third-party presidential campaign with Father Charles Coughlin and Gerald Smith, and in the process parted ranks with cofounder Robert Earl Clements, who had been the organizational genius behind the movement (Pratt 1976, 26–28).

A major source of the decline of the three most influential pension organizations in the late 1930s (Townsend, the American Association for Social Security, the American Association for Labor Legislation) was the overwhelming initial popularity of Roosevelt's Social Security Act among the public. Epstein complained resentfully that the introduction of the act had been accompanied by "an unprecedented barrage of propaganda and ballyhoo" and that activists and supporters of the pension movement had "become so impressed with the bubbling confidence and the prodigious machinery set up that they have mistaken the means for the end" (1938, 761). The American public, however, apparently did not share these reservations about the new Social Security legislation. A 1937 Gallup poll showed that 73 percent of Americans interviewed approved of the Social Security tax on their wages. In a 1941 poll, 91 percent indicated that they were in favor of the old-age pension provision (Gallup 1972, 76, 292–93).

Faced with such effective symbolic reassurance of the American public by policy elites, the old-age pension reform movement lapsed into a dormant phase in the 1940s and early 1950s, which Henry Pratt has called the "dismal years" of the senior rights movement. These years of quiescence were marked by a relative absence of the kind of sustained interest group involvement that had fueled the pension-reform struggles of the 1920s and 1930s.[7] The only significant reform activity during this period was George McClain's Citizens Committee for Old Age Pensions, which claimed thousands of elderly supporters in California, and managed to contribute to increased expenditures on elderly concerns in that state. Most of the organizations that had previously been active in pension-reform efforts, however, were either in an advanced state of organizational atrophy by this point or had turned their attention to other issues (Pratt 1976, 26–30; 1983, 149). By the mid-1940s the AALL and the AASS had ceased to exist, and the once-powerful Townsend organization no longer attracted much attention among the public or on Capitol Hill.

Chapter Five

Coalition Politics and the Struggle for Medicare

Further Elite Concessions and Symbolic Appeasement

> *One of the traditional methods of imposing statism or socialism on a people has been by way of medicine. It's very easy to disguise a medical program as a humanitarian project.*
> *from "Ronald Reagan Speaks Out against Socialized Medicine," a phonograph recording sponsored by the American Medical Association, 1961[1]*

> *The program is not socialized medicine. . . . It is a program of prepayment for health costs with absolute freedom of choice guaranteed.*
> *President John F. Kennedy, 1961[2]*

The "incipiency" phase of the senior rights movement had arisen out of deteriorating economic and social conditions among older Americans in the early decades of the twentieth century, which spawned the old-age pension reform struggles of the 1920s and 1930s. In this early formative stage, the movement's pattern of development corresponded very closely to Herbert Blumer's description of a "general" social movement: "groping uncoordinated efforts" with "little guidance or control" (1951, 200–201). This embryonic phase of the movement reached its peak of momentum in the mid-1930s, and

THE UNDER-THE-BEDSIDE MANNER

Figure 5.1. Herblock cartoon, from *Straight Herblock* (New York: Simon & Schuster, 1964).

Reprinted by permission.

decayed rapidly thereafter, lapsing into temporary dormancy during the forties.

According to Armand Mauss, the second stage in the natural history of a social movement is typically one of "coalescence." In this stage the rather diffuse organization and reform sentiments that characterized the incipiency phase begin to congeal into more permanent organizations. Individual reform groups merge their resources to form common alliances—in response to disappointment over the failure of the host society to adequately address their previous demands and expectations, or in response to overt governmental attempts at co-optation or repression. Movement activities at this stage normally consist of the formation of alliances, ad hoc committees, and caucuses, as well as the development of local and regional formal associations (Mauss 1971, 193).

Renaissance of the Senior Rights Movement in the Late 1950s

The roots of the coalescence phase of the American senior rights movement can be traced to trends that began in the late 1940s and early 1950s, although their impact was not to become fully apparent in national politics until the turbulent decade of the 1960s. The quiescent political mood of the "dismal years" had masked an underlying sense of dissatisfaction and disillusionment among many elderly Americans with Social Security provisions that remained in need of reform. The 1935 Social Security legislation and the 1939 amendments had eased problems of economic insecurity among the nation's elderly but had never actually solved them. The new law remained extraordinarily weak in its provisions in comparison with the standards prevalent in other modern Western nations (Rimlinger 1971, 193–244). In its original form, the act offered workers no protection against the possibility of occupational disabilities forcing early retirement and provided no insurance against illness in old age. It excluded major segments of the working population, such as domestic and agricultural workers. For those who were covered, the emphasis on "social equity" rather than "social adequacy" criteria for benefit distribution meant in practice that the majority of American retirees received an income in old age that was substantially below levels necessary to maintain a decent standard of living. Moreover, the legislation failed to compensate for the erosion of these benefit levels over time by inflation.

Eligibility standards and levels of support also varied widely from state to state. The original proposal, which required that "old age assistance grants must be sufficient, with other income, to provide a reasonable subsistence compatible with decency and health" had been eliminated from the final version of the act as a result of political pressures from southern congressmen, who feared that the clause would obviate local and state practices holding that "Negro persons can have such a reasonable subsistence on less income than a white person."[3]

In the 1950s these and other unresolved old-age policy issues resurfaced on the national political scene. "Senior clubs" had begun to develop throughout the United States in the late 1940s, and in the 1950s these senior-citizen centers proliferated. Their intended purpose was as socializing groups, but they also provided a convenient forum for political discussions, thereby promoting solidarity and raising political consciousness among older Americans. With three out of four American men over 65 no longer participating in the work force owing to forced retirement at a fixed age, a quarter of a million persons had joined these senior clubs by 1960 (Havighurst 1963).

Expressions of mutual frustration with the inadequacy of existing Social Security provisions flourished in these forums, contributing to a sense of commonality of fate and a budding realization of the potential strength of the groups' numbers. The Roosevelt administration's Social Security legislation had imposed an arbitrary definition of old age on American workers, forcing them to retire at a set age regardless of ability to continue in the work force. Passage of the act had fueled elderly expectations that it would henceforth be the duty of society to guarantee economic security in retirement. Inflation and rising costs of old-age health care were, however, leading increasing numbers of the aged to perceive a gap between the lofty rhetoric of Social Security and their personal reality of continued economic insecurity.

This growing perception of social injustice and common political identity among the elderly inspired the formation of a number of influential senior organizations of national scope. The National Retired Teachers Association was formed in 1947, followed by the National Council on the Aging in 1950, the American Association of Retired Persons in 1958, the National Council of Senior Citizens in 1961, and the National Caucus of the Black Aged in 1970. Other related organizations—such as the National Council of Senior Citizens, the National Association of Retired Federal Employees, and the retiree organization of the United Auto Workers—added their political clout and organizational resources to the burgeoning tide of pressure groups on Capitol Hill who could claim to represent hundreds of thousands of American voters.

The Labor-Senior Coalition

During this coalescence phase of the senior rights movement in the 1950s and 1960s, the political fortunes of the elderly were enhanced by the formation of a mutual alliance between the interests of old-age groups and American labor organizations. Earlier in the century this labor-senior alliance had unfortunately been absent. In the pension struggles of the 1920s and 1930s, organized labor had remained on the sidelines—too preoccupied with fundamental issues of union survival and right to organize to exert much pressure on behalf of social security for the elderly (Quadagno 1984a, 639–40). As American labor entered the depression decade, it was weak and ineffectual compared with organized labor in most other Western industrial nations. It possessed little organizational clout with which to extract meaningful concessions from management and the federal court system. The leadership of the American Federation of Labor was inclined to cooperate with management in a "welfare capitalism" arrangement that left the majority of unskilled workers in basic industries without an effective political instrument for genuine reforms. This general atmosphere of deference to management, together with the post–World War I climate of higher employment and political repression of unions, led to declines in AFL membership—from 4.1 million in 1920 to about 3 million in 1930. In the same decade, overall trade-union membership dropped from 5 million to 3.4 million (Axinn and Levin 1975, 161–71). Thus, while the struggle for old-age pensions was gaining momentum in the early 1930s, American unions were busy trying to reverse membership declines and become viable vehicles for the defense of workers' rights.

Eventually American labor organizations were able to regroup and turn the tides. This owed in part to the exigencies of the depression and Roosevelt's New Deal policies. But it took a decade of sustained struggle to extract meaningful concessions from management and government officials, who were often adamant in their determination to prevent unionization. The first real encouragement came with the passage of the Norris-La Guardia Act in 1932, which restricted the ability of federal courts to issue injunctions against unions that engaged in peaceful strikes. Further progress came in July 1935, when President Roosevelt signed into law the National Labor Relations Act (Wagner Act), empowering the newly created National Labor Relations Board to consider union complaints of unfair practices, outlaw company-dominated unions, and supervise union elections.

Each new inroad on behalf of American labor was met with counteroffensives by management and frequent court challenges of the constitutionality of the new laws. Despite these obstacles, by the end of the 1930s labor had managed to establish the right to organize and engage in mediated collective bargaining with management, as well as winning concessions on minimum wages, work hours, and child-labor practices. These symbolic victories in turn stimulated unions to organize and recruit new members, reversing the membership decline. By 1940, total union membership in the United States had rebounded to 10.6 million workers. Organized labor was becoming a major force in American politics, the electoral consequences of which politicians could no longer afford to ignore (Axinn and Levin 1975, 161–71, 172–73).

The relative absence of support from the ailing American Federation of Labor in the early 1930s had resulted in an old-age pension movement that, unlike the pattern in most other Western democracies, was primarily age-based rather than class-based, leaving political elites free to devise a social security package that required no fundamental restructuring of the existing socioeconomic order (Quadagno 1984a, 639–40). By the 1940s, however, the AFL's sympathies had shifted decisively in favor of support for public measures that would ensure the security of workers in retirement. The enactment of the Social Security legislation had inspired interest among American workers and labor leaders in the advantages of publicly administered retirement schemes over private pensions.

During the coalescence period of the modern senior rights movement, from roughly 1950 through 1965, efforts to achieve further old-age policy reforms were strengthened by the formation of a successful coalition between the newly rejuvenated labor organizations and emerging senior organizations. Both stood to gain from the arrangement. Younger workers sought assurances of security in old age. Older workers and retirees found their financial status affected by federal employment and unemployment policies. Medical insurance, pensions, disability insurance, workers' compensation, and unemployment insurance all involved an overlap between the interests of workers and elderly Americans. In the postwar era, United Auto Workers representative Charles Odell emerged as a prominent leader stressing the mutual interests of labor and the elderly, using their combined force to increase political leverage on the national scene. Another advocate of the rights of the aging worker during this era was Ethel Percy Andrus of the National Retired Teachers Association/American Association of Retired Persons (Pratt 1976).

By the early 1960s, the nationwide network of senior organizations was clearly beginning to coalesce into a potent lobby on Capitol Hill. The American Association of Retired Persons, the National Council of Senior Citizens, the National Association of Retired Federal Employees and other senior groups with nationwide clienteles joined forces with the United Auto Workers retiree organization and the AFL-CIO to take on the American Medical Association over the issue of medical insurance for the aged, taxpayer groups over Social Security hikes, and corporations over mandatory retirement provisions. Aided by the liberal climate of the times and public optimism over postwar prosperity, this alliance of the labor lobby and the emerging "gray lobby" in Washington was able to exert enough pressure on policy elites to achieve passage of landmark legislation such as the Medicare program (1965) and the Older Americans Act (1965).

The Legislative Battle for Medicare

The social forces at work during this period can be viewed most clearly in the struggle to achieve congressional approval of the Medicare package.[4] The Medicare legislation that was debated in Congress in the early 1960s was the culmination of a protracted struggle for old-age health insurance that spanned the administrations of five presidents—Roosevelt, Truman, Eisenhower, Kennedy, and Johnson. In Europe the precedent of national health care insurance had already been established by the turn of the century. Germany had provided health insurance for its elderly workers as early as 1883, when it enacted the Sickness Insurance Act in the time of Bismarck. In Great Britain, Lloyd George and the Liberal party passed the National Health Insurance Act in 1911, which provided medical insurance for low-income workers as part of a social security pension program (Rimlinger 1971, 87–136; Marmor 1973, 6–7).

Such advances had not come as easily in the American context, despite popular pressures for government involvement in health care that date back to the early years of the century. Between 1915 and 1918 the American Association for Labor Legislation attempted to secure passage of a medical insurance bill in several state legislatures, but the effort struck a rock. Well-entrenched local medical societies were vehemently opposed to the medical insurance bills. In 1920 the House of Delegates of the American Medical Association voiced in no uncertain terms its opposition to "any plan embodying the system of compulsory contributory insurance against illness . . . which provides for medical service to be rendered to contributors or their dependents, provided, controlled, or regulated by any state or federal government" (quoted in Feingold 1966, 89). The cause was further weakened when the American Federation of Labor, under the leadership of president Samuel Gompers, declined to support the AALL's health insurance proposals (Marmor 1973, 7–8).

The first genuine attempt to move in the direction of public health insurance for the aged came when President Franklin Roosevelt and his advisory Committee on Economic Security briefly considered adding a medical insurance clause to the proposed Social Security bill. The inclusion of a single line in the bill, which suggested that the Social Security Board study the possibility and then report to Congress, caused such an uproar that the clause was promptly withdrawn. As Edwin Witte, executive director of the committee, explained, "That little line was responsible for so many telegrams to the members of Congress that the entire social security program seemed endangered until the Ways and Means Committee unanimously struck it out of the bill" (Feingold 1966, 90).

By 1940 every nation in Western Europe had adopted a national heath care insurance program for at least its low-income citizens, and most of these plans were quite comprehensive in scope (Kudrle and Marmor 1981, 82–83, 103–107). National opinion polls taken in the United States between 1940 and the passage of Medicare in 1965 consistently showed approximately two-thirds of Americans to be in favor of government-sponsored health care (Schwarz 1988, 139). Why, then, in the American context was another quarter of a century required to finally achieve passage of a scaled-down version of hospital insurance, with substantial restrictions on the extent of coverage and benefits?

The answer lies—as it had earlier in the century—in a series of counteroffensives launched by special-interest lobbies on Capitol Hill designed to protect the financial stakes of the medical profession and related hospital and drug industries. Throughout the 1940s bills proposing health insurance coverage for American citizens were regularly introduced in Congress on an annual basis. Despite widespread popular support, frequent Democratic majorities in Congress, and strong endorsement of the idea by President Truman and his advisors, the various national health insurance proposals were invariably "killed in committee" early in the legislative obstacle course, long before they could reach the floor of the House or Senate for serious debate. Intense lobbying campaigns by pressure groups representing the medical-industrial establishment, together with unyielding ideological opposition by congressional Republicans and southern Democrats, succeeded in effectively blocking consideration of any health insurance proposal that might involve government interference with the prerogatives of the private, profit-oriented health care industry in the United States (Marmor 1981, 105–11; Bowler 1987, 202–203).

The prospects for health care reform became even bleaker during the early Eisenhower years. Eisenhower had made it clear during his 1952 campaign that he was opposed to "socialized medicine" in any form. Without the momentum of presidential endorsement, the issue languished during the 1950s, with no realistic chance of receiving consideration on Capitol Hill.

By the late 1950s, however, the legislative equation in Congress working against national health insurance had begun to change. One important element that had changed was the content of the proposed medical care package. Reformers, unable to push a comprehensive national health insurance proposal through Congress in repeated attempts, had shifted to an "incremental" strategy. The new strategy, pioneered in the early 1950s by Federal Security Agency officials Oscar Ewing, Wilbur Cohen, and I. S. Falk, was to "resurrect health insurance" in a narrower, less objectionable form that would limit coverage to beneficiaries of the Old Age and Survivors Insurance program, thereby bypassing enough of the resistance to the national health care idea to ensure an issue majority in Congress for the scaled-down version of the bill. Once passage was achieved, and the precedent of a right of access to public health care established, advocates of the new approach assumed that coverage could then gradually be extended in increments until the entire population was covered. The slow increments in coverage would presumably leave no overt crisis points around which to rally a strong conservative opposition to "socialized medicine." Wilbur Cohen described the revised health insurance plan as "a small way of starting something big."[5] Oscar Ewing surmised that it was unlikely that "anyone with a heart" could oppose a program of limited medical insurance for the aged (Marmor 1981, 107–8).

Another element in the legislative equation that had changed in the interim was the emergence of a new labor-senior alliance in Washington. Between 1958 and 1965 the United Auto Workers retiree organization and the AFL-CIO joined forces with the American Association of Retired Persons, the National Council of Senior Citizens, and other senior advocates in increasingly aggressive lobbying efforts to secure passage of some form of national health insurance. This labor-senior coalition found itself up against the American Medical Association and affiliated health care industry, business, and conservative organizations that, for financial and ideological reasons, were opposed to the idea of federal financing of medical care (Bowler 1987, 202).

With the ascendance of Massachusetts senator John F. Kennedy to the presidency in the 1961, the prospects for passage of a major old-age medical insurance bill began to look brighter. During his campaign, Kennedy had promised to actively promote a compulsory medical plan for Social Security beneficiaries. Shortly after his inauguration, Kennedy asked Wilbur Cohen to head a task force to draft a Medicare proposal for introduction in the first session of the 87th Congress. In his presidential message to Congress of 9 February 1961, Kennedy proposed that social security benefits be extended to cover hospital and nursing home costs of the elderly. Anticipating the probable use of McCarthy-style red-scare tactics by the bill's conservative opponents, Kennedy emphasized to Congress and the American public that the new program was "not socialized medicine" but rather "a new program of prepayment for health costs with absolute freedom of choice guaranteed," in which "every person will choose his own doctor and hospital" (*New York Times* 10 February 1961).

With the issue now a top priority on the domestic agenda of a favorably disposed president, ideological polarization over the merits of the proposed legislation quickly set in on Capitol Hill. A counteralliance was formed between Republicans and conservative southern Democrats to ward off "the entering wedge of the socialized state." Unlike the congressional battle over Social Security earlier in the century, the issue this time was interpreted by both ideological camps as a redistributive one in terms of its potential for altering the allocation of benefits and burdens among socioeconomic groups. Pressure

group alignments on both sides of the issue therefore reflected a high
degree of polarization along class-based lines (Marmor 1973, 107–24).

The battle over the proposed Medicare law rapidly developed into a
classic congressional confrontation between representatives of money-
providing and service-demanding sectors of American society,
between haves and have-nots, which assumed the form of an ideologically charged debate over "socialized medicine" versus "the American
way" (Lowi 1964, 689, 711, 715; Wildavsky 1962, 5–6, 304–5). In a typical exchange, the president of the American Medical Association, testifying before the House Ways and Means Committee, charged that
publicly provided medical care for the elderly would be "dangerous to
the principles underlying our American system of medical care" (quoted in Marmor 1969, 21). The degree of class-based ideological polarization could be plainly seen in the pattern of national interest-group
alignments among organizations actively lobbying for and against the
legislation:[6]

HEALTH INDUSTRY COALITION AGAINST MEDICARE	LABOR-SENIOR COALITION FOR MEDICARE
American Medical Association	American Federation of Labor/ Congress of Industrial Organizations
American Hospital Association	American Association of Retired Workers
National Association of of Manufacturers	National Council of Senior Citizens
Chamber of Commerce	American Geriatrics Society
National Association of Blue Shield Plans	American Nurses Association
American Legion	National Association of Retired Persons
Life Insurance Association of America	National Farmers Union
American Farm Bureau Federation	

Unfortunately for proponents of the legislation, however, Ways and
Means Committee chairman Wilbur Mills was in a position to play a
decisive role in determining the fate of the 1961 Medicare legislation.

Mills, a conservative Arkansas Democrat who was generally hostile to the idea of comprehensive national health insurance, allowed the bill to die a quiet death in committee during that session of Congress—without the issue ever coming up for a vote. President Kennedy, meanwhile, had turned his attention to other pressing priorities of his administration and did not pursue the issue further during the remainder of his tenure.

The Incremental Strategy Backfires

Several years later, with the landslide victory of Lyndon Johnson over Barry Goldwater in the 1964 presidential election, congressional enactment of the Medicare bill finally appeared within reach. Democrats had gained 32 new House seats in the 1964 contest, giving liberals the largest Democratic majority in the House of Representatives since 1936. Not since the early Roosevelt years had nonsouthern Democratic liberals constituted a viable majority in the House and the Senate. Moreover, Johnson was as favorably disposed toward the goal of federal health insurance legislation as Kennedy had been, and the existence of the liberal congressional majority virtually ensured passage of most of his new social agenda.

National senior organizations, frustrated by obstructionist tactics that had bogged down the Medicare bill in committee during the Kennedy years, vowed to make certain the scenario would not repeat itself. Leaders of the National Council of Senior Citizens mobilized 1,400 elderly Americans to attend the opening session of the 89th Congress in 1965 to pressure Speaker John McCormack, a Massachusetts Democrat, to keep his promise to appoint a pro-Medicare majority on the House Ways and Means Committee (Lammers 1983, 157).

With enactment of some form of national health insurance now apparently unavoidable, congressional conservatives and health industry lobbyists abruptly switched strategies, focusing their attention instead on molding the final form of the inevitable health insurance bill. Because the American congressional policymaking process is inherently decentralized and fragmented, with numerous decision points in the shaping of legislation, AMA lobbyists, Republican committee members, and conservative southern Democrats were able to ensure that they would play a formative role in drafting the bill that ultimately emerged from the House Ways and Means Committee (Bowler 1987, 202).

Despite their numerical disadvantage—they now held the smallest proportion of seats in the House since the depression days— Republicans on the Ways and Means Committee were able to work in concert with conservative southern Democrats to force several key compromises in the nature of the final legislation, thereby restricting its scope and limiting future policy options. Conservatives were concerned that the incremental strategy of universal health insurance advocates might work, with Medicare for the elderly becoming only the first installment in what would eventually become a costly comprehensive health-care system covering all segments of the population. In what at first glance appeared to be a charitable change of heart, chairman Wilbur Mills befuddled his liberal opponents on the committee by unexpectedly adding Title 19 to the bill, establishing an additional medical insurance program to be known as "Medicaid" for all low-income persons, regardless of age, who were eligible for public assistance. Mills later revealed, in a 1965 interview, his motives for supporting the revision. Inclusion in the bill of a separate medical program for low-income citizens of all ages would, he predicted, "build a fence around the Medicare program" by successfully undercutting any future incremental proposals seeking to expand the old-age medical insurance provisions to cover other income and age groups (Marmor 1981, 127).

Once again, as in the heyday of Social Security, policy elites favoring dominant societal interests and seeking to preserve the economic status quo had managed to circumvent attempts to achieve fundamental reform through the skillful co-optation of selected portions of the movement's reform program. If conservative congressmen, the AMA, and health industry lobbyists could not prevent the enactment of Medicare, they could nevertheless still use their clout to prevent the loss of vested health industry prerogatives within the American economy. This could be accomplished by effectively dominating the formulation and implementation stages of the new legislation.

That a move was afoot to do exactly that could be seen in the size of AMA lobbying expenditures and media campaigns to alter public opinion during this period. In 1965 alone, the American Medical Association's organizational expeditures totalled over $20 million, including extravagant allocations for lobbying efforts on Capitol Hill, for the AMA's Political Action Committee (AMPAC), and for "public education" campaigns. In the same year AMA lobbyists spent $830,000 for a variety of carefully orchestrated television, radio, and newspaper spots in an effort to mobilize public opinion against the proposed legislation (Marmor 1981, 113–14, 127).

This would be no easy task. National opinion surveys conducted between 1943 and 1965 had consistently shown more than a two-to-one majority of Americans in favor of the idea of government-financed health care (Cantril 1952, 439–44; Schwarz 1988, 139). The American Medical Association's "public education" campaign sought to convince the American public that health-care professionals, as scientific authorities, were best able to judge what should constitute the proper form of administration, regulation, and financing arrangements for health-care practice in the United States. A related strategy involved portraying "the Medicare idea" to the public in such a way as to meet with the widest possible range of objections across different groups in American society. AMA lobbyists sought to combine resistance from business and fraternal groups, health-related industries, professional organizations, taxpayers, agribusiness, and right-wing reactionary organizations, using diverse media appeals designed to associate Medicare in the public mind with higher taxes, bloated bureaucracy, uncontrollable welfare expenditures, loss of freedom of choice, and collectivism (Marmor 1973, 25–26).

While these clarion calls of creeping socialism were sounding in the media, health industry lobbyists were busy on Capitol Hill extracting further concessions from liberal Medicare proponents on the final shape that the bill would take. Lobbyists repeatedly warned legislators that a bill whose terms were too harsh for the medical establishment would lead to widespread noncooperation among American physicians and hospital administrators in implementing Medicare. Fearing that doctors would act on these threats and undermine implementation, the Ways and Means Committee incorporated into its version of the bill Republican John Byrnes's proposal of voluntary and premium-financed physician coverage (Part B of Medicare). The phrasing carefully sidestepped the issue of a set fee schedule for physcans, specifying instead that physicians be reimbursed according to "reasonable charges," and that hospitals be paid on the basis of "cost." Both were to be paid their "usual and customary fee." Because physicians and hospitals would be permitted to bill Medicare patients directly, instead of billing the program, there was no effective limit on the amount that could be charged beyond the government reimbursement level (Bowler 1987, 203; DeSario 1987, 226–28). The success of the American Medical Association, American Hospital Association, and Blue Cross lobbies in extracting this concession on reimbursement provisions further demonstrates the extent to which health industry spokesmen, in conjuction with Republicans and conservative southern Democrats, were able to "rewrite" the Medicare bill that finally emerged from Congress to their specifications—despite a liberal majority in both houses and a liberal Democrat in the White House.

When the altered Medicare-Medicaid bill reached the Finance Committee of the Senate in July of 1965, Senator Clinton Anderson abruptly attacked the reimbursement provisions, pointing out (with considerable foresight) that to pay doctors their "usual and customary fees" for medical treatment of the aged would "significantly and unnecessarily inflate the cost of the program to the taxpayer and the aged." He further protested that this unspecified fee arrangement would amount to an "open-ended payment" scheme. Health industry spokesmen reacted defensively to Anderson's criticisms, arousing sufficient anxiety among Finance Committee members over the potential for a physician's boycott that Senate proponents of Medicare were inclined to drop the volatile issue of physician's fees rather than imperil the entire package.

The revised Medicare package passed the Senate by a margin of 68 to 21, and was then submitted to the joint conference committee. There, more than 500 differences between House and Senate versions were meticulously reconciled. The final version of the Medicare bill that emerged from conference passed in the House on 27 July by a 307 to 116 vote, and in the Senate on 29 July by a 70 to 24 margin (Marmor 1981, 127–29).

The Rhetoric-Reality Gap Revisited

President Lyndon Johnson finally signed the compromise Medicare-Medicaid bill into law on 30 July 1965 at a ceremony in Independence, Missouri, in the presence of former President Harry Truman, who had unsuccessfully attempted to pass a similar law two decades earlier. Reflecting back on a protracted struggle for old age medical insurance that had spanned five administrations, Johnson commented that the remarkable thing was not the passage of the bill "but that it took so many years to pass it" (Marmor 1969, 3). As with the enactment of Social Security 30 years earlier, the successful passage of the

Medicare-Medicaid package would prove to be a bittersweet victory for senior rights advocates. In one sense, it clearly constituted another important step toward realization of the goals of the movement. The labor-senior coalition had demonstrated its effectiveness in lobbying on Capitol Hill for reforms in policies affecting older Americans. This represented a quantum leap in the clout of the elderly as a national political force. Challenging the AMA and health industry interests over the issue of old-age medical insurance had given the new "gray lobby" a degree of credibility, legitimacy, and national exposure that, over the next decade, would enable it to effectively take on major corporations over mandatory retirement provisions and taxpayers over Social Security cost-of-living adjustments.

As had been the case earlier in the century with the Social Security Act, however, the enactment of Medicare was also followed by a growing sense of disappointment with the inadequacies of the law. The credibility gap between rhetoric and reality began to reemerge as attempts were made to implement the flawed legislation. Yale health-policy specialist Theodore Marmor pointed to the restricted scope and idiosyncratic features of the new American medical insurance package, scolding that "were a European to reflect upon this episode . . . his attention would be directed to the narrow range within which government health proposals operated. He would emphasize that no European nation restricted its health insurance programs to one age-group" (Marmor 1969, 60). The federal health insurance law that had finally passed Congress in 1965 as Title XVIII of the Social Security Act was a scaled-down version of limited medical insurance for the elderly (Medicare) and the indigent (Medicaid) only. In its final form it incorporated more than 80 revisions designed to satisfy economic demands imposed by the health industry and conservative lawmakers in the course of the development of the legislation. The AMA and affiliated organizations had marshalled millions of dollars in lobbying and media appeals to ensure that the emergent law would not threaten their continued dominance over the provision of medical services in the United States.

The prolonged and divisive tug-of-war had taken its toll on the bill's provisions. Unlike the comprehensive, cradle-to-grave systems prevalent in other industrialized countries, in which provisions for the elderly were conceived as part of a broad national health-care plan for the entire citizenry, the new American Medicare law was based on a restricted social insurance model designed to partially offset the costs of health care for the elderly and some of the disabled, with Medicaid as a separate "public assistance" program aimed at the indigent. By segmenting the health-care interests of the population in this manner, Ways and Means Committee chairman Wilbur Mills's "Medicaid" strategy had succeeded in its objective of "building a fence around the Medicare program," preempting potential future incremental demands for liberalization and extension of coverage. The "incremental" strategy espoused by comprehensive national health care advocates Wilbur Cohen and Oscar Ewing in the 1950s had clearly backfired. Liberal reformers now found themselves painted into a corner—unable to find justification for subsequent expansion. As with Social Security earlier in the century, political elites representing the interests of privileged segments of the socioeconomic order had again managed to forestall the introduction of European-style redistributive federal programs by carefully preserving the dichotomy between "social insurance" and "public assistance," thereby keeping the various government programs separate, limited, and categorical.

Under an intentionally restrictive and fragmented national medical insurance arrangement of this sort, adequate satisfaction of elderly health-care needs was unlikely, and bureaucratic inefficiency and extravagant costs were all but inevitable in the implementation phase. As with Social Security, many of the problems of effectively administering the program stemmed from the persistence of the private insurance model as a blueprint for implementing the legislation. Congressional insistence on financing Medicare as an adjunct of the Social Security program continued the practice of treating the state as an impartial, nonredistributive administrator in a "contributory" retirement system—avoiding as much as possible the redistributive repercussions of using general tax revenues to fund the program. The modest revenues obtainable through this approach to financing in turn forced Medicare administrators to emphasize cost-containment in the design of policy rather than the original objectives of improving access to care and quality of services for elderly Americans.

Because Medicare was designed to pay only a restricted portion of an elderly person's medical expenses resulting from the most serious illnesses, many of the most common and chronic health-care needs of the elderly were not covered. Even by the mid-1980s, 20 years after its passage, the American Medicare program still did not cover medicine and drugs (with or without a prescription), eye examinations and eyeglasses, hearing examinations and hearing aides, dental care, self-administered injections (e.g., insulin), immunizations, foot care, and full-time nursing in the home. In short, most of the parts of the human body that are prone to deteriorate with age and require frequent and ongoing medical attention were intentionally excluded from coverage as a cost-containment measure.[7] Moreover, the Medicare law placed both a dollar limit and a time limit on coverage for the aged. As a result of these restrictions, many elderly Americans who had assumed they were "covered" by the Medicare program found themselves faced in old age with large, unanticipated out-of-pocket medical bills. After two decades of program development, older Americans and their families still found themselves paying—out of personal financial resources—an average 41.6 percent of nursing home costs, 6 percent of hospital costs, and 31.3 percent of other medical services as a result of these gaps in Medicare. Overall, when deductibles and co-insurance were excluded, the Medicare program was paying for only 38 percent of the total health-care expenses of elderly Americans as of the mid-1980s (Waldo and Lazenby 1984; Sulvetta and Swartz 1986).

Another flaw in the new Medicare law that left senior advocates deeply disillusioned was the tendency of the open-ended reimbursement provisions to encourage escalation in the costs of medical care. In anticipation of the windfall of Medicare-related revenues, physicians' "customary and reasonable" fees more than doubled in the year between the passage of Medicare and its initial implementation. Similarly, between July 1966 and July 1967 hospital charges rose by an unprecedented 22 percent. John Gardner, secretary of the Department of Health, Education, and Welfare, revealed in a 1967 report that the primary source of the increase had been a "re-examination" of hospital charges to patients in anticipation of federal Medicare payments (Marmor 1969, 64).

Ironically, those who had been the most outspoken critics of the Medicare legislation prior to its passage in 1965 became its chief beneficiaries in the implementation phase that followed. The "usual, customary, and reasonable" fees standard for reimbursing doctors and hospitals, which Congress had included in the bill to appease the health-care industry, enabled physicians and hospitals to increase profits by inflating prices for medical procedures and by ordering additional services for elderly patients. This process in turn led to inflationary spirals in the cost of health care that reverberated throughout the health-care system and the economy, contributing to consistently higher rates of inflation in the health care sector than in the economy at large.

Over a period of 10 years following enactment of Medicare, total health care expenditures more than tripled, increasing from $42 billion in 1965 to $133 billion in 1975. Federal health expenditures increased sevenfold during the same period, leaping from $5.5 billion in 1965 to $37 billion in 1975 (Waldo, Levit, and Lazenby 1986, 14). Considered on the individual level, this meant an average yearly health bill for each American of $146.30 in 1960 had escalated to $1,067 in 1980, clearly accelerating at a much faster rate than that of inflation. By the 1980s this dramatic rise in health care costs in the United States was beginning to create formidable financial barriers to health care, not only for the elderly and the poor but for large segments of the American population (DeSario 1987, 226–27). The political instincts of Senator Clinton Anderson—who back in July 1965 had warned the Finance Committee against permitting physicians to charge their "usual and customary fees"—had unfortunately been on target.

Chapter Six

The Institutionalization of Policy Reform

Gray Lobbies, White House Conferences, and the Aging Enterprise

> *The Democratic Party is the only party that gives a damn about your grandmother.*
>
> Hubert H. Humphrey, 1972[1]

> *Your social security payment has been increased by 20 percent, starting with this month's check, by a new statute . . . signed into law by President Richard Nixon on July 1, 1972.*
>
> letter accompanying 24,760,000 Social Security checks several days prior to the 1972 presidential election[2]

The battles for Social Security in the 1920s and 1930s and Medicare in the 1960s had been fought by reform advocates who applied political pressure on reluctant elites from "outside" the established policy-making apparatus. From the mid-1960s on, however, this antagonistic method of accomplishing old-age policy reforms began to give way to a more inclusive, accommodative pattern. The senior rights movement, having earned considerable popular recognition in the course of its earlier struggles, was now entering a more mature phase. According to Mauss, once established political structures have been

forced to officially recognize the legitimacy of a social reform movement and begin to devise routine measures and ongoing structures
for dealing with the social injustices highlighted by the movement,
one can speak of the movement as having entered the "institutionalization" phase. In this more advanced stage of development, the
movement typically has acquired considerable resources with which
to press its demands. By this point it has managed to build a well-
coordinated, broad-based organizational network for social change,
characterized by a sophisticated division of labor and a formidable
membership base. These expanded organizational resources are
used to launch periodic thrusts into the political process, in the form
of lobbying and electoral pressures on policymakers.

Given the movement's enhanced capacity for mounting credible
threats in pursuit of its ends, public officials and the mass media must
now take the movement's demands more seriously, and may even find
themselves competing for its favor. Prominent movement leaders
become frequent invited speakers at universities, community meetings, and media events. In an effort to head off even more fundamental
changes in the social order, policymaking elites find it necessary to
introduce and pass sweeping ameliorative legislation. New commis-
sions, legislative committees, and government agencies representing
the interests of the movement's constituency are created, and some of
the movement's proposed programs of reform are officially adopted. In
the process, policy objectives put forth by movement advocates
become an integral part of the established institutions that had formerly opposed them. A social movement at this stage of development is at
its point of greatest potential influence over the making and implementation of policy, having graduated from being a mere "input" into the
established policymaking apparatus to being a "withinput" (Easton
1965; Heisler and Kvavik 1974).

Ironically for the movement, however, the institutionalization
process also brings with it a number of unwanted side effects, which
tend to co-opt and undermine the vitality of further attempts at
reform. One problem for reformers is that this process of institutionalization of the movement does not automatically imply the concomitant institutionalization of its proposed program of change. Still, it
nonetheless creates the *appearance* that policy change has already
occurred, thereby undermining popular support for additional
reforms—though many problems addressed by the movement may in
fact remain unsolved.

A related dilemma for reform advocates is that turning over the reins of reform to a newly created agency located "within" the official governmental structure requires trusting members of the establishment to carry out the desired policy changes over time. Not only does this bureaucratization of the movement's demands for change rob the movement of its previous basis for popular appeal—its reform agenda—but it also simultaneously creates a condition in which opponents of reform can easily orchestrate symbolic overatures of "progress" for popular consumption while in fact doing little or nothing to ameliorate the social problems that gave rise to the movement. The institutionalization stage in the history of a social movement is therefore paradoxically both the movement's point of greatest potency *and* its point of greatest vulnerability to neutralization of that potency by opponents of reform.

The process of institutionalization of the senior rights movement—which reached critical mass in the mid-1960s and continued through the 1970s—took place concurrently in several overlapping political domains, each of which we shall discuss in turn. These included (1) the development of a coordinated national network of senior advocacy organizations, enabling the movement and its sympathizers to apply continuous electoral and lobbying pressures on lawmakers; (2) the initiation of regular White House Conferences on Aging, to periodically sound out elderly grievances and consider proposals for reform; (3) the creation of a permanent bureaucratic structure, the Administration on Aging, within the executive branch of the federal government, to represent ongoing elderly interests; and (4) the emergence of a nationwide cadre of professionals, in a variety of aging-related fields, with a vested interest in promoting programs and services for older Americans—a group Carroll Estes has aptly dubbed "the aging enterprise."[3]

Consolidation of Electoral and Interest-Group Pressures

One crucial domain in which the clout of older Americans expanded dramatically during the 1960s and 1970s was in their ability to systematically apply organized pressure on political candidates and officeholders. Earlier in the century, during the struggle for old-age pensions, elderly-backed candidate John McGroarty had demonstrated the potential leverage that unified older voters could command—successfully unseating an incumbent congressman in the Long Beach election in California. The outcome of the Long Beach election had sent a clear signal to public officials that the political influence of older voters and elderly sympathizers could pose a significant electoral threat if ignored, and this pressure on elites had been a factor in hastening passage of Social Security. Until the 1960s, however, such episodes of unified voter strength were the exception rather than the rule in local and national electoral contests.

As aging issues increasingly became the focus of national attention and welfare state expansion in the post–World War II era, politicians, political parties, and the media found themselves paying closer attention to elderly voters as a constituency. The Democratic party created a campaign organization in the 1960 election called Senior Citizens for Kennedy (within the broader umbrella organization Citizens for Kennedy) in order to lull older voters into the Democratic camp. (Until the late 1950s, Republican candidates had generally taken the traditional relationship between senior citizens and their party for granted.) The national campaign headquarters of Senior Citizens for Kennedy enthusiastically undertook a variety of political activities, including support for Kennedy's presidential bid, generating publicity in the media, lobbying for age-related causes, and doing educational work within the party.

This symbolic recognition by the Democratic party in 1960, acknowledging that older voters now comprised a significant electoral force, marked an important juncture in the advancement of senior clout and political activism, leading in subsequent elections to enlarged efforts by political elites to court older voters (Pratt 1976, 56–73). During the Great Society era the elderly became a highly visible beneficiary group, resulting in a greater public awareness of, and concern for, their needs and social rights. As federal involvement with old-age issues rapidly expanded in the mid-1960s and early 1970s— with the passage of Medicare, the Older Americans Act, Supplemental Security Income, and other Social Security reforms—both political parties found it increasingly difficult to disregard the potential impact of the elderly vote on their political fortunes. In an electoral appeal characteristic of the period, Senator Hubert Humphrey attempted to persuade citizens to vote for Democratic presidential candidate George McGovern in the 1972 election by raising the politically sensitive issue of government support for the nation's elderly: "Take a good look at these two men [George McGovern and Richard Nixon]. Which one of these two men do you feel would be more likely to sit down with you and discuss the problem of your grandmother? Which one is likely to be sympathetic and understanding about your grandmother? I'll tell you. George McGovern, the Democrat, that's who" (Heffernan and Maynard 1977, 73).

The problems of old age had clearly become pivotal, mainstream concerns in American electoral politics, to which both parties were increasingly addressing their electoral appeals. Republican politicians, too, had discovered during the 1960s and 1970s that they depended on the elderly vote to stay in office. They suddenly found themselves vying with Democrats for the attention and allegiance of a constituency that in the 1950s they had solidly taken for granted. Perhaps the classic instance of Republican attempts to recapture the senior vote from the Democrats was President Richard Nixon's gesture of reassurance to the nation's Social Security recipients just prior to the 1972 election. Nixon, who was running for reelection against Democrat George McGovern, carefully timed a mass mailing of Social Security checks to elderly beneficiaries—containing a recently enacted 20 percent increase in benefits—to arrive shortly before the election. The checks were accompanied by a brief letter explaining that the increase was the result of a new statute "signed into law by President Richard Nixon" (Tufte 1978, 30–36, 39–55). The letter, received by 24,760,000 elderly beneficiaries, went on to say that "the President also signed into law a provision which will allow your social security benefits to increase automatically if the cost of living goes up. Automatic benefit increases will be added to your check in future years according to the conditions set out in that law" (U.S. Department of Health, Education, and Welfare 1972).

Equally revealing of the growing importance of the senior vote was the precampaign tug-of-war between candidates to make political hay out of the benefit increases in that election year. In 1971 President Nixon, with an eye toward the upcoming election, first proposed a 5 percent increase for the 1972 year. (Note that even this minor increase was contrary to his frequently stated economic principles.) The increase easily passed the House, where Wilbur Mills promptly claimed credit for "guiding through" the legislation.

As campaigning for the primaries began in the early months of 1972, Maine Senator Edmund Muskie—who hoped to gain an edge leading into the New Hampshire primary—announced that he was proposing a 15 percent increase in Social Security benefits. Not to be upstaged, Wilbur Mills—himself a candidate in the primaries—then proposed a 20 percent increase. Still prior to the first primary, Muskie then joined Mills in advocating a 20 percent increase. Between the New Hampshire and Wisconsin primaries, Minnesota Senator Hubert Humphrey topped both by offering a 25 percent increase. By the first of July, a 20 percent increase had easily passed both the House and the Senate, despite threats of a possible presidential veto. Lawmakers of both parties and in both bodies rushed to be on record as supporting the legislation in an election year (Tufte 1978, 35–36).

A more recent illustration of the expanded clout wielded by older voters during the institutionalization phase—in many respects paralleling the earlier Long Beach election—could be glimpsed in a 1980 electoral contest in Oregon. Ron Wyden, a young Democrat who was well known as a local leader in the Gray Panthers organization, chose to use symbolic overtures to older voters and their sympathizers as a centerpiece of his campaign strategy. By stressing elderly issues and his ties to the Gray Panthers in his media appeals, Wyden—though a political rookie still in his twenties—was able to defy the odds, winning first an unlikely primary victory and then an upset victory in the general election over six-year incumbent Representative Bob Duncan (Barone and Ujifusa 1982).

Such concerted efforts by political candidates to capture the hearts and minds of older voters attest to the considerable electoral leverage enjoyed by the elderly during the institutionalization stage of the senior rights movement. Yet much of the important old-age legislation of the Great Society period probably owed less to these periodic electoral threats per se than to sustained interest-group pressures on lawmakers. It was, for example, in the period *between* elections that the two major legislative landmarks of the Great Society—Medicare (1965) and the Older Americans Act (1965) became law. These reform packages went into effect not during an election year but sometime afterward. As we saw in Chapter 5, the moving force behind the eventual passage of the Medicare proposal was unrelenting pressure from a cohesive national network of elderly interest organizations and their political allies. Without these ongoing senior advocacy organizations to keep up the pressure on policymaking elites, sporadic electoral threats would have produced few lasting results.

The background against which these electoral forays took place in the 1960s and 1970s, then, was one of greatly increased organizational strength in support of elderly interests. This favorable setting during the institutionalization stage was in stark contrast to conditions that had prevailed earlier in the century. As we observed in Chapter 3, the fledgling senior rights movement that developed in the 1920s and 1930s around the issue of old-age pensions had been fragile and poorly organized. Few of the age-based interest groups that formed in California during that era had managed to survive beyond the end of the 1930s as effective agents for change. Upton Sinclair's End Poverty in California organization withered in the years following his defeat in a 1934 gubernatorial bid. The Townsend organization and the McClain group both declined rapidly in the wake of Roosevelt's legislative coup de grace of 1935. The enactment of Social Security had effectively deprived age-based interest groups of their central reform appeal—at least temporarily.

In the longer view, however, the Social Security Act had also provided age-based groups with a more clearly defined identity around which to unite politically. Subsequent disillusionment among the nation's elderly with the deficiencies of the act supplied a source of common grievances. By arbitrarily pushing older workers out of the work force, it had engendered a new form of socially created dependency. Moreover, by setting an arbitrary retirement age, the Social Security Act had inadvertently circumscribed the problems of persons over 65 as a distinct set of social problems. As such it provided a coherent basis for their solidarity and common identity and gave a newfound sense of legitimacy to elderly demands for social justice.

As the financial deficiencies of Social Security became apparent in the 1940s and 1950s, new organized interests began to coalesce. Among these second-wave senior organizations to emerge in the post–World War II period were the National Association of Retired Persons, the National Council on Aging, the National Association of Retired Federal Employees, the National Council of Senior Citizens, the Gray Panthers, and a number of labor union–related groups. Unlike their counterparts in the 1920s and 1930s, these new groups quickly amassed an impressive national membership base and proceeded to construct a sophisticated nationwide "aging network" of interrelated organizations, many of which maintained effective lobbying arms in Washington.[4]

By virtue of their organizational cohesiveness and their claim to represent millions of older Americans, the component groups in this new aging network were able to exert pressure on lawmakers much more effectively and systematically than had their depression-era forerunners. The legislative victories of the 1960s—Medicare and the Older

Americans Act—as well as the Social Security amendments and cost-of-living increases of the 1970s, were largely the product of intense lobbying efforts by this powerful new "gray lobby" on Capitol Hill. Assessing the effectiveness of this new senior lobby, one Washington observer commented that "to find lobbying skills equal to those of organizations that represent the elderly, you have to go to someone with a gun"—that is, defense contractors, the National Rifle Association (David Hapgood, quoted in Fischer 1979). And in the early 1970s the Nixon administration was so obsessed with the expanding political leverage of the National Council of Senior Citizens that the group was placed on the notorious White House "enemies list."

The American Association of Retired Persons By far the largest interest organization to emerge within the postwar senior alliance was the American Association of Retired Persons (AARP).[5] A retired California high school principal, Dr. Ethel Percy Andrus, founded the parent organization of the AARP—the National Retired Teachers Association (NRTA)—in 1947. The initial concern of the NRTA was to seek legislative reform of tax and pension programs affecting retired educators. By 1955 the NRTA had grown to a membership of more than 20,000. In that year Andrus joined forces with New York insurance agent Leonard Davis in order to offer group life insurance—and eventually also health insurance—to NRTA members. The life insurance option became so popular that the AARP was founded in 1958 to accommodate persons outside the teaching profession who were interested in participating in the benefit program. The combined organization was known as the National Retired Teachers Association–American Association of Retired Persons (NRTA–AARP) until 1982, when the NRTA component became a subdivision of the more inclusive AARP.

The initial attractions of the organization to elderly persons were essentially nonpolitical, as were its goals. The purpose of the group was originally directed toward improving the social image of retirees and raising their status. In addition to the life and health insurance plans, special membership benefits included a bimonthly magazine—*Modern Maturity* (now the most widely circulated magazine in the United States)—newsletters, travel benefits, tax counseling, education and training services, prescriptions, an auto club, and driver reeducation.

Its phenomenal popularity rapidly made the AARP one of the largest voluntary organizations represented on Capitol Hill. In recent years its activities have become increasingly political in emphasis, centering on opposition to compulsory retirement, and efforts to improve pensions and Social Security benefits. To construct a large, unified membership, the AARP has focused on widely shared member goals of this sort, which are unlikely to divide participants. Recruitment has been achieved over the years through a number of devices, including advertisements in the mass media, direct mailings to prospective members, and campaigns in local AARP chapters. The result has been an impressive alliance of the elderly, which by the mid-1990s had become more than 30 million strong and was growing at the rate of approximately 8,000 persons a day. One of every five U.S. voters now belongs to the AARP (Powell 1995).

Given its roots as a professional, rather than labor-based, retiree organization, the AARP has primarily identified with the interests of white-collar, middle-class, professional-status retirees. In contrast to the more ideologically liberal National Council of Senior Citizens and the radical Gray Panthers, the AARP has generally taken nonpartisan stances in national electoral politics. Although the AARP has maintained some informal ties with the Republican party, particularly in its early years, the leadership has generally avoided any implication of close partisan identification. One reason for the neutral stance has been the need to avoid jeopardizing the organization's tax-free status with the Internal Revenue Service by endorsing candidates. Another reason for remaining overtly neutral is the utility for the organization of maintaining a noncommittal strategy that forces the two major parties to compete for its favor (Binstock 1981).

Owing primarily to its colossal membership and revenue base (operating revenues in 1990 were over $295 million), the AARP is able to maintain a sophisticated, full-time lobbying contingent in Washington. Lobbying groups have also been formed in all of the 50 states, and the group has sought to construct a political organization in every U.S. congressional district (Powell 1995a).

The National Council of Senior Citizens The second largest mass-membership group, the National Council of Senior Citizens (NCSC), though officially also nonpartisan, has generally made its political affinities rather more obvious.[6] The NCSC developed out of the Senior Citizens for Kennedy clubs in the 1960 presidential campaign and the early 1960s struggle to pass Medicare legislation. Owing to strong initial ties with labor unions, the NCSC has generally been more working-class than middle-class professional in orientation, and has been (unofficially) pro–Democratic party in electoral politics. The organizational strength of the NCSC tends to be concentrated in the heavily industrial states (Lammers 1983, 58–59). In the early days of the organization, funds were derived largely from labor unions, with Walter Reuther and the United Auto Workers providing organizing assistance (Binstock 1981, 54).

Whereas the AARP has placed greater emphasis on the issue of eliminating mandatory retirement barriers to elderly professionals, the NCSC has focused on issues of primary interest to low-income retirees, such as protection of Social Security benefits and national health insurance. Grass-roots lobbying efforts by the NCSC were particularly instrumental in achieving passage of Medicare in the 1960s and in securing the 1972 Social Security amendments. In the former instance, the NCSC dramatically mobilized 1,400 elderly persons to appear at the opening session of the 89th Congress in 1965 to pressure House Speaker John McCormack into keeping his promise to appoint a pro-Medicare majority on the House Ways and Means Committee (Lammers 1983, 157).

The NCSC launched another major grass-roots lobbying effort in 1972, incessantly reminding incumbent congressmen of the importance of having a favorable record on Social Security benefit increases in an election year. In his analysis of the legislative history of the 1972 amendments, Henry Pratt concludes that the NCSC "played a complex and important role" in the successful passage of the legislation, adding that had it "not intervened, the legislative result would almost certainly have been different." The cumulative grass-roots pressure brought to bear by the NCSC on individual congressmen in that election year was indeed intense. As one participant in the legislative struggle described it, "old-age groups like NCSC had a good case. . . . [T]here were a lot of aged voters who would get furious if we didn't support it. The question wasn't whether we should support it but whether we could afford not to" (Pratt 1976, 166, 168).

The Gray Panthers Though small in comparison to AARP and NCSC, the Gray Panthers organization was perhaps the most effective group during the institutionalization phase in raising the nation's consciousness about ageism and problems of the elderly.[7] From the beginning, the philosophical scope of the organization was broad-based, encompassing a variety of interrelated societal concerns and calling for a bold anti-ageist coalition of young and old persons. A 1974 statement of the organization's principles defined a Gray Panther as a person who "actively promotes the interaction of young and old people and the maximum involvement of all ages in areas of social and political life" (Gray Panthers 1974).

The organization originated in Philadelphia in the early 1970s as an informal discussion group of retirees and young college students, initially called the Coalition of Older and Younger Adults. The grassroots group first gained widespread attention when it took to the streets with picket signs to demonstrate against nursing home abuses. The label "Gray Panthers" was used in jest by a New York television producer, implying that the group played a comparable role within the senior rights movement to that of the militant Black Panthers within the civil rights movement. Newspapers and networks quickly picked up on the label, and when leader Maggie Kuhn appeared on *The Today Show* in May 1972, she was introduced to millions of American television viewers as the leader of the "Gray Panthers" (Rich and Baum 1984, 18–20).

In contrast to interest groups like the AARP and the NCSC, the Gray Panthers have consistently made a point of defining themselves in direct opposition to the political and economic status quo, consciously differentiating themselves from "establishment aging organizations." Robert Binstock (1974) has commented that the Panthers are "the only organization working to solve the problems of human beings rather than those of the profession and the industry." Their 1974 manifesto describes the Panthers as a coalition of aged and youth "concerned with actions for change rather than service" and opposed to social injustice at all levels in American society.

The Panthers began their lobbying operation out of a modest West Philadelphia church office, from which volunteers and a small staff coordinated the affairs of the entire national network, including thousands of members organized into local chapters (referred to as "packs") in cities across the country. Initially, the organization shunned such standard practices as collection of dues and use of formal membership cards as being indicative of "establishment" aging organizations. Asked by a reporter in a 1972 interview about the decentralized nature of the Gray Panthers, Kuhn explained that "we've adopted a purpose—the Panther Manifesto. But a lot of people who have come out of a bureaucracy can't understand why we don't have membership cards and a formal office and letterheads." Over time, however, financial and organizational realities have led to more systematic practices. An organized national network of local groups is now linked by a steering committee, and the Panthers publish a national newsletter called *The Gray Panthers Network.* Initially, the group's income came sporadically from the sale of literature, T-shirts, and Kuhn's speaking fees. At the 1977 Gray Panthers convention a dues structure was imposed to help pay for the organization's activities.

From the early 1970s through the mid-1990s the charismatic personality of Maggie Kuhn has been the focus of the group, and was responsible for most of the publicity accorded the Panthers. Her tactic, and that of the Gray Panthers, was one of local militant action, involving grass-roots organizing in support of selected social causes. Given their aversion to hierarchical organization as a matter of principle, the Gray Panthers have not been a consistent, organized Washington lobby group in the strict sense, as have such organizations as the AARP and the NCSC. Their accomplishments have generally been sporadic and local in nature, although typically highly publicized. In a sense, then, their protest activities are qualitatively different, in that they involve attempts at consciousness-raising through publicized symbolic actions rather than the usual mainstream lobbying tactics practiced by "establishment" aging organizations.

The diverse social causes espoused by the Panthers since their inception have included fostering a new public consciousness of the potential of elderly persons, bringing greater dignity to old age, reform of pension systems, elimination of mandatory retirement, opposition to federal budget cuts in programs for the aged, elimination of poverty, opposition to the nuclear arms race, and national health care. At a 1981 Gray Panthers convention, for instance, resolutions were adopted covering the issues of housing, long-term health care, nuclear energy, legal services, hiring under the Older Americans Act, peace, the Family Protection Act, mental and physical health, Social Security, and the right to die with dignity.

The Emergent Concept of "Ageism" and the Quest to Eliminate Symbolic Barriers to Elderly Empowerment and Well-Being

Yet another sign that the senior rights movement had finally "arrived" as a significant national force during this period was a burgeoning consciousness of the existence of "ageism" and "age discrimination" as a problem within American society, and defiant movement attempts to combat it.[8] There was a growing recognition of the behavioral constraints that this pervasive societal mind-set had imposed on elderly Americans as a social control mechanism—tangibly in the form of overt age discrimination in the workplace, housing, education, and so forth, and less tangibly, in the form of stereotypical portrayals of the aged within American culture and the mass media. Just as the civil rights movement had congealed around the need to combat racism, and the women's movement had united to combat sexism, older Americans now began to self-consciously define the advancement of senior rights in terms of the elimination of "ageism," "ageist stereotypes," and "ageist institutions." That the most visibly "radical" faction of the movement was known as the "Gray Panthers" was certainly no accident. In the context of the times, it signified the same defiance in the face of institutionalized ageism in American society that the Black Panthers had represented as a symbol of the struggle against institutionalized racism (Branco and Williamson 1982).

During the heyday of the the senior rights movement in the 1960s and 1970s, activists increasingly became aware that achieving further movement progress would require a fundamental redefinition of the "proper place" of the elderly within American society—of a need to *de*construct negative, constraining images of the social reality of old age and to *re*construct more positive and empowering images in their stead. Within the academic world this trend was reflected in two seminal books, which did much to facilitate the growing awareness of the societal phenomenon of ageism, and crystalized attempts by progressive reformers to combat it. In 1972 Simone de Beauvoir's *The Coming of Age* became available in English translation. The book was a scathing indictment, based primarily on literary sources, of modern society's indifference toward the fate of its older members. Then in 1975 appeared Robert Butler's widely read *Why Survive? Being Old in America*, for which he later received a Pulitzer prize. These two pathbreaking examinations of the phenomenon of ageism helped to define the concept, to raise consciousness about it as a chronic social "problem" requiring policy "solutions," and to bring to the subject a newfound legitimacy as a respectable area of academic inquiry within the social sciences. Following this lead, historians began developing theories of how and why this "ageism" had developed within modern industrialized societies, arguing that the process of modernization had led to a shift in the social roles and treatment of elderly persons—

although substantial scholarly disagreements rapidly emerged as to the exact timing and the causes of this shift. As other historians began to examine the evidence more closely (e.g., Fischer 1977; Achenbaum 1978), their analyses indicated that an attitudinal shift in societal images of the aged had apparently already begun to occur *prior* to the economic and technological changes that accompany modernization, thus raising the additional possibility that cultural or ideological forces had been at work in undermining reverence for the aged in traditional societies. Other social scientists suggested that it was primarily the development of medical science and the associated definitions of aging as a "disease" and a "social problem" that had cultivated negative societal attitudes toward the aged.

Within the movement, "wrinkled radical" Maggie Kuhn and the Gray Panthers were quick to seize on the "ageism" theme as a powerful symbolic lever for achieving social change in the status and treatment of older persons. Testifying before the House Select Committee on Aging in 1977, for example, Kuhn described the "empowerment" mission of the Gray Panthers, vis-à-vis the dominant social order, in the following terms:

The Gray Panthers are a national coalition of old, young, and middle-aged activists and advocates working to eradicate ageism and all forms of age discrimination in our society. We define ageism as the arbitrary discrimination against persons and groups on the basis of chronological age. . . . Old people constitute America's largest untapped and undervalued human energy source, yet I have observed only token effort to give us a chance to be self-determining. . . . We find the process demeaning and calculated to make us wrinkled babies rather than mature, responsible adults concerned about helping ourselves and healing the ills of our sick society. (U.S. House of Representatives 1977)

Though movement activists continued to inveigh against the ageist tendencies within American society during the institutionalization phase, real progress was, in fact, forthcoming in the legal treatment of elderly persons, particularly in combating workplace discrimination. Senior "rights" in the area of employment opportunities were substantially expanded during this period, beginning with the passage of the Age Discrimination in Employment Act of 1967, which (as later amended) prohibited age discrimination and protected applicants and employees 40 years of age or older from discrimination on account of age in hiring, promotion, discharge, compensation, terms, conditions, or privileges of employment. The new law was designed to cover applicants to and employees of most private employers, state and local governments, employment agencies, labor organizations, and educational institutions.

The White House Conferences on Aging: Last Line of Defense against Change

Another milestone in the institutionalization stage of the senior rights movement was the initiation of regular White House Conferences on Aging.[9] Political scientist Henry Pratt has argued that the tendency to convene such conferences at regular 10-year intervals (1950, 1961, 1971, 1981, 1991) suggests that they "have taken on the character of political institutions" (1978, 67). Electoral and interest-group pressures on public officials, though much better organized in the postwar period than they had been earlier in the century, nevertheless remained limited in their capacity for producing policy change. The "pressure" or "lobbying" approach still lacked direct access to administrative structures and the inner dynamics of policymaking at the highest levels of government. With the advent of the White House Conferences on Aging, however, elderly advocates from across the nation were brought one step closer to direct participation in old-age policymaking processes—"inside" the system at the federal level. Emergent grievances and proposals for reform could now be presented to the executive branch of the federal government at an officially recognized national forum in Washington, with reasonable assurances that the resultant ideas for reform would receive serious consideration from the current administration.

Of course the other side of the coin, as always, was that opportunities for establishment co-optation of the reform process also increased in these national forums. As with the movement-establishment confrontations over Social Security and Medicare, the successive White House Conferences on Aging were punctuated by a series of symbolic gestures and countergestures between representatives of elderly interests and staunch defenders of the status quo. Advocates for the elderly came to these national forums seeking tangible benefits for older Americans. But incumbent administrations were generally more interested in heading off incipient social change by preempting it, if possible, using elaborate displays of symbolic reassurance, or, if that was not feasible, through restricted, tangible concessions on specific aging programs.

The first government-sponsored National Conference on Aging (the "White House Conference" label had not yet been adopted) was convened in August 1950 by Oscar Ewing, head of the National Security Agency under President Truman. Truman, who at the time was casting about for a compelling new issue to restore confidence in his leadership, asked Ewing to assess the conditions of the nation's elderly, which led to the decision to convene a national conference in Washington to discuss the problem and give it greater visibility.

In 1950 the senior rights movement had not yet emerged from the "dismal years." The American Association for Labor Legislation and the American Association for Social Security had ceased to exist, and the Townsend and McClain movements were in an advanced state of decay. With the senior rights movement temporarily in disarray, administration planners were free to design the format of the conference to suit their own political ends, without concern about organized resistance. Conference planners were thus able to adopt a "divide and conquer" strategy of inviting guests and experts to the conference as individuals rather than as representatives of organizations. Emphasis was intentionally placed on inviting local aging advocates, rather than the leaders of national associations. The official explanation for this curious procedure was that it would presumably result in "a more informed group of delegates" and that "most of the work with the aging will always be done by various groups at the local and state levels." As Henry Pratt has observed, however, the administration's real concern appears to have been that "an assembly of essentially atomized individuals, not beholden to any outside institutions, could be more readily controlled and channeled" (1978, 68–69).

As one might expect under such carefully orchestrated conditions, President Truman's and Mr. Ewing's addresses to the conference delegates were filled with "a grandiloquence of rhetoric" that, on closer scrutiny, turned out to be devoid of any substance. Amid the numerous accolades to the "dignity" of the nation's elderly—who, it was repeatedly pointed out, deserved more "respect" than they were getting—not a single concrete action or policy reform was proposed by the national forum. The delegates were divided into 10 working sessions to discuss various aging issues, but no resolutions or recommendations for action were forthcoming. If one considers this lopsided dominance of the conference agenda by the administration, the absence of any concrete policy concessions, and the administration's success at reassuring the nation's elderly that their problems were being addressed in the highest national circles, it is clear that the Truman administration had achieved a masterstroke in what political psychologist Murray Edelman calls "the construction of gestures as solutions" (1988, 24).

Beginning with the 1961 White House Conference on Aging, however, this one-sided power equation between established order and movement slowly began to shift. In the intervening decade, the national network of senior organizations had rebounded, which in turn gave senior advocates an improved bargaining position leading into the conference. Moreover, lingering disappointment with the lack of any concrete results from the 1950 conference had strengthened the resolve of reformers to see to it that this time rhetoric would be matched by government action on behalf of the nation's elderly.

The 1961 White House Conference on Aging occurred at an awkward time for the Eisenhower administration. At the time of the conference, the second week in January, Eisenhower was a lame duck president with only a week remaining before he was to be replaced by President-elect John F. Kennedy. Eisenhower and his advisors apparently decided that it would not be wise to again scheme behind the scenes to undermine the efficacy of the delegate selection process and conference proceedings, as had Truman. Rather, they approached the conference with caution, hoping to hold the line on old-age policy changes while projecting a willingness to "consider all sides" on elderly issues (Pratt 1978, 70).

This cautious stance reflected the administration's awareness of a growing restlessness among representatives of aging organizations and their memberships for *tangible* policy responses to the unsolved social ailments of older Americans. The American Association of Retired Persons had been organized since the previous conference, and was already 100,000 strong. The National Council on the Aging had also become a prominent organization in the interim. Although ostensibly apolitical in their early stages, the burgeoning clout of these senior organizations was beginning to make its presence felt in the proceedings. And the AFL-CIO made sure that delegates representing its interests were included in the conference deliberations, which created additional pressure on elites for policy reform. Other sources of outside pressure came from Senator Patrick McNamara's newly created Senate Subcommittee on Aging and the Aged, and the recent introduction of elderly health-care bills by Aine Forand and John Kennedy in Congress.

The 1961 White House Conference represented a turning point in the power balance between reluctant Washington elites and aging-policy reform advocates. The White House and opponents of change began to lose control over the ideological composition of the delegates and the direction of the proceedings. As a result, there emerged several concrete policy recommendations that clearly were a rebuff to Eisenhower's stated positions on aging issues. The delegates voted to endorse the idea of Medicare through the Social Security program (in the conference's Section on Income Maintenance), as well as the idea of new federal categorical grants (in the Section on State Organization). Both policies had been consistently opposed by the Eisenhower administration.

The conference also placed a great deal of pressure on Eisenhower's successor, John Kennedy, to pursue major aging policy initiatives during his administration. The 1961 White House Conference is generally credited with having contributed to the enactment of Medicare and the decision to establish the National Association of State Units on Aging (NASUA), and with having crystallized support for the founding of the National Council of Senior Citizens. It also appears to have inspired Kennedy's "Elderly Citizens of Our Nation" message to Congress in February 1963, in which he appealed for categorical grants in aging, calling for "a five-year program of assistance to State and local agencies . . . for planning and development services; for research, demonstration, and training projects leading to new or improved programs to aid older people" (Pratt 1976, 111–13).

By the time the next White House Conference was convened, in November of 1971, the power balance had shifted decisively in favor of aging-policy reform advocates. National media accounts of the White House conferences now began to speak of the "clout" of the new "gray lobby" in Washington. Organizations such as the AARP, NCSC, and NCOA were not only widely recognized but *feared* by those who stood opposed to further old-age policy reforms and their costs. By this point the National Council of Senior Citizens boasted three million members, organized into about 3,000 local chapters. The American Association of Retired Persons had also expanded rapidly, and as a result now maintained a well-financed Washington lobbying contingent. Moreover, the Senate aging subcommittee chaired by McNamara had become a permanent legislative fixture—called the Senate Special Committee on Aging. Depicting the altered political climate as the White House Conference convened in November 1971, a *Washington Post* reporter observed that "this conference reflects a willingness on the part of some segments of society for substituting action for rhetoric. If rhetoric is to be translated into action it will probably be because of the enormous clout of the elderly."[10]

Even before the conference began in that year, the newfound power of the senior coalition could be felt on Capitol Hill. In March 1971, in testimony for hearings of the Senate Special Committee on Aging, leaders of major nationally based senior groups expressed outrage at the apparent intention of Nixon's Administration on Aging to exclude them from participation in the pre–White House Conference gatherings. They also accused the Nixon administration of attempting to impose a political test on delegates to the conference in order to exclude proponents of radical reform. The national press, of course, found this all very interesting, and the negative media coverage became increasingly embarrassing to the Nixon White House. Democratic senators were depicted sympathizing with senior groups' complaints, and the chairman of the National Caucus and Center on Black Aged threatened to boycott the conference and convene instead a "Black House Conference on Aging."

Nixon arranged for the appointed conference chairman, Arthur Flemming, to hold a series of prior meetings with senior group leaders in an attempt to undercut the protests by making some concessions on ground rules for the upcoming conference. Concessions were made on the number of delegates who would be representatives of senior organizations, and a task force—half of which would be composed of senior group leaders—was created to monitor planning for the 1971 White House Conference. With senior advocates temporarily appeased, the wave of protest subsided.

This attempted stage-managing of the proceedings by Chairman Flemming continued on into the conference in November. Flemming held a number of closed-door meetings with senior group representatives in which prior agreements were reached on sensitive points that threatened to erupt into open conflict and lead to escalating demands for change. Flemming, sensing that patience with administration rhetoric as a substitute for action was low, scrupulously avoided rhetoric in his public pronouncements, emphasizing instead the need for concrete action. He remarked, for example, on one occasion that "proposals that are not backed up by sound programs are nothing more than sounding brass."[11]

The predominant mood of senior advocates was suspicious and impatient, demanding that action—not merely flowery rhetoric or symbolic reassurance—be forthcoming from political elites. In a typical exchange during the conference, Secretary of Housing and Urban Development George Romney conveyed the administration's preferences at a luncheon meeting, suggesting that the conference should emphasize "voluntary action" and "self-help" solutions to problems of the elderly. He was abruptly challenged by Jean Meyer, chairman of the committee on nutrition, who asked incredulously, "What the hell does that mean? . . . [W]hen you are talking about someone who is arthritic? who is deaf? who is partially blind? whose children have moved away?"[12]

In order to survive the ordeal politically, Nixon administration representatives were forced to shift from a strategy of what Murray Edelman calls "the politics of reassurance"—where policy change is forestalled by fostering a climate of quiescence—to "the politics of specific benefits"—in which support for government initiatives is restored by dealing in a limited way with concrete, specific problems of needy groups (Edelman 1964). In his closing address to the conference delegates, Nixon avoided rhetoric and focused on tangible benefits of interest to elderly groups.

Although Nixon administration officials had been able to limit the political damage, advocates for the senior rights movement had clearly been successful in utilizing their newfound clout to force policy elites to make commitments to old-age policy change. In all, more than 700 policy recommendations were produced by the conference. The majority of the members of Congress praised the recommendations, interpreting them as a statement of national aging policies and seeking to develop legislation to implement them. By the end of the decade most of the recommendations had in some way been translated into laws: Medicare was expanded, a nutrition program was developed, Social Security benefits were raised, and cost-of-living adjustments were added. Senator Frank Church described the old-age legislation that occurred in the wake of the 1971 White House Conference as "ranking only behind 1935, when Social Security was enacted, and 1965, when Medicare became law" (Fischer 1979, 64).

From Input to "Withinput": The Older Americans Act and the Administration on Aging

The senior rights movement's shift during the institutionalization phase from being a mere "input" into the policymaking process to being a "withinput" can be seen most clearly in the construction of the Administration on Aging as a federal agency designed to deal with problems of the elderly on an ongoing basis, as mandated by the Older Americans Act. Location *within* the established structure of the federal government for the first time gave reform advocates a niche from which to initiate and consolidate policy advances on behalf of the interests of older Americans. The monopoly on technical information, the implied legitimacy, and the considerable resources available to federal agencies all invested the promotion of elderly concerns with a "withinput" status in the policymaking process, thereby considerably improving their overall political leverage as a constitutency vis-à-vis other competing societal concerns.

The Administration on Aging was a product of the Older Americans Act, which was enacted by the 89th Congress during the heyday of the Great Society.[13] The Senate bill to establish a separate federal agency to deal with aging concerns was first introduced in 1963, as an outgrowth of President Kennedy's interest in the problems of the elderly. Well aware of the growing political visibility and organizational strength of the nation's elderly, Kennedy's "Elderly Citizens of Our Nation" address in February of that year declared that "it is not enough for a great nation merely to have added new years to life—our objective must also be to add new life to those years" (1963, 2693). At the time, the secretary of the Department of Health, Education, and Welfare, Anthony Celebrezze, was opposed to the idea of creating a new federal agency, arguing that a new agency would be superfluous because the existing department could adequately provide for elderly needs. A majority of members of the Senate—with one eye on the ballot box—disagreed, however, maintaining that older Americans' problems needed to be dealt with separately.

A compromise between the two positions was eventually reached in an amended bill that proposed to create an Administration on Aging as a new division within Celebrezze's DHEW. The legislation did not come up for consideration before the 88th Congress adjourned, but it was immediately reconsidered by the strongly liberal Democratic 89th

Congress, owing in part to intense lobbying by the National Council of Senior Citizens and other senior advocates. When the Older Americans Act (HR 3704) was introduced again early in 1965, it expeditiously made its way through the House of Representatives, passing by an overwhelming 394 to 1 margin by 31 March. The act then went on to pass unanimously in the Senate by 27 May of the same year, and shortly thereafter it was signed into law by President Johnson (Rich and Baum 1984, 25–29).

In its original form, the Older Americans Act was funded at such a minimal level that it had little impact on the lives of the aged. The initial appropriation was a meager $7.5 million—minuscule in comparison to other federal government allocations. With subsequent amendments to the act and increased funding levels, however, it soon evolved into a major source of ongoing support for services to the nation's aged, as well as a major within-system lobby on behalf of elderly interests. By the early 1980s the annual budget allocation had expanded to nearly three quarters of a billion dollars (Lammers 1983, 179).

The stated goals of the Older Americans Act, as specified in Title I of the act, were to provide all elderly Americans with the following:

1. An adequate income in retirement in accordance with the American standard of living.

2. The best possible mental and physical health that science can make available and without regard to economic status.

3. Suitable housing, independently selected, designed and located with reference to special needs and available at costs that older citizens can afford.

4. Full restorative services for those who require institutional care.

5. Opportunity for employment with no discriminatory personnel practices because of age.

6. Retirement in health, honor, and dignity—after years of contribution to the economy.

7. Pursuit of meaningful activity within the widest range of civic, cultural, and recreational opportunities.

8. Efficient community services that provide social assistance in a coordinated manner and that are readily available when needed.

9. Immediate benefit from proven research knowledge that can sustain and improve health and happiness.

10. Freedom, independence, and the free exercise of individual
    initiative in planning and managing their own lives.

These were impressive objectives, and at first glance it appeared that most of the problems of the nation's elderly were at last well on their way to being solved by committed policy elites in Washington. As Carroll Estes has trenchantly pointed out in her critique of American old-age policies, *The Aging Enterprise* (1979), however, the lofty goals outlined in Title I were for the most part merely inflated political rhetoric. Precisely how these stated objectives were to be translated into realities for the nation's aged was not spelled out. Although a new administrative agency representing the interests of the aged had indeed been created, the Older Americans Act had given the Administration on Aging neither sufficient new administrative authority nor sufficient financial support to make implementation of the rhetorical ideals a possibility. On closer scrutiny, what political elites had actually created for the nation's elderly was a cornucopia of symbolic reassurances, mixed with enough token policy concessions to appease an increasingly restive and politically influential senior rights movement. Fortunately for the movement, one of those concessions was a new federal base for senior advocacy, which could henceforth be used in the struggle to narrow the gap between the rhetorical ideals and the social realities of aging in America.

Chapter Seven

Old Age and the New Right

Resisting Attempts to Delegitimize Social Security

> *Put bluntly, the old have come to insist that the young not only hold them harmless for their past profligacy, but sacrifice their own prosperity to pay for it. . . . A fairer distribution of both necessary sacrifices and ensuing benefits of American life is required.*
>
> Phillip Longman, research director,
> Americans for Generational Equity, 1982[1]

> *There's a contrived effort to set the old against the young, to persuade the young people that old people are getting too much, that we're all rich and well-endowed and that they're getting robbed, which is not true. . . . The classic effort, which was so dangerous, was [Reagan's] effort to privatize the Social Security system.*
>
> Maggie Kuhn, founder and leader of the Gray Panthers, 1988[2]

The 1960s and 1970s had been a period of growing institutionalization of the senior rights movement. Senior advocacy organizations such as the American Association of Retired Persons, the National Council of Senior Citizens, the National Council on the Aging, and the Gray Panthers had come to play an increasingly prominent role in national politics, serving as focal points for age-related issues and actively promoting elderly causes through congressional lobbying, electoral pressures, and media exposure. Moreover, the promotion of senior rights had increasingly become embedded "within" the established legal and policymaking structure itself, via such landmark legislation as the Older Americans Act and Medicare, and through the creation of bureaucratic structures such as the Administration on Aging and the National Institute on Aging.

In the Reagan-Bush era that followed, however, the senior rights movement was to be confronted with its most formidable political challenge. In the 40 years between the mid-1930s and the mid-1970s the United States had experienced a continuous liberalization in its federal policies toward the aged—the landmark Social Security Act of 1935 and the amendments to the act introduced over the years that added dependents' and survivors' benefits, disability insurance, Medicare, and automatic benefit adjustments for inflation. Starting in the mid-1970s, however, the momentum of this liberalization process began to slow, and by the end of the decade an anti–welfare-state backlash was clearly under way, finding expression in a middle-class "tax revolt" and the election of a right-wing conservative, Ronald Reagan, to the presidency (Reeves 1985; Kuttner 1980).

During the 1980s the American political landscape changed even more dramatically, as a new reactionary countermovement—often referred to as the "New Right"—was able to ascend to political power and aggressively assert its imperatives. In that decade the strength of the senior rights movement was to be measured more by its ability to resist cutbacks imposed by New Right political elites than by its ability to obtain new programs and extend benefits. The movement suddenly found itself pitted against other welfare constituencies for a share of the shrinking social services pie, as each group scrambled to resist political attempts to delegitimize its stake in the welfare state. Ironically, the programmatic successes that had been achieved during the 1960s and 1970s now made the elderly more vulnerable politically, undercutting their legitimacy as a policy constituency (Hudson 1978). As the perceived well-being of the elderly had "improved" in the public mind relative to other segments of the population, there had emerged a dialectical response from other policy constituencies. In a slow-growth, "zero sum" society (Thurow 1980), the stronger the gray lobby became, and the greater its success in obtaining an increasing share of the federal budget, the stronger became the opposition from those constituencies who resentfully questioned the legitimacy and fairness of generous federal old-age entitlements.

This chapter examines the political struggle that emerged during this period—between the senior rights movement and supporters of the New Right countermovement. We consider the ideological basis and political strength of the New Right, the election of Ronald Reagan as a symbolic embodiment of its political objectives, the efforts of senior advocacy organizations to resist its hostile agenda of social program retrenchments, and the partial success of the Reagan and Bush administrations in shifting the context of debates over old-age justice away from issues of adequacy, need, and fairness between classes to issues of cost-containment, merit, and fairness between generations. We continue to pay particular attention to emergent definitions of fairness and justice and the rhetorical themes used by senior advocates and their adversaries to frame the public debate.

The Gathering Political Storm

The Great Society era of the 1960s had been a time of economic expansion for business and improved standard of living for most Americans. In that optimistic epoch it seemed possible to sustain a generous domestic "Great Society" agenda while simultaneously building up an expensive military campaign in Vietnam. As we have seen, it was in this period that the senior rights movement moved rapidly toward institutionalization of its imperatives. In a less robust economy, opposition to institutionalization might have been considerably stronger, and legislative proposals such as Medicare and the Older Americans Act might never have been passed. The economy was so hardy and the nation so militarily dominant on the international scene, however, that it appeared the classic economic choices between "guns and butter" need not be made.

That notion was seriously challenged in the 1970s, when America's economic optimism ran headlong into "stagflation"—a combination of stagnated economic output and high rates of inflation. The recession that ran from late 1973 through the spring of 1975 was the worst downturn in the economy to occur since the Great Depression. The rate of unemployment doubled between 1970 and 1981 (Burghardt and Fabricant 1987, 13). By the mid-1970s "double-digit inflation" had become a household phrase. There was also unsettling news on the political front. Disclosures of rampant corruption and deception at the highest levels of power in the Watergate scandal led to a loss of faith and confidence in governmental authority among many Americans.

And the humiliating American withdrawal from Vietnam had shaken the nation's pride that the U.S. military could defeat any enemy, anywhere. The taking of American hostages in Iran in 1978 added further insult to the Vietnam injury. America in the late 1970s increasingly appeared to be a nation adrift and in decline.

At the close of the decade another recession stalled the economy, and the Democratic president Jimmy Carter's feeble response was to characterize the nation as being in a state of "malaise." This inadequate stance left him vulnerable to charges that his policies in particular, and New Deal–Great Society liberalism in general, were responsible for the economic and military decline into which the nation had slipped (Hamby 1985, 353). The perceived lack of political leadership and failed economic management created a temporary power vacuum into which a new group with ideas heretofore considered too extreme and out of the mainstream of American politics could step—namely, the right wing of the Republican party and the corporate sector (Myles 1991, 300–304). The diverse elements of this group had been coalescing throughout the late 1960s and 1970s and had long prepared for the opportunity that Carter had created. Their principal public spokesman, former screen actor Ronald Reagan, could now be heard as he argued skillfully, via network television, that America was "still great" and if only we could "get Big Government off our backs" the economy would again flourish and the country's previous standing as a military power not to be trifled with would again be proudly restored (Dalleck 1984; Denton 1988).

As Walter Dean Burnham (1981, 123) has astutely observed, "1980 is the election in which the empire strikes back." When Ronald Reagan, the charismatic "Great Communicator" for these newly emergent conservative forces, took office in January 1981, he did so with the claim that the election represented a clear "mandate" from the American people to implement a sweeping new conservative agenda, including social-program cutbacks, tax cuts, a balanced budget, and a military buildup. Not only was Reagan the first president in a half century to come to office without some plan to improve the situation of the nation's aged, but as a spokesman for the ascendant New Right, he came as leader of a countermovement that openly advocated dismantling the country's social-welfare system, claiming that extravagant overfunding of that system was a primary cause of the nation's economic woes. This new anti–welfare-state agenda proved seductive to many Americans, tapping a nostalgia for the individualistic strengths of a mythic American past. For the nation's aged, however, returning to that "past" implied a return to less government assistance and to the "traditional values" of an earlier epoch in which the quality of life in old age was seen as reflecting the extent to which one had been frugal and hardworking during one's younger years. While the "good old days" were symbolically seductive, they would have meant a return to higher poverty and lowered quality of life for many of America's elderly.

Ascendance of the New Right as a Hostile Countermovement

A dramatic shift was taking place in American political symbolism, and that change was no accident. As Benjamin Ginsberg observes, "Successful . . . or at least widely held political ideas are usually the products of carefully orchestrated campaigns by organized groups and interests rather than the result of spontaneous popular enthusiasm" (1986, 111). A look at the origins of New Right advocacy is instructive. The ascendance of the New Right had begun in the 1960s, as a response to the perceived threat to the interests of "intellectuals and businessmen driven into political exile after the crushing defeat of Barry Goldwater in 1964" (Reeves 1985, 23). Following the Goldwater loss, right-wing conservatives reorganized to mount a more effective campaign of persuasion to spread their ideas and political symbols throughout American culture. By the late 1960s this effort had begun to bear fruit. Conservative think tanks such as the Heritage Foundation, the American Enterprise Institute, and the National Conservative Research and Education Foundation were becoming generously endowed centers of conservative political thought and writing. William F. Buckley, Jr., emerged as the intellectual media kingpin of the revived conservative movement, with his television program, *Firing Line,* and his conservative journal, *National Review.* In the 1970s former Nixon Treasury Secretary William Simon encouraged corporations to fund "books, books, and more books" (Saloma 1983, 65–66) that promoted the view that political liberty and pure free-market enterprise were inextricably bound. Corporate elites responded generously to the cause. The chemical industry's Olin Fund and the pharmaceutical Smith Richardson Foundation, for example, were each providing $3 million annually by the late 1970s. These funds contributed to the publication of *The Way the World Works,* a popularized reification of supply-side theory, and to the Reagan "bible," George Gilder's *Wealth and Poverty*. The petro-chemical industry's Scaife funds helped finance the Heritage Foundation, the *Public Interest* journal, the conservative Law and Economics Center at Emory University, and media projects such as Accuracy in Media, the *American Spectator*, and economist Milton Friedman's television program, *Free to Choose* (Ferguson and Rogers 1986, 88; Rothmyer 1981).

All of these concerns contributed their resources toward the goal of accomplishing a rightward redefinition of American public issues. Their common thrust toward reduced social-welfare expenditures, tax reductions for upper-income groups and corporations, less environmental regulation, and opposition to the recent gains of minorities and women tended to unite them ideologically, if not organizationally (Ferguson and Rogers 1981, 25). By the late 1970s this New Right countermovement had reached the stage of coalescence and was poised to mount an attempt to institutionalize its policy agenda—in opposition to, and at the expense of, the goals of the senior rights movement and other related progressive social-change movements that had prospered in the United States since the New Deal.

Declaration of a Social Security "Crisis" to Justify Impending Retrenchments

This success of the New Right in reframing the debate over the nation's economy was central to its assault on the welfare state in general and programs for the aged in particular. Proposed shifts in social policy during the Reagan years were rationalized in terms of ideas about the performance of the economy, and, not surprisingly, they tended to favor the economic interests of the economic elites that had underwritten both the intellectual popularization of the New Right agenda and the 1980 election campaign of Ronald Reagan.

For his "solution" to the persistent economic problem of stagflation, the newly elected president drew on the "supply-side" theories of economist Arthur Laffer. Laffer argued that Keynesian economic theory, which had been the dominant approach to domestic policy since the 1930s, had failed to adequately consider the importance of the supply of capital to business in producing economic growth. He contended that the supply of capital comes predominantly from the investments of persons in the upper-income brackets. President Reagan embraced Laffer's idea that a drop in the supply of capital to business was the primary cause of the economic problems the United States had experienced during the 1970s. Accordingly, he believed that the nation's economic problems could best be solved through tax cuts, especially for corporations and those at the upper end of the income spectrum, who were in a position to invest. Reagan also maintained that deficit spending was a "liberal" policy that had long been a drag on the economy. The primary cause of these ballooning deficits, he argued, was gross overspending on social programs.

Framing the problems in the economy as a "supply of capital" issue enabled New Right politicians to advocate a solution that they had long desired—namely, tax reductions for upper-income brackets and extensive cuts in social-welfare programs. The Reagan administration's economic nostrum for the nation's ills was to enact supply-side policies, which were presented to the public as the "only way" to stimulate economic recovery and thereby improve the well-being of all Americans. While this bitter economic medicine would require extensive cuts in social spending, the charismatic new president symbolically reassured wary Americans that a "safety net" would protect the "truly needy," that these cuts were a necessary part of improving overall economic performance, and that any negative effects of the cuts would soon be offset, as the greatly improved economy would produce enough new wealth to "trickle down" to those at the bottom of the income hierarchy. Thus "Reaganomics" promised a brighter future for all Americans in the long run, in exchange for short-term sacrifices (Reagan 1981, 1982).

In the summer of 1981 this aggressive new economic policy agenda was introduced as legislation in the form of the Omnibus Reconciliation Act (OBRA), which achieved many of the social-spending cuts sought by the administration. The act sought a $40 billion decrease in social-spending in 1982 and an additional $50 billion decrease by 1984. This was to be achieved by eliminating 57 programs. The need created by the elimination of these programs was to be met through more meagerly funded block grants. In addition to the programs eliminated by OBRA, deep cuts in means-tested programs were to be made, and eligibility levels for programs such as food stamps, Aid to Families with Dependent Children programs, and unemployment insurance were to be altered (Estes 1984, 244; Cohen 1981).

Thus within only six months of Reagan's taking office, the implementation of his new economic agenda was well under way. The administration's budget director, David Stockman, strongly urged the president to include cuts in elderly entitlement programs in this initial legislation. He pointed out that Social Security and Medicare made up a large portion of domestic spending and could therefore not be left untouched if the administration was to achieve its fiscal goals. Stockman advocated "huge bites that would have to be taken out of Social Security. I mean really fierce, blood and guts stuff, widow's benefits, and orphan's benefits, things like that" (Greider 1981, 40).

Reagan officially declared that a Social Security "crisis" existed through his secretary of health and human services, Richard Schweiker, who announced to the public in May of 1981 that there was a "crisis in financing and in public confidence in the system. The old-age and survivors insurance program will not have enough funds to pay benefits after mid-1982. Band-aid approaches will not work. . . . The root of the problem is over-expansion of Social Security over the years. . . . We must be economically mature and not fool the American people by financing Social Security through general revenues." The "causes" of, and possible "solutions" to, the crisis were thus defined by the administration as involving ever-increasing numbers of government-dependent older Americans, receiving ever-increasing benefit levels. These "uncontrolled" increases were represented as not only driving the Social Security system into "bankruptcy" but as contributing substantially to the economic woes that the nation was experiencing (Bethel, 1981; *U.S. News & World Report,* 27 July 1981).

The periodic financial difficulties that had existed in the Social Security system since the mid-1970s provided an irresistible vehicle to carry the New Right's anti–welfare-state agenda. To build popular opposition to social welfare expenditures it was necessary to first create a sense of resentment among those contributing the taxes that funded the programs. The new conservative movement had already cultivated considerable taxpayer resentment during the "tax revolt" of the late 1970s—including Proposition 13 in California and Proposition 2 in Massachusetts. The manner in which they now framed the Social Security "crisis" was aimed in particular at building resentment among younger workers, who were increasingly led to believe that they were paying into a system that would not be able to provide them with benefits when *they* reached old age. A report out of the conservative Heritage Foundation, for instance, charged that Social Security was a "gigantic, government-operated, Ponzi scheme, in which earlier, smaller investors are paid off with the receipts from later, larger investors" (McAllister 1980).

As far back as the mid-1970s, conservative economists and intellectuals had begun to promote the idea that there was a "crisis" in Social Security, repeatedly parading the system's fiscal weaknesses before the American public in conservative journals such as the *Public Interest* and in books and technical reports coming out of the Heritage Foundation, the Hoover Institution, the American Enterprise Institute, and the Cato Institute. The "crisis" concept was also aggressively promoted in business press publications such as *Forbes, Fortune, Business Week,* and the *Wall Street Journal* and in popular news magazines and newspapers. Supply-side economist Arthur Laffer argued in 1976 that Social Security "will be unable to deliver on its promises," as expenditures would inevitably grow faster than revenues (Laffer and Ranson 1977, 133). In addition to this argument that Social Security was drifting toward "bankruptcy," New Right intellectuals had also begun promoting the view that contributing to Social Security was a "bad investment" for workers. Conservative economist Martin Feldstein argued in the late 1970s that investing the same amounts in private pension funds and savings accounts would produce a much better return (Feldstein 1977; Feldstein and Pellechio 1979).

Sociologist Carroll Estes (1983) observes that during the early 1980s the Social Security "crisis" was ingeniously constructed in the national media by the New Right in such a way that the implied "solution" was dictated from the outset. Thus the goal of the new conservative movement and the Reagan administration was not, as the American public had been told, to "solve" the financing problem through benefit cuts but to reduce benefits through focusing on the financing "problem" as a rhetorical pretext. Nor was this an unusual political strategy. Political psychologist Murray Edelman (1988, 21) has extensively studied "the construction of problems to fit solutions" throughout the twentieth century, and he notes that, typically, "those who favor a particular course of government action are likely to cast about for a widely feared problem to which to attach it in order to maximize its support." The Social Security financing "problem" thus fit nicely with the administration's plan to cut social spending as much as possible. By defining the problem as having reached a "crisis" stage, a convenient context had thereby been created within which the public would be more willing to make required sacrifices and endure new forms of deprivation, ostensibly for the good of the larger society.

The New Right's declaration of a Social Security "crisis" also performed the useful symbolic function of *re*defining old people as a "burden" to American society, as an unproductive group that was draining off needed resources, "busting the budget," and "robbing younger generations" (Estes 1983, 450–51). This represented a major shift in the way old age had been viewed in American culture since the New Deal. In this new view, the aged became scapegoats for the economic problems the nation was facing. Prior to the mid-1970s, the major stereotypes of the elderly had been ones of poverty, frailty, political impotence, and deservingness of assistance. By the late 1970s, however, the nation's elderly were increasingly being characterized in the national media as financially well-off, as politically powerful, and as using that power to ruthlessly monopolize an ever-growing share of the federal budget (Binstock 1983a; Minkler 1991).

These cumulative efforts to delegitimize the elderly as deserving recipients and undermine public confidence in Social Security were apparently working. In 1978 a Harris poll indicated that 43 percent of Americans had "hardly any" confidence that Social Security would be able to pay promised benefits. By 1981 the figure had increased to 61 percent. Thus the stage had been set for the administration's political assault on Social Security—the linchpin of the American welfare state. In the spring of 1981 the administration confidently proposed the following as an opening salvo: (1) a reduction in the early retirement benefit (age 62) from 80 percent of full benefits to 55 percent of full benefits; (2) a reduction in benefits for all new beneficiaries, beginning in 1982; (3) stricter disability criteria that would have reduced disability costs by one-third; and (4) a six-month delay in the cost of living allowance, beginning in 1982 (Kingson 1984).

Senior Lobby Responses

In its ideologically charged haste to reduce social expenditures and benefits, however, the administration had underestimated one very important factor—the strength of the "gray lobby" on Capitol Hill, which had slowly been accumulating clout over the past half-century. Within hours after Reagan's plan was announced, elderly organizations and their supporters began mobilizing to block the proposed retrenchments. The National Council of Senior Citizens fired off 10,000 "seniorgrams" to its national network of 4,000 clubs. The American Association of Retired Persons sent out "legislative alerts" to 14,000 volunteer leaders, asking them to contact public officials voicing their opposition to the proposals and urging them to recruit friends and relatives willing to do the same. The Gray Panthers, led by "wrinkled radical" Maggie Kuhn, held vigils across the street from the White House and staged public demonstrations around the country, including a 21 July rally at the Capitol. Save Our Security (SOS)— a coalition of 141 senior interest groups, unions, and liberal organizations—held a press conference in May 1981 in which they reminded lawmakers that, in all, they stood for 40 million Americans, represented by some 90 organizations, who were united in their steadfast opposition to the proposed cuts. Describing the coalition's straightforward lobbying methods, SOS executive vice chairman William Driver explained that "we make mention of our size and the fact that it's the group of people from which you get the largest percentage of the vote. We also impress upon congressmen that we're urging our members to oppose anyone who favors the cuts." House Ways and Means Committee chairman Dan Rostenkowski described them as "like paratroupers—they can drop in on you at any time."

On Capitol Hill, outspoken advocates of elderly programs, such as Congressman Claude Pepper, went on the offensive. Other Democratic congressmen—who had up to that point meekly accepted the idea of a Reagan mandate to cut spending on other programs— now began to rail indignantly against the administration's proposals to sacrifice programs serving the aged, accusing the president of going back on his word. House Speaker Thomas ("Tip") O'Neill organized Democratic members of the House in support of a resolution that accused the administration of an "unconscionable breach of faith" (Clark 1981, 1053).

Republican senators quickly recognized that these proposals were politically "dangerous," and they joined Democrats in a vote of opposition, even before they could formally be introduced as legislation. Acknowledging the power of the Washington senior lobby, Republican Senator Bob Dole commented wryly that "voting to cut Social Security benefits is the last thing you do on your last day in the Senate."[3]

As a result of the organized political opposition to the cuts, the Reagan administration had to settle for substantially less in the summer of 1981. The 1981 Omnibus Budget Reconciliation Act did, nevertheless, manage to achieve some of the desired cuts in Social Security, by permanently eliminating the benefits that would have been available to students aged 18 to 21 (survivor's benefits) and temporarily eliminating the Social Security minimum benefit. (The minimum benefit allocated $122 a month to anyone eligible for Social Security, regardless of

past earnings or taxes.) This latter cut affected some three million people, primarily aged women, and rekindled fierce opposition from
Democrats in the House and Senate. Republicans in the House found
themselves pressured into voting for a Democratic resolution to
"insure that social security benefits are not reduced for those currently
receiving them." Senate Republicans followed, restoring the minimum
benefit in October (Stockman 1986; Light 1985, 124, 130).

Owing to the intense lobbying effort by senior advocates, public
opposition to President Reagan's handling of Social Security was considerable by this point. To add to his problems, the 1981 White House
Conference on Aging was just over the horizon, convening from 30
November through 2 December. The Leadership Council of Aging
Organizations, a coalition of senior groups, was formed in the months
prior to the conference to act as a united "advocate for the rights and
opportunities for older people." The Leadership Council on Aging
brought together the following senior advocacy organizations:

American Association of Retired Persons/National Retired
  Teachers Association
Gray Panthers
National Council of Senior Citizens
National Council on the Aging
Gerontological Society of America
Association for Gerontology in Higher Education
Western Gerontological Society
National Association of State Units on Aging
National Association of Area Agencies on Aging
Urban Elderly Coalition
Social Security Department, AFL-CIO
Retired Members Department, United Auto Workers
National Senior Citizens Law Center
National Association of Retired Federal Employees
National Caucus and Center on Black Aged
Asociacíon Nacional Pro Persona Mayores
National Pacific/Asian Resource Center on Aging
National Indian Council on the Aging
Older Women's League

National Interfaith Coalition on Aging

Concerned Seniors for Better Government

National Association of Mature People

National Association of Meal Programs

National Association of Nutrition and Aging Services Programs

American Association of Homes for the Aging

National Association of Retired Senior Volunteer Program (RSVP)
  Directors

National Association of Senior Companion Project Directors

National Association of Foster Grandparents Program Directors

Reagan administration officials feared that the conference would
give these senior rights organizations a highly publicized forum from
which to criticize the president's proposals on Social Security and
other aging issues. Thus the administration began positioning itself to
"manage" the conference and the political fallout that might result
from it. The executive director, the associate executive director, and
all but 11 of a 56-member advisory committee were replaced. The new
advisory committee changed the rules of the convention so that delegates would be limited to one vote—to either accept or reject the recommendations of each of the 14 working committees as a
package—rather than voting on each committee's proposal separately.
An additional 400 "presidential" delegates were appointed. Finally, the
Republican National Committee financed a preconference "survey" of
delegates, the ostensible purpose of which was to "see what the concerns of the seniors were." This survey questioned delegates on,
among other issues, their views on the role of government in care of
the aged, the kinds of cuts in federal aging programs they would
accept, their view of the president and his performance, and their
organizational affiliation and leadership positions (Rich and Baum
1984, 20–21).

Incensed senior rights advocates charged that the survey's real purpose was to intimidate and control the delegates. The Senate
Committee on Aging, dismayed by the administration's thinly dis-
guised attempt to manipulate the conference, responded by ordering a
congressional investigation. The House Select Committee on Aging,
chaired by Claude Pepper, also wanted answers. Pepper scolded that
"if the purpose of this effort was to gather information to stack the

important committees that will be considering President Reagan's Social Security and budget cuts, it would amount to an outrageous attempt to politicize what has historically been a bipartisan function" (Stockman 1986, 62).

The Leadership Council of Aging Organizations pressed Health and Human Services Secretary Schweiker, who was in charge of the conference, to revise the rules so that the delegates could exercise broader privileges of discussion and voting. Schweiker refused. Jacob Clayman, president of the National Council of Senior Citizens, charged that this would mean that "about 7.5 percent of the delegates, about 156 in each of the fourteen sessions, will make the ultimate decisions for the entire 2,200. . . . That, we think, is a perversion of the democratic process."[4]

On 30 November the conference finally opened to a warmly received address by Congressman Pepper, who promised the delegates that Social Security would be "preserved" by the Congress. Secretary Schweiker, speaking on behalf of the Reagan administration, called for a "bipartisan spirit of cooperation." The delegates then broke into committees. It quickly became apparent that such a spirit of cooperation was unlikely, at least within the Committee on Economic Well-Being, when Bert Sideman, director of the AFL-CIO's Social Security Department, soundly criticized the president's spring Social Security proposals. Defending the administration's position, conservative economist Michael Boskin countered that the serious financial problems in Social Security should be solved by reducing the growth of the system.[5] On the evening of the first conference day a meeting of delegates was called by representatives of the senior organizations to report what was going on in the committees. Delegates complained that they had not been allowed to speak, that their recommendations were ruled out of order, and that administration delegates were receiving special treatment. One delegate even called for Congressman Pepper to intervene.

On the second day of the conference a crowd formed outside the Committee on Economic Well-Being, chanting "We Want Pepper!" Shortly thereafter, Congressman Claude Pepper and several staff members arrived and attempted to gain entrance to the committee. As the news cameras rolled, Pepper, an honorary chairman of the conference, was refused entry by security guards, who said that only official delegates or observers could be admitted. The crowd responded with chants of "Let Pepper In!" The Congressman left, but after brief negotiations between his staff and security forces, he returned and was finally escorted into the room.

Also on the second day of the conference, President Reagan chose to address the delegates. Moving to limit potential political damage, the Great Communicator quickly attempted to establish himself as one of the aged. He opened by saying that, "We are of the same generation," explaining that he had been wrongly cast by his opponents "during the campaign and now in this office I hold, . . . as an enemy of my own generation. Most of this attack has been centered around one issue, Social Security. There has been political demogoguery and outright falsehood, and as a result many of those who rely on Social Security for their livelihood have been needlessly and cruelly frightened." The president went on to argue that the "state of aging" was tied to a "healthy economy" and made references to "run away government spending," dependency ratios, and the 28 percent of the federal budget that was allocated to the 11 percent of Americans over 65. Perhaps most important, however, for the first time he publicly withdrew his May recommendations and declared that "the needy elderly, like all needy Americans . . . have a government, and a citizenry, that cares about them and will protect them" (*New York Times,* 2 December 1981, 24).

President Reagan was clearly trying to distance himself, and the Republican party, from the increasingly unpopular stance on Social Security cuts. He continued this strategy of symbolic reassurance when, in December 1981, he appointed a blue-ribbon commission on Social Security, whose charge it was to study the issue and produce "bipartisan recommendations." Fearing that the Social Security issue would hurt Republicans in the upcoming 1982 congressional elections, Reagan shrewdly arranged for the commission to report its findings shortly *after* those elections. Although the outward appearance was one of bipartisanship and impartiality, the makeup of the commission in fact assured that it would be reasonably sympathetic to Reagan's preferences, with five members appointed by the president, five members chosen by the (Republican-controlled) Senate leadership, and five by the House leadership. By appointing a commission, Reagan had hoped to bypass the intense public scrutiny and lobbying pressures that the aging coalition could bring to bear. As Gray Panther leader Maggie Kuhn later recalled, however, the fact that they "weren't invited" did not detour senior advocates from making their preferences known to the commission members: "There was a commission established and we weren't invited, but we came and demonstrated every time it met. We talked a lot individually to members of the committee. We told them that the Social Security system constituted a contract between the American people and the U.S. Government that couldn't be broken. It was set aside, no matter how Ronnie would try to bankrupt it" (Lyman 1988, 30).

The two declared goals of the National Commission on Social Security Reform were "to propose realistic, long-term reforms to put Social Security back on a sound financial footing; and to forge a working, bipartisan consensus so that necessary reforms can be passed into law" (Clark 1981). Reagan said that he was open to any proposals that the commission might offer for "fixing" Social Security, with the major exceptions of funding out of general revenues and increased Social Security taxes. In its final report, the commission recommended that early retirement benefits (at age 62) be eliminated, and that the age for receiving benefits be raised to 68. They also recommended taxing benefits of those persons whose income exceeded $20,000, with the taxes so collected going back into the Social Security trust fund (Jannson 1988).

With the bipartisan commission having made its recommendations, the "crisis" was finally "resolved" through the 1983 amendments to the Social Security Act. This act permanently moved the cost-of-living allowances (COLAs) from July to six months later, in January. This was included in the legislation not only because it led to substantial "savings" but also because it enabled Republicans to argue that benefits were not actually being cut, but rather the rate of increase in benefits was simply being slowed. A second feature of the amendments put in place a mechanism that would reduce the COLAs when the trust funds were running low and increase COLAs when the trust funds were greater. A third amendment increased payroll taxes at a faster rate than had been provided for in the earlier 1977 amendments. A fourth subjected up to one-half of Social Security benefits to taxation if total income exceeded $25,000 for a single retiree or $32,000 for a couple. Finally, the age of eligibility for full benefits was raised. This amendment would not go into effect until the year 2000, and then would gradually raise the retirement age until it reached 67 in the year 2026 (Kingson 1984).

This set of political compromises effectively ended the "crisis" within the financing framework set out by the Reagan administration, at least for the short term. Other debates over the fairness and long-range financial soundness of the Social Security system were to follow, however, throughout the Reagan and Bush administrations, as senior rights advocates and their New Right opponents continued to face off over the future of the system.

Rhetorical Themes Used by the New Right to Delegitimize Aging Programs

As had been the case during the Roosevelt era a half century earlier, in the Reagan-Bush years the national debate over the fairness of old-age policies once again became highly polarized and emotional. This time, however, it was the opponents of aging-program expansion who had managed to seize the rhetorical initiative, placing senior rights advocates on the defensive. Taking advantage of anti–welfare-state sentiments in the late 1970s and 1980s, conservative interests that had long opposed the principles underlying Social Security, Medicare, and related programs now sensed a rare opportunity to undermine the legitimacy of those programs in the public mind.

The central motif around which opponents of Social Security organized their new public relations campaign was "the failure of public solutions." Their core assertion—that "public" solutions to problems of old age had "failed"—was two-pronged. First, neoconservatives claimed that Social Security and related programs had proven to be *fiscal* failures—that existing programs were economically unworkable in their present "public" form. As the senior vice president of Guardian Life Insurance of America put it in a 1980 *Forbes* critique, "Our present Social Security system ignores basic economics. . . . Social Security as practiced in this country now is an attempt both to eat the cake and to have it later. Even a child can see that won't work" (Bladen 1980, 40). The other prong of the "failure" argument was the idea of *moral* failure. Even if one could somehow defend them on economic grounds, publicly financed programs for the elderly remained fundamentally unethical. They had created unacceptable "inequities" between taxpayers and recipients and between young and old. Economist Peter Peterson wondered in a widely read 1982 article, "What then does it mean to say that the patterns and trends of today's benefits are sacred and untouchable? It means that people retiring today . . . will inevitably shortchange their children and grandchildren. I see no ethical logic in that position" (1982a, 53).

If, as those who subscribed to this rhetorical frame insisted, meddlesome "public" programs for the elderly had raised "staggering questions of both solvency and fairness," it followed that the solution to this quandary could only be found in a return to the time-worn principles of private thrift and personal responsibility. Neoconservative economists pointed out that the latter principles might easily be realized through strategies such as privatization and individual retirement accounts.[6] From the late 1970s through the early 1990s this core message—of privatization as the only alternative to failed public solutions—was aggressively sold to the public by conservative opponents of the senior rights movement, using a variety of images and arguments presented in the media.

The chief exponents of this reactionary frame included prominent New Right think tanks, business and insurance industry spokesmen, Reagan and Bush administration officials, interest groups such as Americans for Generational Equity, and a host of neoconservative economists, intellectuals, journalists, and politicians. These interests shared a common desire—to dismantle the federal aging programs that senior rights movement advocates had fought for half a century to build. If that did not prove possible because the American public could not be persuaded to part with those programs, their more modest objective was to at least achieve substantial cutbacks in existing programs and benefit levels and to shift some of the responsibility for old-age care away from the federal government and back onto local government, individuals, and families.

The most poignant symbolic weapon within the New Right's "failure of public solutions" arsenal was a clever appeal to fears that the Social Security system might go bankrupt. The "crisis and impending collapse" theme painted a frightening picture of the future of Social Security, Medicare, and related publicly financed old-age programs. The operative message was that prudent Americans should desert Social Security before it deserted them. Social Security could no longer be trusted to be there when they reached old age, so the time had come for Americans to withdraw their support for the failed public system and begin investigating private retirement alternatives offered by private insurance companies. Opponents of Social Security hoped that fear of an impending "collapse" in the public retirement system would become a self-fulfilling prophecy. As more and more citizens were persuaded to opt out of the public system in favor of private

Figure 7.1. Cartoon by Pat Oliphant in the 16 June 1980 *Business Week*.

arrangements, popular support for federal Social Security and Medicare expenditures would be undermined, and the system would then, in fact, collapse.

Beginning in the mid-1970s, a steady stream of neoconservative journal articles, newspaper editorials, and magazine features proclaimed the seriousness of this impending catastrophe with such anxiety-provoking headlines as "Social Security Fund's Problems Take on a New Urgency," "Fresh Scare over Social Security," "Facing the Social Security Crisis," "Why Social Security Is in Trouble," "Social Security: Don't Count on It," "The Shocking Shape of Things to Come," "Social Security: The Coming Crash," "Will Social Security Go Broke Soon?" and "Talk of Revamping the Social Security System." The credibility of this version of economic reality received a major boost when Ronald Reagan decided to lend the authority of the presidency to the New Right's crisis scenario. In a televised 24 September 1981 address to the nation, he told the American public that "for many years we've known that an actuarial imbalance existed and that the program faced an unfunded liability of several trillion dollars. . . . The Social Security retirement fund has been paying out billions of dollars

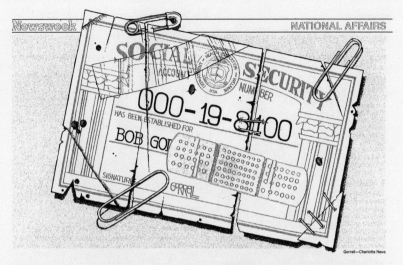

Figure 7.2. "Band-Aid solutions for the hemorrhaging program: By 2010, 'deficits so large we won't be able to handle them.'" Cartoon by Bob Gorrell in the 24 May 1982 *Newsweek*.

Reprinted by permission of Bob Gorrell and the *Charlotte News*.

more each year than it takes in and could run out of money" unless "something is done" (1982, 127). This pessimistic definition of the situation was also peddled aggressively on Capitol Hill, where Budget Director David Stockman warned the House Ways and Means Committee that they did not "fully understand the magnitude of the crisis facing Social Security" (quoted in Bethel 1981, 44).

In the print media, the "crisis and collapse" theme was driven home to the American public with a barrage of powerful visual images. A 1976 political cartoon featured in newspapers and magazines across the country depicts the Social Security edifice (originally intended to symbolize the soundness of institutionalized citizen protection) as a cracked, crumbling structure soon to collapse on the heads of the elderly (see Figure 7.1). Cleverly embedded in the image is the prescription for appropriate citizen action. The cartoon implies that the only way for older Americans to escape the consequences of fiscal collapse is to "get out" of the unstable Social Security system as soon as possible. A similar visual critique of the system's instability (see Figure 7.2) shows a tattered Social Security card precariously held

Figure 7.3. Cartoon by MacNelly from the 20 July 1981 *U.S. News & World Report*.

Reprinted by permission: Tribune Media Services.

together by a makeshift combination of tape, paper clips, staples, a safety pin, and a Band-Aid, symbolizing federal policymakers' numerous "failed" attempts to fix the program and place it on a sound fiscal basis. The caption reads "Band-Aid solutions for a hemorrhaging program: By 2010, 'deficits so large we won't be able to handle them.'" Another persuasive cartoon, appearing in *U.S. News & World Report* in 1981, likens the Social Security system to the sinking *Titanic*, with the nation's elderly presumably still on board and in danger of drowning in a sea of red ink (see Figure 7.3). Juxtaposed to the image of the sinking luxury liner is the foreboding headline "The Battle to Save Social Security: The Nation's Premier Pension System Is in Danger of Going Broke." Again, the implied response is for citizens to "get out" before it is too late (1981, 41).

Social Security's critics tried just about everything in their attempt to stampede Americans into abandoning the "collapsing" federal system. If the appeal to fear of drowning failed to strike a deep psychic chord, then perhaps the opposite would—fear of diving into an empty pool. In a widely circulated Pat Oliphant cartoon (see Figure 7.4), the

Figure 7.4. Cartoon (1980) by Pat Oliphant from the *Washington Star.*

looming possibility that the Social Security trust fund might run "dry" is dramatized in the form of a retired couple contemplating a dive from a Social Security–card "diving board" into an empty retirement-fund "pool." In yet another metaphor of impending disaster, a headline in *Business Week* cautioned readers that "The Social Security Time Bomb Is Still Ticking" (9 January 1978). Playing on the same image, a 1982 political cartoon by Borgman (see Figure 7.5) features a gigantic Social Security time bomb, which neither Democrats nor Republicans in a congressional "bomb squad" can muster the political courage to defuse.

Frequently invoked in conjunction with this collapse scenario was a related theme—that the "bureaucratic nightmare" conservatives had long warned about had now materialized. Critical articles in the popular media conjured up a specter of rampant mismanagement, inefficiency, waste, and fraud. Citing selective examples of inefficiency in the administration of Social Security and Medicare, these accounts appealed to the habitual American skepticism about governmental solutions to human problems and implied that private-sector insurance companies could handle the task more efficiently. A typical article, written in 1982 by the associate editor of *U.S. News & World Report,*

Cartoon by Borgman. Copyright 1982, King Features.

Figure 7.5. Cartoon (1982) by Jim Borgman from the *Cincinnati Enquirer*.
© 1982, King Features Syndicate.

sermonized against the "growing mountain of administrative foul-ups bedeviling the nation's 160-billion dollar pension system," which the editor attributed to the agency's "antiquated, patchwork computer system," its "monumental backlog," its "mammoth files," and mounting problems of "fraud" and "morale" among workers (Hildreth 1982, 92:67–68). A 1981 *Los Angeles Times* editorial, adopting an analogy reminiscent of the 1930s "Chock Full of Genii" image, concluded that the "Social Security system hovers . . . like the ghost of budgets future" over any hope of reforming the federal bureaucracy (22 February 1981).

Another theme that echoed anti-pension rhetoric of the 1930s was the idea that Social Security and related old-age programs were "too expensive for taxpayers." The 18 February 1980 cover of *Forbes* magazine asked readers rhetorically, "America's Elderly: Can We Afford Them?" The article inside worried that "the bite is going to go deeper—much deeper. . . . Where will the money come from—not just the short-term dollars needed in the 1980s, but the sums in the trillions needed in a couple of decades?" (Flint 1980, 53). Highlighting the

Cartoon by MacNelly. Reprinted by permission: Tribune Media Services, Inc., 1982.

Figure 7.6. Cartoon (1982) by MacNelly from the *Chicago Tribune*.
Reprinted by permission: Tribune Media Services.

unfairness of this tax "burden" in a 1981 televised address, Ronald
Reagan indignantly reminded Americans that "for the nation's work
force, the Social Security tax is already the biggest tax they pay. In
1935 we were told the tax would never be greater than 2 percent of the
first $3,000 of earnings. It is presently 13.3 percent of the first $29,700
and the scheduled increases will take it to 15.3 percent of the first
$60,600" (1982, 127). This conservative message of "runaway spend-
ing" on the nation's elderly was captured in a 1982 MacNelly cartoon
in the *Chicago Tribune* (see Figure 7.6), which depicts an old woman
in a wheelchair speeding past a congressional "squad car," while
Democratic and Republican "policemen" look on apathetically, unwill-
ing to arrest her for the violation. In another portrayal of "excessive"
federal spending—appearing in a 1988 *National Journal* piece entitled
"The Elderly's Limit" (not shown)—an old man sits smugly in a rocking chair shaped like a huge dollar sign. Playing on the same cost
symbolism, a 1989 *Dallas Morning News* cartoon (not shown), later
reprinted in the *Boston Herald*, has an elderly man standing behind an
X-ray machine. The X-ray of the old man's chest reveals not a normal
human rib cage but a grotesque dollar-sign–shaped skeleton, repre-

senting the exorbitant cost to taxpayers of federal Medicare and Medicaid programs (*Boston Herald,* 22 July 1990, 35). All of these images conveyed essentially the same message to the public. It was, as a 1988 *Forbes* piece cogently summarized, that "this is a luxury the nation can no longer afford" (Chakravarty and Weisman 1988, 225).

Even if the public could be persuaded to accept the crisis scenario as fact, to view Social Security as a bureaucratic mess, and to resent its exorbitant cost, the problem, however, remained that most Americans were unlikely to support major cutbacks in programs as long as the aged continued to be perceived as needy and deserving. The "compassionate stereotype" of the elderly constructed by movement activists in the 1920s and 1930s had legitimized Social Security to the public by presenting it as a just reward for frail, long-suffering elders, who had worked hard all of their lives only to be cast into poverty by economic forces beyond their control. This sympathetic image of the aged as helpless victims had served to justify their "right" to generous federal treatment for nearly 50 years. With the resurgence of conservatism during the Reagan-Bush era, however, New Right critics sensed an opportunity to reframe the context within which Americans viewed the elderly and their federal entitlements. Conservative commentators began to recast the nation's elders in the mass media as "greedy geezers" and "savage grannies" whose powerful "geriatric juggernaut" in Washington shamelessly protected their extravagant legislative gains at the expense of the needs of the rest of American society (Binstock 1983a; Minkler 1991).

For those whose agenda included reducing government services to the elderly, this image reversal served an important purpose. The various proposals for reduction or withdrawal of federal support would inevitably cause hardship and dislocation for at least some dependent elders, and public qualms about this needed somehow to be desensitized if retrenchment proposals were to gain widespread popular acceptance. To be willing to tolerate potential harm to members of any group, the public must first be able to rationalize the action to themselves. During times of war, for example, people in all cultures stereotype their "enemies" as greedy, evil savages with monsterlike qualities—people who therefore "deserve" to be treated with moral indifference (Keen 1986; Levine and Campbell 1972). To a lesser extent, this symbolic dehumanization process also occurs in the stereotyping and scapegoating of "enemies" in domestic political conflicts (Edelman 1988, 66–89). During the Reagan-Bush years, conser-

GREEDY GEEZERS

Figure 7.7. Cover illustration by Ben Sargent for the 28 March 1988 *New Republic*.

Reprinted by permission of Ben Sargent.

vative opponents of the senior rights lobby sought to redefine the popular image of the elderly in a negative light—as resented "enemies" of the rest of society—in order to justify proposed retrenchments in aging programs that might otherwise be regarded by the public as too cruel and heartless. The new profile drawn by opponents was of a wealthy, homogeneous class of elderly parasites, voraciously feeding off the nation's budget in ever-increasing numbers. *Forbes* magazine titled a 1981 article on the elderly "The Monster That's Eating Our Future." Similarly, economist Peter Peterson complained in a 1982 critique of old-age programs that "we have created a fiscal Frankenstein monster" that, if not stopped, would "devour immense amounts of available savings" (Peterson 1982, 36). A 1988 *Newsweek* feature called

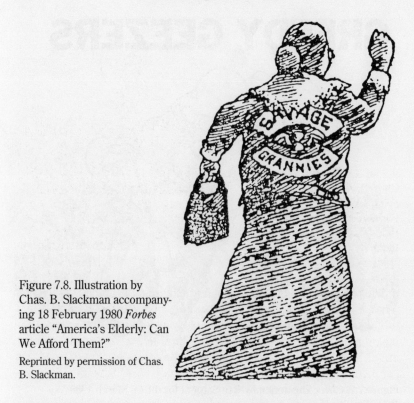

Figure 7.8. Illustration by
Chas. B. Slackman accompanying 18 February 1980 *Forbes*
article "America's Elderly: Can
We Afford Them?"

Reprinted by permission of Chas.
B. Slackman.

Social Security "The Trust Fund That Ate America." In visual form, the
classic expression of this redefined image of America's aged appeared
on the 28 March 1988 cover of the *New Republic* (see Figure 7.7),
which depicts approaching hordes of sinister-looking "greedy
geezers," armed with golf clubs, bearing down on the viewer. Their
features are subhuman, with bulging eyes and predatory teeth, symbolizing an avaricious economic enemy and implying that there are
"too many of them" to support.

A variant on this negative stereotype, the "savage granny" image,
also became a staple of anti–Social Security media caricatures during
the 1980s. Savage grannies were usually shown traveling in gangs and
wielding canes, golf clubs, or purses that they used aggressively to
force their will on others—clearly symbolic of the "ruthless" organized
political clout of the aging lobby on Capitol Hill. Figures 7.8 and 7.9,
which appeared as illustrations in the 1980 "Can We Afford Them?"

Figure 7.9. Illustration by Chas. B. Slackman accompanying 18 February 1980 Forbes article "America's Elderly: Can We Afford them?"

article in *Forbes*, are typical. In the first example the choice of the label "savage" on Granny's back is particularly noteworthy. It implies that the elderly are subhuman, barbaric enemies of civilized society (thus making it easier to rationalize treating their needs with moral indifference). The latter example, in which Granny's unrestrained greed has "broken the bank," illustrates the commonly used tactic of scapegoating the aged for the nation's economic difficulties (Flint 1980).

The 1980 *Forbes* article also made a concerted attempt to reverse the prevailing image of elderly impoverishment, arguing that "the myth is that they're sunk in poverty. The reality is that they're living well. The trouble is there are too many of them. . . . Why then does everyone believe the elderly are trapped in real poverty?" The old depression-era image of innocent, frail, deserving elders was ridiculed with selectively chosen anecdotes, cynically noting that "you don't get to be 65 without learning to play the system. . . . [T]here are police and firemen who retire with large tax-free pensions for finger injuries; indeed a New York fireman, retired with a 'back injury,' won a footrace to the top of the Empire State Building. Truck drivers who have never been in a mine can get black lung pensions" (Flint 1980). The intended cumulative impact of these counterimages was to achieve a reversal of the "compassionate stereotype" of deserving elders in the public mind.

Closely intertwined with the "greedy geezer" and "savage granny" stereotypes was the image of the aged as a "lazy, unproductive elite,"

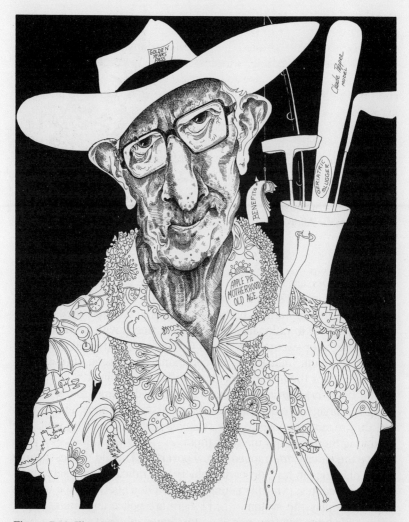

Figure 7.10. Illustration by Vint Lawrence from the 28 March 1988 *New Republic.*
Reprinted by permission of the *New Republic.* © 1988, the New Republic, Inc.

taking an extended late-life vacation at taxpayer expense. Conservatives in the 1920s and 1930s had warned that public pensions, if established, would "encourage idle dependency." Now, their Reagan-era counterparts argued, that prophecy had come to pass. An article by journalist Tom Bethel, entitled "Social Security: Permit for Idleness?," complained that "for years Americans have been encouraged to believe that they do not have to save much because government checks will come to their rescue at age 65" (1981, 40). Henry Fairlie, in his 1988 "Greedy Geezers" article, was less tactful: "The pampered ones, increasingly numerous, are rather pathetic to observe, some riding around in golf carts even on the streets, instead of taking an invigorating walk. . . . Everything is provided. For the first time in their lives, in effect, they have servants" (1988, 21). Robert Samuelson (1990a, 61; 1990b, 58) sounded the same theme in two critical *Newsweek* editorials on "Pampering the Elderly," in which he decried this kind of special treatment as "age discrimination in reverse." The theme was also a popular subject in anti–Social Security cartoons. A classic example, a caricature of senior rights champion Claude Pepper in the *New Republic* (see Figure 7.10), is replete with conspicuous symbols of leisure and privilege, including a Hawaiian shirt with lei, the ever-present golf clubs, a "golden years pass," and miscellaneous "benefits." Another drawing, appearing in a 1983 *Reader's Digest* piece entitled "Unfair to Taxpayers" (not shown), depicts a retiree lounging lazily in a lawn chair and reading a book, supported by a Social Security–card magic carpet, while a grimacing young worker-taxpayer, briefcase in hand, stoically shoulders the entire heavy burden beneath.

While all of these rhetorical themes proved somewhat effective in undermining public confidence in the integrity of the Social Security system, the most potentially divisive argument to emerge during the 1980s was the idea of "generational inequity." Originating in the same circle of neoconservative think tanks and journals that had spawned anti-progressive rationales like "reverse discrimination," "preferential treatment," and "political correctness," the generational-inequity theme quickly found its way into the mainstream media in the form of articles with such titles as "Cry Baby: The Intergenerational Transfer of Wealth," "Young v. Old," "The Coming Conflict as We Soak the Young to Enrich the Old," "Age Wars: The Coming Battle between Young and Old," "Justice between Generations," and "Lines Drawn for Intergenerational Battle." Exponents of the generational-inequity theme portrayed the generations within American society as having inherently divergent and incompatible interests. Generations were defined as being independent, opposed, and in conflict. Relationships between the generations were characterized as a zero-sum game in which one generation's gains automatically implied losses to other generations. The possibility that common interests might exist across generations was downplayed and rarely mentioned.

Within this zero-sum interpretive context, generous public spending on the aged gave the impression of being inherently unfair to future generations. Hence the act of committing a substantial portion of society's resources to the elderly became the moral equivalent of stealing from helpless children. A *Forbes* piece moralized that "we are witnessing nothing less than a massive transfer of income and wealth from the younger generations to the older. . . . Simply put, in economic terms we are consuming our children" (Chakravarty and Weisman 1988, 222). Phillip Longman, research director for the Washington-based lobby Americans for Generational Equity (AGE), protested in a widely read 1982 article that Social Security was inequitable because it resembled "a pyramid game in which those who arrive early get far more than they pay in. Later arrivals face the prospect of getting much less, or nothing at all." Republican Senator Dave Durenberger of Minnesota, the founder and chairman of AGE, worried that "we have entered an era in which the date of one's birth has become the prime determinant of one's prospects for realizing the American dream." Another veteran politician, former Colorado governor Richard Lamm, carried this generational inequity argument even further, criticizing society's use of expensive technologies to artificially keep elderly patients alive: "We've got a duty to die and get out of the way with all our machines and artificial hearts and everything else like that and let the other society, our kids, build a reasonable life" (Cooperider 1987, A13).

Some of the most dramatic statements of this inequity theme were visual. An illustration appearing on the November 1982 cover of *Washington Monthly* (see Figure 7.11) compared the inequity between generations to a poker game, in which the odds were heavily stacked in favor of the elder player. The drawing, which depicts a retiree and a young man on either side of a card table, is replete with symbols of generational unfairness. Nearly all of the winnings are on the old man's side of the table, including a house with a paid mortgage, generous Social Security and Medicare benefits, and tax breaks from the federal government. An ace surreptitiously tucked in the pantleg of the retiree implies that the old are cheating the young in a loaded budgetary game. The discrepancy between the casual sneakers worn by the old man and the young man's working shoes further highlights the theme of generational unfairness. The caption beneath reads "What the Old Are Doing to the Young." Another powerful visual statement of generational injustice (not shown), appearing in a November 1988 *Forbes* article, depicts successive generations of older

What The Old Are Doing To The Young

Figure 7.11. Cover illustration by Ray Diver from the November 1982 *Washington Monthly*.

persons precariously balanced on the shoulders of younger genera-tions in an unstable human pyramid, with a single child at the bottom bearing the cumulative burdens of the older generations.

This message of financial servitude of younger generations to older ones found its clearest expression in an AGE pamphlet entitled *Indentured Servants*: "We are raising a generation of young Americans who will live in financial slavery amidst a deteriorating environment and a crumbling infrastructure. . . . And like slaves everywhere they'll eventually revolt" (Cooperider 1987, A13). Hoover Institution economist and Reagan advisor Michael Boskin warned that "this could cause the greatest polarization in the U.S. since the Civil War. It would be age warfare" (*Time,* 24 May 1982, 22). In a provocative 1986 *Futurist* article entitled "Age Wars: The Coming Battle between Young and Old," AGE research director Phillip Longman sketched a hypothetical future scenario of the coming youth revolt, to be led by "Jesus Garcia," fictional charismatic leader of "the Youth Machine," in the year 2030. According to Longman's scenario, the revolt of the young against the elderly would begin with a series of anti–Social Security rallies around the country, in which thousands of younger workers would protest by burning their Social Security cards in front of the television cameras, shouting slogans like "Bash the Boomers." Longman continues the revolt scenario:

Tax evasion was already rampant, but once Garcia had elevated it in his speeches and videos into a high cause of youth, virtually the entire economy went underground. Within six months, the Social Security trust funds, which were already running trillion-dollar deficits, were completely exhausted. . . . The government had no choice but to yield to the demands of the Youth Machine. Social Security and Medicare payments to all but the very poorest senior citizens were sharply reduced. . . . Meanwhile, the government used the money freed up by the old-age benefit cuts to . . . allow young people affordable housing and a chance for a college education. (Longman 1986b, 9)

As with the "impending collapse" theme, purveyors of the generational-inequity idea hoped that their warnings of a coming conflict between generations would become a self-fulfilling prophecy, undermining support for the public retirement system among the younger generation and thereby clearing the way for privatized alternatives to Social Security.

To summarize, we have seen that the overall "failure of public solutions" frame used to delegitimize aging programs in the public mind during the Reagan-Bush era was made up of the component themes of "crisis and collapse," "bureaucratic nightmare," "too expensive for taxpayers," "greedy geezers," "lazy, unproductive elite," and "generational inequity," and that these variations on the central theme were mutually reinforcing in anti–Social Security rhetoric. The New Right's prescribed alternatives to the "failed" public solutions of Social Security and Medicare invariably called on policymakers to return to principles of private thrift and responsibility in devising future old-age programs. Ashby Bladen concluded a 1980 *Forbes* article with the advice that "sometime, somehow and fairly soon, Social Security is simply going to have to be financed just like private pensions . . . or else our standard of living will really go to pot and Social Security benefits will ultimately prove to be unsustainable" (1980, 40). In similar fashion, Phillip Longman concluded his 1986 "Age Wars" article with the observation that "like their Victorian forebears who built up America into a great industrial power, the baby boomers will have to rediscover an ethos of thrift and sacrifice for the future" (1986a, 11). The "solution" offered by Social Security's opponents in the Reagan-Bush era was thus remarkably similar to what it had been 50 years earlier, when Calvin Coolidge had admonished that "unless real reform comes from within, the problem will never be solved."

Rhetorical Themes Used by Senior Rights Advocates to Defend Movement Gains

Whereas the opponents of Social Security had woven their rhetoric around ideas of private responsibility for old-age care, stressing the divergent interests of generations competing with one another for resources in a zero-sum game, the rhetoric of senior rights advocates reflected diametrically opposed assumptions, emphasizing society's continuing obligation to provide for old-age care and the convergent interests between generations working together to solve problems of mutual interest.

During the Reagan-Bush years supporters of senior rights for the first time found themselves uncomfortably placed on the defensive, forced to justify the continued existence of federal programs whose sanctity had theretofore been taken for granted. Their rhetorical objective was therefore to frame the public debate over old-age justice in such a way as to reinforce the legitimacy of Social Security in the public mind, thereby protecting against opponents' attempts to justify retrenchments in old-age programs. Senior advocates constructed their new defensive posture around a motif of "preserving American social progress." The core assumption around which this interpretive package revolved was the idea that growth of Social Security and related federal old-age programs since the 1930s had constituted "progress" toward a more just and civilized society. As liberal economist Lester Thurow reminded Americans in a 1981 editorial, Social Security was "the crown jewel of American social legislation. . . . Instead of focusing exclusively on the problems of financing social security, the country should hold a victory celebration. We have created a just society where the elderly are treated almost as well as the rest of the population. That is something to take pride in" (Thurow 1981, 71).

It followed that any attempt to withdraw these humane social supports would represent a step backward to a more primitive society. Efforts by conservative opponents to scale back the gains achieved by the senior rights movement in half a century of political struggle were therefore characterized as barbaric attempts to dismantle the foundations of the modern social order. "Without these public and private intergenerational transfers," the executive director of the National Council of Senior Citizens warned, "the very continuity and progress of society and families would cease" (Hutton 1989, 84). Cuts in benefits and programs would, according to this frame, irreparably damage the interdependent social fabric of the United States as an advanced industrial society. Senator Joseph Biden captured this view in a moving 1981 congressional address, in which he defended elderly Americans against proposed Reagan administration retrenchments:

Let us not forget that the people who retire in 1982 . . . spent their adolescence in the midst of the Great Depression. The generation which retires next year was also the generation that fought the Second World War. Those that came back alive spent much of the 1940s and 1950s building the prosperity which we, their children, have come to enjoy . . . and all of a sudden they are being told we can no longer afford them. . . . I firmly believe that the best measure of the humaneness of a society is the way in which a society treats its elderly. The Social Security Act marks America's commitment to itself. It is the bedrock of a great task ahead of us to preserve and strengthen that foundation. We have a commitment morally as well as financially to maintain that system. (Biden 1981)

One of the most compelling elements within this overall "preserving social progress" package was the notion of "generational interdependence"—the idea that a "common stake" exists between generations. The theme was developed by senior advocates as a rhetorical antidote to the New Right's generational inequity arguments and found its clearest expression in a 1986 report entitled *Ties that Bind: The Interdependence of Generations*. The report—sponsored by the Gerontological Society of America, with support from the AARP and the National Institute on Aging—sought to "assist with the reformulation of the generational equity debate . . . and with the search for an appropriate framework for the aging society." The authors of the report identified what they called "flaws and misunderstandings" in the generational-inequity approach, countering each "misunderstanding" with relevant facts and arguments that supported their generational-interdependence perspective. Calling for a renewed commitment to strengthening family and community bonds, they argued that instead of attempting to incite conflict between young and old generations, Americans ought to adopt a "multigenerational" social-policy agenda stressing the "common stake" between generations that were, in fact, highly "interdependent":

By concentrating on what joins rather than divides the interests of generations . . . we focus on the common stake because we believe the interdependence of generations is at the root of the progress and continuity of society. An approach to public policy that does not build on this understanding—or, even worse, that threatens to strain the bonds between generations—does not represent a realistic framework from which to prepare for the future. (Kingson, Hirshorn, and Cornman 1986, 164)

Although popularized during the 1980s, this generational interdependence idea can be traced back to the activities of the Gray Panthers during the early 1970s. Prior to being dubbed the Gray Panthers, the membership had originally called themselves the "Coalition of Older and Younger Adults." In an interview featured in the *Progressive*, founder Maggie Kuhn explained that the theme of cooperation between generations had developed because "when we started the Gray Panthers in 1970 our first issue was the war in Vietnam. And that was the occasion for our becoming intergenerational. You see, we're not an old folks' lobby. We never have been. . . . In the Gray Panthers, probably 65 percent of the people are fifty and older. The rest are young" (Lyman 1988, 29).

Other senior activists traced the inspiration for the generational interdependence idea back even further—to the New Deal era. In "The Young and the Old Are Not Enemies," William Hutton of the National Council of Senior Citizens argued that "perhaps the greatest danger posed by AGE and others is that they encourage us to . . . ignore the history of respect for the compact of mutual responsibility between generations. In our highly interdependent society it is both normal and expected that individuals experience personal needs that only other individuals and social institutions can meet. Franklin Roosevelt realized this over 50 years ago, relating social insurance to what he identified as the 'hazards and vicissitudes of life'" (1989, 65).

Visual images used to convey the generational-interdependence theme usually depicted idyllic scenes of harmony and mutual support between generations. The cover of the *Ties that Bind* report, for example, showed a young boy and his grandfather eagerly running toward each other with open arms, anticipating a warm hug. The rear cover showed the same two figures strolling off together, arm in arm, engaged in pleasant conversation. Similarly, the Gerontological Society of America's "Common Stake" report featured an abstract drawing of a harmonious extended family—overlapping human figures of different ages, each enveloped within the protective support of the others (Kingson, Hirshorn, and Harootyan 1986).

As evidenced in these examples, the idea of preserving the integrity of home and family against the "hazards and vicissitudes of life"—a theme dating back to the 1930s—was a central part of the generational-interdependence appeal. Defenders of Social Security pointed out that conservative critics had conveniently ignored the fact that senior-assistance programs provide economic advantages to all members of society, regardless of age, and not just to persons over 65. If Social Security were to be scaled back or withdrawn, they argued, elderly poverty rates would increase phenomenally. Without Medicare, the burden of hospital and medical expenses would be overwhelming. Without a public pension to encourage older workers to retire, employment opportunities for younger workers would diminish. In short, without the economic independence that federal programs provided for older Americans, an enormous burden of support would fall on the shoulders of younger family members. As Robert Kuttner put it in a 1982 *New Republic* article, "The claim that today's workers are therefore a 'gypped generation' overlooks the immense value to middle-aged workers of their parents' financial security. Anybody with an aged parent on Social Security, rather than in the spare room, knows that Social Security prevents more 'inter-generational class wars' than it creates" (1982, 20).

New Right critics of Social Security had also conveniently overlooked the nature of the spending that goes on within families. John Rother, director of legislation, research, and public policy for the AARP, noted in a *Modern Maturity* article that "when you look at these kinds of private outlays—between parents and children and grandparents and parents—you find that there's a greater flow of resources down the age ladder than many people realize" (Carlson 1987, 39). Similarly, former National Institute on Aging director Robert Butler

Figure 7.12. "Have a heart! . . . Artificial or whatever!" Cartoon (1982) by Paul Conrad.

complained in 1983 that the generational inequity argument deceptively "overlooks . . . the income transfers that go on from elderly to the young" (1983, 37).

Senior rights activists also found objectionable the unrealistic picture that New Right inequity arguments had painted of static generations, seemingly frozen in time. Supporters of the interdependence perspective lampooned the naïveté of this assumption with the common-sense reminder that "everyone ages." They argued that the young and the old could not realistically be defined as having separate,

Figure 7.13. Cartoon (1974) by Paul Conrad.

permanent age-related interests if, over time, the young were themselves destined to become the old. "We're all doing it," Maggie Kuhn
coyly observed in a 1988 interview (Lyman 1988, 29). The idea that
everyone ages rendered the New Right's invidious comparisons
between the relative resources of different generations meaningless in
the long run. Old age was ultimately a shared fate, part of the human
condition. The aging process was involuntary, so it was cruel to pre-
tend that dependent elders could somehow be held morally responsi-

ble for their condition. The absurdity of doing so was driven home in a political cartoon that appeared during the early years of the Reagan administration, which depicted a miserly bureaucrat behind a Social Security office desk, moralistically scolding an elderly recipient because "in spite of all the warnings, in spite of all the efforts of our President . . . you went right ahead and got old!"

Another major theme employed by senior rights activists during the Reagan-Bush era was an appeal to sympathy for the "abandoned" elderly. Although not quite as effective in the context of the 1980s as it had been in the heyday of the depression, the specter of poverty and abandonment by an uncaring social order still retained much of its persuasive power. Senior advocates, fighting to preserve the integrity of besieged federal programs, argued that it would be heartless and cruel to withdraw support to helpless aged persons. They implied that for the federal government to permit older Americans to languish in poverty would amount to an indirect form of elder abuse. While conceding that the situation of the nation's elderly had improved considerably since the depression era, senior activists argued that there were nevertheless "growing holes in the safety net" and that many were still in danger of "falling through" if overzealous Washington budget-cutters ever succeeded in scaling back benefits. House Select Committee on Aging chairman Claude Pepper, sounding the "abandonment" theme, sermonized in 1980 that "the new panacea for the budget-cutters is the slashing of benefits for America's aged. . . . In light of the disproportionate incidence of poverty among the elderly, it is cruel and callous to suggest that older people are luxuriating in unearned and undeserved benefits. Our Federal policy toward the elderly leaves little margin for survival, much less for extravagance" (Pepper 1980). Similarly, Gray Panthers leader Maggie Kuhn railed against the injustice of a "society that throws people away, that views old age as a disease, that says if you don't have a job, you're nobody" (Lyman 1988, 29). In response to threatened cuts in elderly benefits in 1981, House Speaker Tip O'Neill chastised Reagan administration officials for their insensitivity, saying, "I'm not talking about political issues. I'm talking about the decency of it. It was a rotten thing to do" (*Newsweek,* 25 May 1981). Ohio Senator Howard Metzenbaum agreed, commenting that "I see no logical reason why the burden of balancing the budget should be placed upon people who are receiving Social Security. How cruel and inhumane that would be!" (*U.S. News & World Report,* 10 May 1982, 81). New York Senator Daniel Patrick Moynihan

"BLESS US, O LORD, AND THESE THY GIFTS WHICH WE ARE ABOUT
TO RECEIVE FROM WHAT IS LEFT OF OUR SOCIAL SECURITY CHECK..."

Figure 7.14. Cartoon (1973) by Paul Conrad.

called it "political terrorism" against the old (*U.S. News & World Report,*
20 July 1981, 42). Figures 7.12 through 7.14 illustrate the use of this
"abandonment" theme in visual form. Note that Figures 7.12 and 7.13,
in particular, recall vividly the depression-era image promulgated by
Father Townsend of the "haggard, very old women, stooped with great
age, bending over the barrels, clawing into the contents."

Figure 7.15. Cartoon (1984) by Ben Sargent from the *Austin American Statesman*.
Reprinted by permission of Ben Sargent.

Closely related to this abandonment theme was the idea of threatened cutbacks as "broken promises." Defenders of Social Security argued that any retrenchments in federal aging programs would represent a grave moral injustice to the elderly because promises of support made to them in good faith by their government would thereby be broken. During his 1980 campaign and in his initial budget proposals Ronald Reagan had promised to keep old-age programs like Social Security and Medicare intact as part of the "safety net." When subsequent Reagan administration plans to make cuts in Social Security failed to live up to this early rhetoric, advocates of senior rights immediately cried foul, accusing President Reagan, Budget Director Stockman, and Health and Human Services Secretary Schweiker of an "unconscionable breech of faith." Former Health Education and Welfare Secretary Wilbur Cohen (who, as a research assistant in the 1930s, had helped Roosevelt's committee draft the original Social

Figure 7.16. Cartoon (1989) by Paul Conrad.

Security Act) moralized that "the thrust of the proposals, in addition to violating the President's promise, would break the promises made by 20-odd Congresses and seven past presidents from both parties to those who have paid in earmarked contributions to the system over the past 43 years" (1981, 5). Others were equally outraged by the proposed cuts. Claude Pepper complained that with administration talk of $40 billion in cutbacks coming on the heels of presidential assurances, "People must be in a grave quandary. . . . What are people to believe?"

(*Time,* 24 May 1982, 27). Senator Howard Metzenbaum of Ohio commented that "you don't lead people down a primrose path, tell them
they're going to get retirement benefits they paid for and then suddenly tell them they aren't going to get it" (*U.S. News & World Report,*
10 May 1982, 81).

Nor did Reagan's bipartisan commission or the 1983 amendments
do much to stop these charges of betrayal. When in March 1984
Reagan made a careless reference to "revamping" the Social Security
program to make it fair to young workers, the reaction by pro–Social
Security forces was again swift and virulent. House Speaker Tip O'Neill
charged that "President Reagan has had a lifelong itch to tamper with
Social Security. This week he started scratching again" (*Washington
Post,* 8 May 1984). And Senate Minority Leader Robert Byrd quipped
that "Trusting the Reagan administration to protect Social Security
after the November election is like hiring a self-proclaimed pyromani-
ac to guard your firewood" (*Washington Post,* 1 July 1984). Pro–Social
Security political cartoons also sounded the "broken promises" theme,
with moving visual portrayals of the effects on elderly Americans of
Reagan administration proposals to cut back on food stamps, Social
Security benefits, and disability (see Figures 7.15 and 7.16).

This argument that the New Right's proposed retrenchments represented "broken promises" was in turn based on two underlying
premises: the idea that a sacred, inviolable "contract" existed between
the government and the elderly, and the idea that federal old-age benefits were an earned "right." Unless those bedrock assumptions could
somehow be discredited by conservatives, it would be difficult to rationalize making major permanent cuts in aging programs. Gray
Panthers leader Maggie Kuhn laced her speeches, interviews, and
writings with references to the "fact" that Social Security was "a *contract* between the American people and the U.S. Government" (Lyman
1988, 30). Similarly, former HEW Secretary Wilbur Cohen (1981, 5)
defended the sacrosanct status of elderly programs against proposed
Reagan administration cuts by arguing that "the entitlement to these
benefits is a *compact* the elected representatives of the people have
written into a law. . . . The millions of people who have contributed to
this insurance system for many years have done so believing it would
pay them the stipulated benefits as a matter of legal *right*." Ohio
Senator Howard Metzenbaum's defense of cost-of-living adjustments
in 1982 employed the same argument: "I believe that a *contract* was
made with the people when they entered the Social Security system.

Figure 7.17. Cartoon (1981) by Paul Conrad.

This is their money. They had it deducted from their wages" (*U.S.
News & World Report,* 10 May 1982, 81). The director of the AARP's
Public Policy Institute, Marilyn Moon, added an intergenerational
twist to the contract argument, pointing out in a *Modern Maturity* article that the Social Security system constituted "a 'social *contract*' in
which the *promise* is made that the working generation help support
the old. . . . The promise is that the next generation will act in the
same way. And as long as everyone observes the contract, then I think
we have a pretty fair way to go about meeting this particular social
obligation" (1987, 39).

Relegitimizing Social Security in the public mind as an earned
"right," guaranteed by a "contract" between citizens and government
proved to be a useful strategy for deflecting many of the New Right's

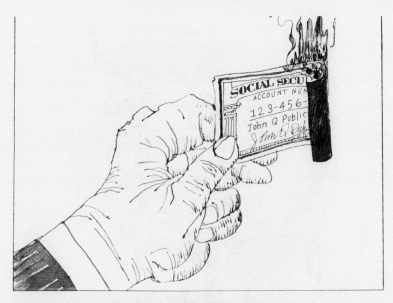

Figure 7.18. Illustration from the 1 June 1981 *New Leader.*
© 1981, the *New Leader.* Reprinted by permission.

rhetorical ploys. The problem remained, however, that the public's view of the elderly themselves was being tarnished by the recurrent "greedy geezer" portrayals in the media, which were rapidly undermining sympathy for the aged as a deserving constituency. The senior rights movement's rhetorical response to the "greedy geezer" image was the "truly greedy vs. truly needy" image. This class-oriented theme was best captured in a 1981 *Los Angeles Times* cartoon (see Figure 7.17) that depicts a "truly greedy" corporate executive (complete with cigar and briefcase) shamelessly competing for public alms on a city street with a rumpled, homeless "truly needy" old man.

Whereas neoconservatives had chosen to focus on generational differences, thereby diverting attention away from the widening resource gap between haves and have-nots in American society, senior rights advocates adamantly insisted that class-related differences remained central to any conception of fairness, and accused the Reagan and Bush administrations of further aggravating class divisions by unjustly diverting the nation's financial resources away from programs helping the "needy" and into the already-overstuffed pockets of the "greedy."

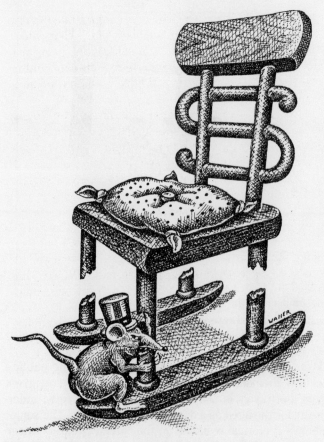

Figure 7.19. Illustration by Charles Waller from the February 1983 *Progressive*.

Reprinted by permission of Charles Waller.

Ronald Pollack, director of the Washington-based Villers advocacy group, complained in an article in *Generations* that "under the banner of 'intergenerational equity,' we hear much about the alleged maldistribution of resources between old and young. But . . . it is the growing disparity between rich and poor, not between old and young, that tears at the fabric of America. The 'intergenerational equity' debate is a diversionary and dangerous sideshow" (1988, 14). Similarly, William Hutton of the National Council of Senior Citizens warned that

"I'M IN THE SAME AGE BRACKET AS YOU"

Figure 7.20. Herblock cartoon, from *Herblock through the Looking Glass* (New York: W. W. Norton & Co., 1984).
Reprinted by permission.

although New Right critics claimed to be promoting fairness between generations, "they promote divisiveness, not equity. . . . [W]e should not fall victim to the trick of pitting one generation against the other for funds in a mythical competition to see who is worse off" (1989, 64).

This class-conflict–oriented "truly greedy vs. truly needy" theme, especially as it was expressed in visual form, had much in common

Figure 7.21. Illustration by Giora Carmi from the 16 January 1988 *Nation*.
Reprinted by permission of Giora Carmi.

with the "fat cats vs. the frail elderly" theme used by pension advocates in the 1930s. As in that era, a ruthless greedy economic elite was
portrayed as unfairly monopolizing the wealth and resources of the
nation at the expense of the common man, the little guy, the elderly
poor (see Figures 7.17–7.22). A 1981 drawing in the *New Leader* (see
Figure 7.18), for example, shows a man in an expensive pin-striped
suit setting fire to "John Q. Public's" Social Security card. Another
class-oriented portrayal (see Figure 7.19), appearing in the *Nation*, features a rat in a top hat fiercely gnawing away at the supports of a dollar-sign–shaped rocking chair. A December 1981 Herblock cartoon
(see Figure 7.20) mocks Reagan's statement to the White House
Conference on Aging that "we are of the same generation," comparing
Reagan's $515,878 income with the $2,043 a year Social Security mini-

Figure 7.22. Herblock cartoon from 1990.
© 1990 by Herblock in the *Washington Post*. Reprinted by permission.

mum benefit received by persons retiring at age 65. The theme of "fat cats" hoarding resources at the expense of the "frail" elderly was also stressed in a 1983 *Nation* drawing (see Figure 7.21), which depicts a corpulent man, whose plate is already full, reaching rudely across a dinner table to steal the few remaining crumbs from the nearly empty plate of an emaciated old man. This image of New Right "thievery from the aged" surfaced as well during the Bush administration, when a 1990 *Washington Post* cartoon (later reprinted in *Newsweek*) showed

Bush administration officials attempting to "steal" from the Social Security trust fund to pay off the federal deficit (see see Figure 7.22).

As in the imagery of the 1930s, "truly greedy" fat cats were cast as evil enemies and contrasted with "truly needy" elderly martyrs. Greed and excess were associated with corpulence. Elderly need and innocence were associated with physical emaciation. The intended rhetorical effect of such images was clearly to achieve a reversal in the public mind of the "greedy geezer" image, transferring public attributions of blame for the nation's economic problems from the greed of the old to the greed of the well-to-do and mammoth corporations. As senior advocate Ronald Pollack put it in a 1988 *Generations* article, the strategy of the movement's "rhetorical response to inter-generational-strife provocateurs" was to "refocus social debates on the inequitable divisions among the rich and poor, instead of imaginary differences between young and old" (1988, 14).

Chapter Eight

Framing the Equity Debate in an Era of Mass-Mediated Political Realities

The temptation always exists for political actors to propose magical solutions and fantastic political scenarios through the use of myths, stereotypes, scapegoats, and other symbolic devices. When the media legitimize such techniques and in the process condition the public to accept them, there are no restraints on the fabrication of political reality.

W. Lance Bennett[1]

At the outset of this inquiry we suggested that in order to understand how the debate over American old-age policy is being framed today, and what form it might be expected to take in the years ahead, one must be familiar with the dynamics of how aging policy struggles and their associated rationales have developed historically. We therefore made it our task in the intervening chapters to trace some of the salient disputes that have been waged between progressive and conservative elements in American society over definitions of social justice in old age, as these have expressed themselves through successive eras of the American experience.

We observed that from colonial times through the end of the nineteenth century the problems of elderly Americans were usually viewed as a residual component of the more general public debate over appropriate government policy toward the poor. This residual status of aging issues was particularly evident during the Jacksonian period, when restrictive public-assistance reforms—aimed at reinforcing work norms among the non-elderly poor—inadvertently affected the living conditions of the elderly as well, forcing many to spend their last years in squalid poorhouses.

In the twentieth century, however, struggles over appropriate policies for the nation's elderly increasingly began to take center stage, becoming the context within which larger debates over national welfare priorities and the proper role of the state were to be played out. Here one can begin to speak of "senior power" and the gradual emergence of a "senior rights movement" in the United States. During the incipiency phase of this emerging senior rights movement in the 1920s and 1930s, the issue of "social security" for elderly Americans became the focal point of national debates over federal welfare priorities and eventually the centerpiece of Franklin Roosevelt's New Deal legislation. As the senior rights movement further coalesced during the Great Society period, national debates over whether the state should provide national health insurance to its citizens once again centered on services to the aged. And in the era of social-policy retrenchment that followed, in the late 1970s and the 1980s, policies affecting elderly Americans again became a major focus of national attention—this time as attempts by conservatives to scale back the "welfare state" pointed to Social Security and Medicare expenditures as major culprits in America's fiscal woes. Clearly, public debates over what constitutes social justice in old age have come to occupy center stage in the construction (and *de*construction) of American social policies for the better part of this century. One needs only to look at the hefty portion of annual federal expenditures devoted to Social Security and Medicare in recent decades, or at the vast membership of the AARP, to see the importance aging politics has come to assume in American life.

The Growing Influence of Mass-Media Symbolism on Political Outcomes

As we return to the present and consider the future of old-age politics in the United States, what overall insights might be drawn from the foregoing analysis of past struggles that would better equip us to understand aging politics in coming years? Certainly one recurrent observation in this analysis of past trends has been that the alternative social constructions and symbolic portrayals of elderly conditions advanced by various political factions have often proven to be as important—sometimes more so—than the "objective" realities. In each historical context we have examined, those social forces most successful in their efforts to construct and "sell" to the public their images of what would be fair with respect to aging policy—that is, those who were victorious in framing the debate—also proved successful in exerting a preponderant influence on policy outcomes.

It seems reasonable to extrapolate from this general trend that just as alternative definitions and constructions of elderly conditions have been pivotal in determining aging policy outcomes in the American past, they can be expected to become even more so in an age of electronic mass-mediated political realities. Political pundits and practitioners increasingly agree that the American political process has in recent decades come to be more and more dominated by sophisticated telecommunications wizardry and the concomitant growth industries of "public relations" and "image management." Daniel Boorstin, reflecting on this change, observes that "two centuries ago when a great man appeared, people looked for God's purpose in him; today we look for his press agent."[2] This qualitative shift in how political battles are fought has thus far taken a number of forms, most notably the rise to prominence of political consultants and ideological think tanks, the "staging" of political events for network news consumption, and increasing reliance by political actors on such techniques as "spin control," "sound bites," focus groups, perception analyzers, sociodemographic targeting, computer-aided direct mail, and campaign videos to sway public opinion on issues and win elections.[3]

Two aspects of this qualitative shift in how American politics is conducted are likely to have an impact on elderly rights struggles in coming decades: the shift from substance to symbolism in political discourse, and the shift from labor-intensive to capital-intensive political organizing.

With respect to the former, the past 30 years in American politics have seen a steady erosion of traditional forms of political expression by a new politics of symbol generation. Most analysts of political communication attribute this shift to the introduction and diffusion of television. In the decades since its introduction into American homes, political contests fought out in the public arena have become more concerned with public relations and image management than with substantive discussion of the merits of alternative public policies. In the first presidential debate to be disseminated by the new technology of television, for example, image clearly triumphed over substance. In 1960, candidates Richard Nixon and John Kennedy both held popular positions on policy issues of the day. Kennedy and his advisors, however, proved much more effective in exploiting the potential of the new technology of television for symbolic packaging of a political candidate and for selling political ideas to the public. The latter carried the day, and the presidential election.[4]

American politics would never be quite the same again. Impressed with the image Kennedy had projected and its effectiveness in influencing millions of voters, politicians in subsequent campaigns were quick to see the advantages of television as a medium of mass public persuasion, and increasingly turned to symbolic packaging and advertising advisors to create a salable television image. Over the next several decades, Madison Avenue advertising techniques that had been used to sell toothpaste, detergents, and beer to consumers were applied by political influentials to the task of "selling" policies, candidates, and political ideas to the public. As this shift from substantive political dialogue to image manipulation has accelerated in recent years, it has become easier and easier, as political scientist W. Lance Bennett (1988, 170) puts it, "to propose magical solutions and fantastic political scenarios," playing skillfully on the hopes and fears of mass publics, in an atmosphere in which "restraints on the fabrication of political reality" have largely disappeared.

In this brave new political world, mastery of the art of mass public persuasion via television has come to assume unprecedented importance. One need merely consider the monumental success of screen actor and television personality Ronald Reagan, whose rapid political ascent first to the governorship of California and then to the presidency is widely acknowledged to have been a function of his exceptional skills as a "Great Communicator" rather than his knowledge of the intricacies of public administration. Reagan's unsuccessful challenger in the 1984 presidential election, Walter Mondale—a more traditional-style politician—aptly summarized the political sea change that has been taking place when he attributed his landslide 1984 loss to Reagan (he carried only his home state) to the fact that he had "never warmed up to the camera." In this revised climate of public discourse—with its altered game rules and sophisticated opinion-manipulation technologies—political forces that continue to rely on the more traditional forms of public argumentation and organization are likely to find themselves left behind by the emerging politics of media image management and "manufacturing consent," just as earlier in this century many silent film stars became cinematic dinosaurs when they failed to adapt to the new communications technology of the "talkies."

Given the reality of this shift from substance to symbols in public debate, one can anticipate that in coming years the social construction of images of aging will become even more pivotal to the outcomes of old-age policy struggles than it has been in the past. Modern telecommunications technologies tend to magnify the importance of popular images and impressions and to downplay the role of rational argumentation (Postman 1984; Bennett 1988; Mitroff and Bennis 1993; Powell and Robinson 1996). It follows that both the advocates and the opponents of further expansion of old-age rights will find it necessary to concentrate much more heavily on strategies of symbolic persuasion, on projecting salable images of their cause, and on psychologically convincing the public to support it.

Concomitant with this shift from substantive public discourse to symbol manipulation, the past 30 years have also witnessed an equally dramatic shift from labor-intensive to capital-intensive political organizing techniques. Traditionally in American politics, lobbying efforts and electoral contests have been carried out primarily by interest organizations and party coalitions, which exercised political influence by mobilizing large numbers of citizens in favor of political causes. In this political game, there was great political clout in numbers. Declines over the past several decades in citizen affiliation with political parties and mass organizations such as labor unions, together with the development of expensive communications and information technologies, have, however, rendered political competition in the United States less labor-intensive and more capital-intensive. Thus far this trend has fallen largely to the benefit of the political Right, the sympathizers of which are in a better position to supply the large sums of capital needed to compete effectively in the new public relations campaigns required to win political battles in an era of mass electronic media (Ginsberg 1986, 149–80; Bennett 1992).[5]

The potential implications of this latter shift for future elderly-rights struggles are profound. Because labor-intensive political organizing is no longer sufficient to win political battles, the massive memberships commanded by organizations such as the AARP will constitute less of a political advantage than was the case earlier in this century. The real political danger for such organizations lies in the illusions of power and security fostered by such massive numbers, which do not necessarily translate into political clout in the new era of image management and expensive capital-intensive political struggle. With organization and sheer numbers becoming secondary to image management and the ability to afford sophisticated communications technologies, it would be prudent for elderly advocates to pay more attention to the latter in conducting future political battles. In fact, the large numbers and clout of senior organizations on Capitol Hill might even conceivably be used *against* the gray lobby if they can be skillfully manipulated by their political adversaries to create a sense of injustice among the nonelderly. Advocates for the aged will have to learn how to spot such attempts and deflect them promptly with effective "counterpropaganda" appeals via mass media, making efficient use of their organizational resources to conduct effective image-management and damage-control campaigns.[6]

The Emerging Conflict over Definitions and Appropriate Models of Aging

If our analysis of the history of senior-power struggles has been on track, and if we are correct in assuming that the telecommunications revolution has magnified the importance of public image management in winning political battles, then one can anticipate that in coming years the power to determine the course of American aging policies will become more and more a matter of "who defines." Political conflicts over aging policy objectives are likely to assume the form of intense public skirmishes over conflicting *images* of the problems of elderly Americans, over who should and should not be responsible for solving those problems, and over what would constitute "appropriate," "equitable," or "feasible" solutions.

We know from our survey of past conditions that spokespersons for the more affluent, privileged elements of American society have usually attempted to frame the public debate over appropriate social policies in such a way as to justify keeping public assistance benefits to disadvantaged groups low and "welfare" programs minimal in scope. The incentive to invent plausible rationales justifying "cost-containment" measures has been particularly strong during periods of economic contraction, which have increased the tax burden on the more privileged sectors of society and threatened their accustomed standard of living (Galbraith 1985). Two prominent examples of this pattern noted in the foregoing historical account were the early 1800s backlash in New England cities and the Reagan-era public-assistance retrenchments. Despite the fact that these examples are separated by a century and a half, when they are juxtaposed the pattern appears remarkably similar. In both instances one finds that anti–public-assistance rationales were constructed by representatives of privileged groups to legitimize social-program retrenchments and expenditure reductions to the public, with an eye toward reducing tax burdens on more affluent Americans (Powell and Williamson 1985b).

This rhetorical strategy of recasting public definitions of the situation so as to justify cost-containment measures has tended to work best for conservative elites when the middle class believes it is more likely to benefit from a reduction in taxes than from an increase in benefits from the state (Sears and Citrin 1985; Kuttner 1980). In the 1980s retrenchment phase, for example, the well-crafted rhetoric of Ronald Reagan (and his advisors, image consultants, and speechwriters) proved highly effective in persuading voters that tax reduction was the better solution to their woes. A similar pattern would appear to have been at work in the mid-1990s "Republican revolution"/ "Contract with America." Political leaders who during these periods attempted to frame the debate in such a way as to link the well-being of middle-class Americans with expansion of benefits to citizens—for example Walter Mondale, Michael Dukakis, Edward Kennedy, Bill Clinton—proved considerably less articulate and persuasive in their public posturing and generally failed to carry the day.

Throughout the present century, those social reformers and progressive politicians who have sought to improve the lot of low-income Americans have typically been most successful in their public appeals when socially disadvantaged groups could plausibly be included as beneficiaries of programs designed to meet the needs of the broad middle class. This has especially been the case in justifying aging programs to the public, such as Social Security and Medicare. The strategy that has worked best in rationalizing reforms designed to improve the lot of the less affluent elderly has been to frame the policy debate in such a way as to benefit as wide a segment of the elderly population as possible. Conversely, those who have sought to achieve policy goals chiefly benefitting the more affluent echelons of American society—elderly and nonelderly alike—have proven most persuasive when it has been possible to frame policy issues in such a way as to differentiate between what is in the interest of the upper middle class and what is in the interest of the lower middle class. The catastrophic health insurance legislation enacted (and later repealed) in the 1980s was a notable example of how this kind of divisive strategy can work.

What these general observations suggest is that the emerging battle over definitions and models of American aging policy is likely to be largely one of public perceptions of *divergent* interests versus perceptions of *convergent* interests. One can anticipate, for example, that in coming years conservative opinion-makers will be able to convince many Americans to accept the idea of minimizing federal commitments to the elderly if the debate can somehow be framed so as to clearly differentiate what is in the interest of the lower-middle-class elderly from what is in the interest of the upper-middle-class elderly. Those seeking to reduce support levels for elderly programs, and for the welfare state more generally, can be counted on to try to discover ways to split the middle class elderly into two opposed camps—those who are heavily dependent on Social Security pensions for their sustenance and those who are not—with the objective of influencing the latter category to defect and withdraw their support.

One possible way to do this would be to expand the fraction of the middle class covered by "private" or "independent" retirement options. A harbinger of this "divide and conquer" strategy was initiated during the Reagan administration years, when American retirees were offered special financial incentives to persuade them to contribute to individual retirement accounts (IRAs). If IRAs were to be made more widely available, and taxpayers were allowed to make substantially larger contributions to them, such a program might, over time, succeed in substantially eroding the extent of support from the more affluent segment of the middle-class elderly for Social Security.

Besides the strategy of dividing elderly Americans along lines of economic status, there is the additional promising strategy of *generational* division. Those seeking to limit or cut back on spending for aging programs are likely to prevail over the next several decades to the extent that they are able to get the policy debate framed in a way that will persuade young and old Americans to view their interests as being incompatible. In recent years, the concept of "intergenerational equity" has been developed and sold to the public by Americans for Generational Equity (AGE), Lead . . . Or Leave, and a number of conservative political organizations critical of Social Security spending and the welfare state generally. Essentially these groups have attempted to divert the focus of the public debate away from previous issues of the needs and social rights of elderly Americans by arguing that less of society's resources ought to be devoted to the aged so that more will be available for use by future generations—for example, poor children and young adults who are trying to build a new life for themselves.

Not surprisingly, on closer inspection these new conservative generational politics organizations appear to be more interested in reducing federal spending on the aged than in their professed goal of increasing social benefits to poor children and young adults. What IRAs and intergenerational equity have in common is that they are well-targeted symbolic devices aimed at persuading Americans— primarily middle-class Americans—to perceive their relationship with others in society as a *zero-sum* game and then to act on the basis of that perception. Forces seeking to scale back Social Security and other elderly benefits, then, can be expected to prevail in coming years to the extent that they are able to "divide and conquer," stressing images of divergent interests between population categories, downplaying possible convergent interests among these groups, and persuading the public to think about aging issues primarily in zero-sum terms.[7]

By contrast, those whose objective is to preserve or expand elderly benefits can be expected to do quite the opposite. The progressive perspective will be successful to the extent that proponents of elderly rights are able to get the public debate defined around perceptions of a "common stake" among all categories of elderly Americans, as well as among younger and older generations. Instead of divergence, progressives can be expected to stress *convergence* of interests. Instead of a zero-sum game, progressives will prevail in defining American old-age policies to the extent that Americans can be persuaded to see the interests of upper-middle-class and lower-middle-class elderly, and young and old, as a *non–zero-sum* game.[8]

Human history is an immensely complex process, and the authors of this volume certainly do not presume to be soothsayers. All of the foregoing observations do appear to converge, however, on one central conclusion: that the future of old-age policies in the United States is likely to depend heavily on who frames the public debate over what is equitable. As has so often been the case in the American past, one can expect that future efforts to control the direction of elder service policies will continue to center on competing definitions of what would constitute a fair relationship between generations and classes in American society. Our analysis demonstrates that contemporary concerns over the issues of "intergenerational equity" and what to do about the "crisis" of the Social Security system, on closer scrutiny, turn out to be only the most recent polemical manifestations of a recurrent struggle to define the context of public discourse over social justice in old age. If the New Right succeeds in its recent rhetorical attempts to redefine public discussion around images of "getting Big Government off the taxpayer's back," cost-containment, privatization, and intergenerational (rather than interclass) equity, it is conceivable that the centerpiece of twentieth-century aging reforms, Social Security, could be scaled back or even substantially dismantled based on popular acceptance of these rationales. If, on the other hand, senior rights advocates, liberal policy analysts, and professionals with vested interests in the "aging enterprise" are able to keep the policy debate consistently focused on problems of adequacy, elderly needs, citizen rights to old-age security, and issues of class equity, one can expect that Social Security and other hard-won accomplishments of the twentieth-century senior rights movement will be preserved and perhaps even expanded in coming years. Whichever scenario ultimately unfolds, one thing is clear: it will be the success of political influentials in selling one or the other of these interpretive packages to the public that will primarily determine the course of old-age politics in the United States.

Notes

Chapter One

1. *Political Science and Politics* 18, no. 1 (1985): 10.
2. For prominent examples of "Social Security crisis" and "generational inequity" perspectives developed over the past several decades, see Martin Feldstein, "Social Security, Induced Retirement and Capital Formation," *Journal of Political Economy* 82 (1974): 905–26, and "Facing the Social Security Crisis," *Public Interest* 47 (1977): 88–100; Nathan Keyfitz, "Why Social Security Is in Trouble," *Public Interest* 58 (1980): 102–19; Jerry Flint, "The Old Folks: Can We Afford Them?" *Forbes*, 18 February 1980, 51–56; Alvin Rabushka and Bruce Jacobs, "Are Old Folks Really Poor?" *New York Times*, 15 February 1980, A29; Peter Ferrara, *Social Security: Averting the Crisis* (Washington, D.C.: Cato Institute, 1982); Peter Peterson, "Social Security: The Coming Crash," *New York Review of Books*, 2 December 1982; Phillip Longman, "Justice between Generations," *Atlantic Monthly* 256 (1985): 73–81; Michael Boskin, *Too Many Promises: The Uncertain Future of Social Security* (Homewood, Ill.: Dow Jones-Irwin, 1986); Phillip Longman, "Age Wars: The Coming Battle between Young and Old," *Futurist* 20, no. 1 (1986): 8–11; P. Hewitt, *A Broken Promise* (Washington, D.C.: Americans for Generational Equity, 1986); Phillip Longman, *Born to Pay* (Boston: Houghton Mifflin, 1987); Henry Fairlie, "Greedy Geezers: Talkin' bout My Generation," *New Republic*, 28 March 1988, 19–22; S. N. Chakravarty and K. Weisman, "Consuming Our Children? The Intergenerational Transfer of Wealth," *Forbes*, 14 November 1988, 222–32; and Laurence Kotlikoff, *Generational Accounting: Knowing Who Pays, and When, for What We Spend* (New York: Free Press, 1992).

3. Examples of this perspective on old-age justice can be found in Robert Binstock, "The Aged as Scapegoat," *Gerontologist* 23 (1983): 136–43; Eric Kingson, B. Hirshorn, and L. Harootyan, *The Common Stake: The Interdependence of Generations—a Policy Framework for an Aging Society* (Washington, D.C.: Gerontological Society of America, 1986); Elliot Carlson, "The Phony War: Exploding the Myth of Generational Conflict between Young and Old," *Modern Maturity*, February 1987, 34–46; Theodore Marmor and J. Mashaw, *Social Security: Beyond the Rhetoric of Crisis* (Princeton, N.J.: Princeton University Press, 1988); Ronald Pollack, "Serving Intergenerational Needs, Not Intergenerational Conflict," *Generations* 13 (1988): 14–18; J. R. Gist, *Social Security and Well-Being across Generations* (Washington, D.C.: AARP Public Policy Institute, 1988); Robert Hudson, "Social Policy and Aging: Renewing the Federal Role," *Generations* 13 (1988): 23–26; Jill Quadagno, "Generational Equity and the Politics of the Welfare State," *Politics and Society* 17, no. 3 (1989): 353–76; William Hutton, "The Young and the Old Are Not Enemies," *USA Today Magazine*, March 1989, 63–65; Elizabeth Binney and Carroll Estes, "The Retreat of the State and Its Transfer of Responsibility: The Intergenerational War," *International Journal of Health Services* 18, no. 1 (1988): 83–96; and Maggie Kuhn and J. E. Bader, "Old and Young Are Alike in Many Ways," *Gerontologist* 31, no. 2 (1991): 273–74.

4. Murray Edelman's "political spectacle" approach to the study of symbolic politics weaves together crossdisciplinary insights from George Herbert Mead, Alfred Schutz, Kenneth Burke, Edward Sapir, Lev Vygotsky, Nelson Goodman, Harold Lasswell, Jacques Ellul, Ludwig Wittgenstein, Noam Chomsky, Jacques Derrida, Michel Foucault, Jurgen Habermas, and Jean Baudrillard, among others. See *The Symbolic Use of Politics* (Urbana, Ill.: University of Illinois Press, 1964); *Politics as Symbolic Action* (Chicago: Markham, 1971); *Political Language: Words That Succeed and Policies That Fail* (New York: Academic Press, 1977); and *Constructing the Political Spectacle* (Chicago: University of Chicago Press, 1988).

Chapter Two

1. *The Writings of Thomas Paine, 1779–1792* [1792], vol. 2, ed. Moncure D. Conway (New York: AMS Press, 1967), 487.

2. "On the Laboring Poor—Communicated to the Editor of a Newspaper, April, 1768," in *Essays on General Politics, Commerce, and Political Economy* [1768], vol. 2 (New York: Augustus M. Kelley, 1971), 368.

3. Similarly, in a Concord, Massachusetts, meetinghouse a century later (1774), historian David Hackett Fischer finds that the order of seating was determined first according to age, then by wealth within each age group, and then by social status within wealth groups. See his chapter "Growing Old in America," in *Aging: The Individual and Society* (New York: St. Martin's Press, 1980), 47. The evidence does not, however, necessarily point to the existence of a colonial gerontocracy. Some historians have argued, for instance, based on the same meetinghouse records, that they instead indicate the priority of wealth over age in the seating plan. See John Demos, "Old Age in Early New England," in *The American Family in Social-Historical Perspective,* ed. Michael Gordon (New York: St. Martin's Press, 1978), 245–47.

4. British dominance during the colonial period led to adoption of the English poor laws as a basic model for American relief policies. The main features of the Elizabethan Poor Law of 1601 and the Law of Settlement and Renewal of 1662 were therefore emulated and adapted to American conditions. The Poor Law of 1601 had established the principle of state responsibility for indigent persons and required that poor relief be organized at the community level and funded by a local poor tax. See Blanche Coll, "Public Assistance in the U.S.: Colonial Times to 1860," in *Comparative Development in Social Welfare,* ed. E. W. Martin (London: Allen & Unwin, 1972).

5. Quoted in R. E. Pumphrey and M. W. Pumphrey, eds., *The Heritage of American Social Work* (New York: Columbia University Press, 1961), 22.

6. Cotton Mather, *Diary of Cotton Mather* [1713], vol. 2 (Boston: Massachusetts Historical Society, 1912), 208.

7. Quoted in Alfred J. Kutzik, "American Social Provision for the Aged: An Historical Perspective," in *Ethnicity and Aging,* ed. Donald Gelfand and Alfred Kutzik (New York: Springer, 1979), 37.

8. Note the parallels to official rhetoric used to justify retrenchments during the Reagan era a century and a half hence. See Lawrence A. Powell and John B. Williamson, "The Reagan-Era Shift toward Restrictiveness in Old Age Policy in Historical Perspective," *International Journal of Aging and Human Development* 21, no. 2 (1985): 81–86.

9. As Murray Edelman points out, "A particular explanation of a persisting problem is likely to strike a large part of the public as correct . . . if it reflects and reinforces the dominant ideology of that era" (see *Constructing the Political Spectacle*, 17).

10. For descriptions of the conditions that obtained in nineteenth-century American poorhouses, see Matthew Carey, *Letters on the Condition of the Poor* (Philadelphia: Hasswell & Barringon, 1835); and New York State Senate, "Report of the Select Senate Committee to Visit Charitable and Penal Institutions, 1857," New York Senate Document No. 8 of 1857, in *Public Welfare Administration in the United States: Selected Documents* [1857], ed. S. P. Breckinridge (Chicago: University of Chicago Press, 1938).

11. It should be kept in mind, however, that despite this succession of liberalizing reforms and increasing expenditures, large segments of the American elderly population remained excluded from coverage. Immigrants who came to the United States after the war, most southerners, and blacks were ineligible, as were many low-income workers.

12. Similar legitimizing functions had been performed by Malthusian population doctrines accompanying industrialization in Europe. See Gaston V. Rimlinger, *Welfare Policy and Industrialization in Europe, America and Russia* (New York: Wiley, 1971), and John Kenneth Galbraith, "How to Get the Poor off Our Conscience," *Harper's,* November 1985, 17–20.

13. The account in this section owes much to W. Andrew Achenbaum's excellent analysis of declines in elderly social status and opportunity in *Old Age in a New Land: The American Experience since 1790* (Baltimore: Johns Hopkins University Press, 1978), 47–106. See also his article "The Obsolescence of Old Age in America, 1865–1914," *Journal of Social History* 8 (1974): 45–64, and David Hackett Fischer, *Growing Old in America* (New York: Oxford University Press, 1977), 77–195.

Whether the decline in elderly status from a "golden age of aging" can be attributed primarily to forces of modernization and industrialization or is better explained by other factors (e.g., cultural values, new ideas) remains a subject of considerable disagreement among scholars. See Donald Cowgill and L. Holmes, eds., *Aging and Modernization* (New York: Appleton-Century-Crofts, 1972); W. Andrew Achenbaum and Peter Stearns, "Essay: Old Age and

Modernization," *Gerontologist* 18 (1978): 307–12; Brian Gratton, "The New History of the Aged: A Critique," in *Old Age in a Bureaucratic Society: The Elderly, the Experts, and the State in American History*, ed. David Van Tassel and Peter Stearns (Westport, Conn.: Greenwood Press, 1986), 1–29; Patricia Passuth, "Reconsidering the History of Old Age," *Contemporary Sociology* 13, no. 6 (1984): 676–77; Carole Haber, *Beyond Sixty-five: The Dilemma of Old Age in America's Past* (New York: Cambridge University Press, 1983); Jill Quadagno, *Aging in Early Industrial Society* (New York: Academic Press, 1982); Peter Stearns, *Old Age in Preindustrial Society* (New York: Holmes & Meyer, 1982); Gerald Grob, "Explaining Old Age History: The Need for Empiricism," in Van Tassel and Stearns, *Old Age in a Bureaucratic Society,* 1–29; and Thomas R. Cole, *The Journey of Life: A Cultural History of Aging in America* (Cambridge: Cambridge University Press, 1992).

Chapter Three

1. "What Rabbi Wise Said," *Old Age Security Herald* 4, no. 5 (May 1930): 12.

2. "Coolidge and Self-Respecting Security," *Old Age Security Herald* 5, no. 4 (1931): 2.

3. Curiously, Hering had decided to involve the Eagles in the issue of old-age pensions not for political reasons but as a means for increasing membership, since it had begun to fall off sharply immediately after World War I. See Jill Quadagno, *The Transformation of Old Age Security: Class and Politics in the American Welfare State* (Chicago: University of Chicago Press, 1988), 66–72.

4. The Eagles pamphlet from which these quotes are taken is reprinted in Lamar T. Beman, *Selected Articles on Old-Age Pensions* (New York: H. W. Wilson, 1927), 241.

5. *Santa Rosa Press-Democrat*, 12 October 1938, quoted in Phil Hamilton, "$30 a Week for Life!" *California: Magazine of the Pacific* 36 (1938): 13. See also John Canterbury, "Ham and Eggs in California," *Nation* 147, no. 17 (1938): 408–10.

6. With the support of Ham and Eggs, as well as Sinclair's EPIC and the Townsendites, Downey went on to defeat incumbent senator William McAdoo in that year's Democratic party primary—this

despite Roosevelt's public endorsement of McAdoo. In the November election that followed, Ham and Eggs–backed candidates Sheridan Downey, Ellis Patterson, and Culbert Olson were all victorious. Unfortunately, the Ham and Eggs ballot initiative did not fare as well; it was narrowly defeated in the same election by a vote of 1,143,670 to 1,398,999. This, however, did not seem to discourage Ham and Egg members from continuing their quest to enact the plan. See Joseph Alsop and Robert Kintner, "Merchandizing Miracles: Sherican Downey and the Pension Business," *Saturday Evening Post,* 16 September 1939, 5–7, 85–87, 89–90; Max Knepper, "Scrambled Eggs in California," *Current History,* October 1939, 58–64; Sheridan Downey, *Pension or Penury?* (New York: Harper, 1939), 26–27.

7. Winston Moore, *Out of the Frying Pan* (Los Angeles: De Vorss, 1939), 185.

8. *Proceedings of the Fourth National Conference on Old Age Security* (New York: American Association for Old Age Security, 1931), 83.

9. "The Townsend Plan," song, in *The Records of the Committee on Economic Security,* (Washington, D.C.: National Archives, 1934), Box 43, Group 47.

10. Quoted in the *American Labor Legislation Review* 17, no. 3 (1927): 286.

11. Quoted in the *Old Age Security Herald* 4, no. 2 (1930): 5.

12. Ibid., vol. 4, no. 3 (1930): 1, 8.

13. Ibid., vol. 4, no. 9 (1930): 3.

14. Ibid., vol. 4, no. 3 (1930): 11.

15. *American Labor Legislation Review* 19, no. 1 (1928): 78, and 20, no. 2 (1930): 213. A typical article of this kind in the *Review,* guest authored by a member of the Canadian House of Commons in 1934, sought to soften American prejudices against the idea of federal government intervention by quoting from one of Prime Minister Bennett's radio addresses on "the crash and thunder of toppling capitalism." In the address, Bennett had exhorted his audience to consider the fact that "the old order is gone . . . reform means government intervention. It means government control and regulation. It means the end of laissez faire." See J. S. Woodsworth, "Social Insurance in Canada: Program and Prospects," *American Labor Legislation Review* 24, no. 1 (1934): 61–66.

16. Descriptions of the propaganda campaign launched in California to disrupt Sinclair's gubernatorial aspirations can be found

in his *I, Candidate for Governor, and How I Got Licked: The Inside Story of a Political Campaign, the EPIC Plan, and How Big Business Raised Millions of Dollars and Beat it by Millions of Lies* (Pasadena, Calif.: Sinclair, 1934), and Greg Mitchell, *The Campaign of the Century: Upton Sinclair's Race for Governor of California and the Birth of Media Politics* (New York: Random House, 1992).

17. *Old Age Security Herald* 5, no. 12 (1931): 1, 4, 6.

Chapter Four

1. "Are Old Age Pensions Worth Their Cost?," *American Labor Legislation Review* 26, no. 1 (1936): 10, 14.

2. *Insecurity: A Challenge to America: A Study of Social Insurance in the United States and Abroad* (1938; New York: Agathon Press, 1968), 732, 761.

3. See Arthur Altmeyer, *The Formative Years of Social Security* (Madison: University of Wisconsin Press, 1966), 10.

4. See U.S. Senate, Committee on Finance, *Economic Security Act: Hearings on S. 1130, a Bill to Alleviate the Hazards of Old Age Unemployment, Illness, and Dependency*, 74th Cong., 1st Sess. (Washington, D.C.: U.S. Government Printing Office, 1935), 104–105.

5. Quoted in Arthur M. Schlesinger, *The Coming of the New Deal* (Boston: Houghton Mifflin, 1958), 308–309.

6. See Martha N. Ozawa, "Income Redistribution and Social Security," *Social Service Review* 50 (1976): 216–17, and Jerry R. Cates, *Insuring Inequality: Administrative Leadership in Social Security, 1935–54* (Ann Arbor: University of Michigan Press, 1983).

7. Although the primary reason for the pension-reform movement's loss of prominence after 1935 was the host society's successful co-optation of its reform agenda, another contributing factor may have been a change in the composition of the population during the 1940s and 1950s. Because fertility rates affect the age composition of the population, when the birthrate rises the proportion of older Americans falls. Historian David Hackett Fisher has suggested that "it is no accident" that the dismal years of the senior movement "coincided almost exactly" with the so-called baby boom that began in the mid 1940s. See D. H. Fischer, "The Politics of Aging: A Short History," *Journal of the Institute for Socioeconomic Studies* 4 (1979): 61.

Chapter Five

1. Quoted in Max J. Skidmore, *Medicare and the American Rhetoric of Reconciliation* (University of Alabama: University of Alabama Press, 1970), 126.

2. Quoted in the *New York Times,* 10 February 1961.

3. See U.S. Senate, Committee on Finance, *Economic Security Act: Hearings on S. 1130, a Bill to Alleviate the Hazards of Old Age Unemployment, Illness, and Dependency,* 74th Cong., 1st Sess. (Washington, D.C.: U.S. Government Printing Office, 1935), 489.

4. The account in this section is based in large part on Theodore Marmor's excellent legislative history of the political struggle to pass Medicare, *The Politics of Medicare* (Chicago: Aldine, 1973). See also his "Enacting Medicare," in *The Aging in Politics: Process and Policy,* ed. Robert Hudson (Springfield, Ill.: Charles C. Thomas, 1981), 105–34; and Eugene Feingold, *Medicare: Policy and Politics* (San Francisco: Chandler Publishing, 1966).

5. Quoted in Richard Harris, *A Sacred Trust* (New York: New American Library, 1966), 55.

6. The listing of Medicare interest group alignment patterns is based on Marmor, "Enacting Medicare," 112.

7. For examples of rhetorical arguments accompanying this ongoing "cost-containment vs. needs" debate, see Daniel Callahan, *Setting Limits: Medical Goals in an Aging Society* (New York: Simon & Schuster, 1987); Robert L. Barry and Gerard V. Bradley, eds., *Set No Limits: A Rebuttal to Daniel Callahan's Proposal to Limit Health Care for the Elderly* (Urbana: University of Illinois Press, 1990); Peter J. Ferrara, "Catastrophic Health Benefits Translate into Catastrophic Taxes," *Consumers' Research Magazine* 72, no. 4 (1989): 11–14; Robert J. Samuelson, "Pampering the Elderly," *Newsweek,* 26 November 1990, 58; Elizabeth A. Binney and Carroll L. Estes, "Setting the Wrong Limits," in *A Good Old Age? The Paradox of Setting Limits,* ed. P. Homer and M. Holstein (New York: Simon & Schuster, 1990); Stephen Crystal, "Health Economics, Old-Age Politics, and the Catastrophic Medicare Debate," *Journal of Gerontological Social Work* 15, no. 3–4 (1990): 21–31; Phillip Longman, "Catastrophic Follies: The Old Folks Outfox Themselves," *New Republic,* 21 August 1989, 16–17; Amitai Etzioni, "Spare the Old: Health Care Generation War," *Nation,* 11 June 1988.

Chapter Six

1. Speech at the 1972 Democratic National Convention, quoted in Robert Heffernan and Charles Maynard, "Living and Dying with Dignity: The Rise of Old Age and Dying as Social Problems," in *This Land of Promises*, ed. A. Mauss and J. Wolfe (Philadelphia: J. B. Lippincott, 1977), 73.

2. U.S. Department of Health, Education, and Welfare, "Higher Social Security Payments," letter, DHEW Publication No. (SSA)73-10322/October (Washington, D.C.: Social Security Administration, 1972).

3. See Carroll L. Estes, *The Aging Enterprise: A Critical Examination of Social Policies and Services for the Aged* (San Francisco: Jossey-Bass, 1979), and "The Aging Enterprise Revisited," *Gerontologist* 33 (1993): 292–98.

4. On the emergence and rapid development of elderly interest groups in the postwar period, see Michael Carlie, "The Politics of Age: Interest Group or Social Movement?" *Gerontologist* 9 (1969): 259–63; Robert Binstock, "Interest Group Liberalism and the Politics of Aging," *Gerontologist* 12 (1972): 265–80; Henry Pratt, "Old Age Associations in National Politics," *Annals of the American Academy of Political and Social Science* 415 (1974): 106–19, and *The Gray Lobby* (Chicago: University of Chicago Press, 1976); John Williamson, Linda Evans, and Lawrence Powell, "The Political Influence of Older Americans," *Journal of Sociology and Social Welfare* 8 (1981): 771–95; Robert Binstock, "The Politics of Aging Interest Groups," in *The Aging in Politics,* ed. Robert Hudson (Springfield, Ill.: Charles C. Thomas, 1981); Henry Pratt, "National Interest Groups among the Elderly: Consolidation and Constraint," in *Aging and Public Policy*, ed. William Browne and Laura Katz Olson (Westport, Conn.: Greenwood Press, 1983), 145–79; Christine Day, *What Older Americans Think: Interest Groups and Aging Policy* (Princeton, N.J.: Princeton University Press, 1990); and Jill Quadagno, "Interest Group Politics and the Future of U.S. Social Security," in *States, Labor Markets, and the Future of Old-Age Policy*, ed. John Myles and Jill Quadagno (Philadelphia: Temple University Press, 1992).

5. On the history and political activities of the AARP, see Henry Pratt, "National Interest Groups among the Elderly: Consolidation and Constraint," in *Aging and Public Policy*, ed. Browne and Olson,

145–79; Lawrence Powell, "The American Association of Retired Persons," in *United States Health Interest Groups*, ed. Craig Ramsay (Westport, Conn.: Greenwood Press, 1995); *How Legislative Policy Is Made at AARP* (Washington, D.C.: AARP National Legislative Council, 1992); M. Hornblower, S. Holmes, and M. Riley, "Gray Power! AARP Emerges as the Nation's Most Powerful Special-Interest Lobby," *Time*, 4 January 1988, 36–37; *Toward a Just and Caring Society: The AARP Public Policy Agenda* (Washington, D.C.: AARP, 1995); Janet Novack, "Strength from Its Gray Roots: The American Association of Retired Persons," *Forbes*, 25 November 1991, 89–94; and Lee Smith, "The World According to AARP," *Fortune*, 29 February 1988, 96–98.

6. On the history and political activities of the NCSC, see Pratt, "National Interest Groups among the Elderly"; Lawrence Powell, "The National Council of Senior Citizens," in *United States Health Interest Groups*, ed. Ramsay; John W. Edelman, "National Council of Senior Citizens, Inc.," *Senior Citizen* 13, no. 3 (1967): 15–18; *National Council of Senior Citizens Progress Report* (Washington, D.C.: NCSC, 1995).

7. See C. Offen, "Profile of a Gray Panther," *Retirement Living*, December 1972, 33; the *Gray Panthers Pamphlet* (Philadelphia: Gray Panthers, 1974); Dicter Hessel, *Maggie Kuhn on Aging* (Philadelphia: Westminster Press, 1977); Ruth H. Jacobs and Beth B. Hess, "Panther Power: Symbol and Substance," in *Aging, the Individual, and Society*, ed. Jill Quadagno (New York: St. Martin's Press, 1980), 407–13; Ron Wyden, "Inside Congress: A Gray Panther's View," *Generations* 9 (1984): 31–32; John Zinsser, "Gray Panthers: Fighting the Good Fight for 15 Years," *Fifty-Plus* 26 (July 1986); Jan Fisher, "Maggie Kuhn's Vision: Young and Old Together," *Fifty-Plus* 26 (July 1986): 22; Francesca Lyman, "Maggie Kuhn: A Wrinkled Radical's Crusade," *Progressive* 52 (January 1988): 29–31; Maggie Kuhn, *No Stone Unturned: The Life and Times of Maggie Kuhn* (New York: Ballantine, 1991).

8. On the phenomenon of ageism and its political implications, see Robert N. Butler, "Ageism: Another Form of Bigotry," *Gerontologist* 9 (1969): 243–46, and *Why Survive? Being Old in America* (New York: Harper & Row, 1975); Simone de Beauvoir, *The Coming of Age*, trans. P. O'Brien (New York: G. P. Putnam's Sons, 1972); Jack Levin and William C. Levin, *Ageism: Prejudices and Discrimination against the Elderly* (Belmont, Calif.: Wadsworth,

1980); Erdman B. Palmore, "Attitudes toward the Aged," *Research on Aging* 4 (1982): 333–48; Lawrence Powell, "Mass Media as Legitimizers of Control," in *Aging and Public Policy: Social Control or Social Justice?*, ed. John Williamson, Judith Shindul, and Linda Evans (Springfield, Ill.: Charles C. Thomas, 1985), 180–205; and Kenneth Branco and John Williamson, "Stereotyping and the Lifecycle: A Focus on Views of the Aged," in *In the Eye of the Beholder*, ed. Arthur G. Miller (New York: Praeger, 1982), 411–65.

9. For a creative application of Edelman's symbolic politics perspective to analysis of the White House Conferences, see Henry Pratt's "Symbolic Politics and White House Conferences on Aging," *Society*, July–August 1978, 67–72. This section owes much to Pratt's perceptive analysis. See also Harold Johnson, George Maddox, and Jerome Kaplan, "Three Perspectives on the 1981 White House Conference on Aging," *Gerontologist* 22 (1982): 125–28.

10. Quoted in Pratt 1978, 70–71.

11. Ibid.

12. Ibid.

13. For an overview of the development of the OAA since its inception in 1965, see Robert H. Binstock, "From the Great Society to the Aging Society: 25 Years of the Older Americans Act," *Generations*, Summer–Fall 1991, 11–18.

Chapter Seven

1. "Taking America to the Cleaners," *Washington Monthly*, November 1982, 24.

2. Francesca Lyman, "Maggie Kuhn: A Wrinkled Radical's Crusade," *Progressive* 52 (January 1988): 29–30.

3. Quoted in the *Los Angeles Times*, 9 May 1981, 5.

4. Quoted in the *New York Times*, 28 November 1981, 10.

5. Quoted in the *New York Times*, 1 December 1981, 24.

6. Examples of these "privatization" arguments can be found in E. Laffer and D. Ranson, "A Proposal for Reforming Social Security," in *Income Support for the Aged*, ed. G. S. Trolley and R. V. Burhauser (Cambridge, Mass.: Ballinger, 1977), 130–50; Peter J. Ferrara, "Social Security and the Super IRA: A Populist Proposal," in *Social Security: Prospects for Real Reform*, ed. Peter J. Ferrara (Washington, D.C.: Cato Institute, 1985), 193–220; Peter G. Peterson, "The Salvation of Social Security," *New York Review of Books*, 16 December 1982, 54;

Michael J. Boskin, "Social Security: The Alternative before Us," in
The Crisis in Social Security: Problems and Prospects, ed. Michael
Boskin (San Francisco: Institute for Contemporary Studies, 1977),
173–86, and "The Financial Impact of Social Security by Cohort under
Alternative Financing Assumptions," in *Issues in Contemporary
Retirement*, ed. R. Ricardo-Campbell and E. P. Lazear (San Francisco:
Institute for Contemporary Studies, 1988), 207–32.

Chapter Eight

1. *News: The Politics of Illusion*, 2d ed. (New York: Longman,
1988), 170.
2. Daniel Boorstin, *The Image, or What Happened to the
American Dream* (New York: Antheneum, 1962).
3. For perceptive analyses of this sea change in American poli-
tics, see Larry Sabato, *The Rise of Political Consultants* (New York:
Basic Books, 1981); Gary Mauser, "Marketing and Political
Campaigning: Strategies and Limits," in *Manipulating Public Opinion*,
ed. Michael Margolis and Gary Mauser (Pacific Grove, Calif.: Brooks
Cole, 1989), 19–46; W. Lance Bennett, *The Governing Crisis: Media,
Money, and Marketing in American Elections* (New York: St. Martin's
Press, 1992); Larry Sabato and David Beiler, "Magic . . . or Blue
Smoke and Mirrors? Reflections on New Technologies and Trends in
the Political Consultant Trade," in *Media Technology and the Vote: A
Sourcebook,* ed. Joel Swerdlow (Washington, D.C.: Annenberg
Washington Program, 1988), 3–17; Stephen Ansolabehere, Roy Behr,
and Shanto Iyengar, *The Media Game: American Politics in the
Television Age* (New York: Macmillan, 1993); Shanto Iyengar, *Is
Anybody Responsible? How Television Frames Political Issues* (Chicago:
University of Chicago Press, 1991); Edwin Diamond and Stephen
Bates, *The Spot: The Rise of Political Advertising on Television*
(Cambridge, Mass.: MIT Press, 1992); Terence H. Qualter, *Opinion
Control in Democracies* (New York: St. Martin's Press, 1985); Ian
Mitroff and Warren Bennis, *The Unreality Industry: The Deliberate
Manufacturing of Falsehood* (Oxford: Oxford University Press, 1993);
Ben Bagdikian, *The Media Monopoly*, 4th ed. (Boston: Beacon Press,
1992); Shanto Iyengar and Donald Kinder, *News That Matters*
(Chicago: University of Chicago Press, 1987); and Douglas Kellner,
Television and the Crisis of Democracy (Boulder, Colo.: Westview
Press, 1990).

4. The impact of the "new" medium of network television on the outcome of the 1960 presidential contest is described in Theodore H. White, *The Making of the President, 1960* (New York: Antheneum House, 1961), 317–34; Erik Barnouw, *Tube of Plenty: The Evolution of American Television*, 2d ed. (New York: Oxford University Press, 1990), 270–75; and Kathleen H. Jamieson, *Packaging the Presidency: A History and Criticism of Presidential Campaign Advertising*, 2d ed. (New York: Oxford University Press, 1992), 158–61.

5. Murray Edelman notes in *Constructing the Political Spectacle* (Chicago: University of Chicago Press, 1988) that "the privileged benefit more than the underprivileged from spectacle construction" via mass-media images, adding that such images are "typically expressions and vivid reinforcements of the dominant ideology that justifies extant inequalities. They divert attention from historical knowledge, social and economic analysis and unequal benefits and sufferings." Similarly, Benjamin Ginsberg observes in *The Captive Public: How Mass Opinion Promotes State Power* (New York: Basic Books, 1986) that the "marketplace of ideas" in Western democracies such as the United States "effectively disseminates the beliefs and ideas of upper classes while subverting the ideological and cultural independence of the lower classes" (86). In a related vein, Edward Herman and Noam Chomsky assert in *Manufacturing Consent: The Political Economy of the Mass Media* (New York: Pantheon, 1988, xi) that mass media in the United States "serve to mobilize support for the special interests that dominate the state and private activity."

While the systematic bias in access to media technologies cited by these analysts unquestionably gives privileged elites a definite political advantage, it is important not to lose sight of the fact that in recent decades non-establishment, progressive reform groups have at times also succeeded in manipulating television images to sway public opinion in favor of their desired policies, particularly in the case of the civil rights and anti–Vietnam War organizations of the 1960s and environmentalist groups in the 1980s. Presumably, similar "guerrilla media" techniques could also be applied in coming years in advancing elderly rights struggles. See, for example, the methods described by political consultant Tony Schwartz in *Guerrilla Media: A Citizen's Guide to Using Electronic Media for Social Change*, videorecording (Princeton, N.J.: Films for the Humanities, 1989).

6. See Michael Pfau, *Attack Politics: Strategy and Defense* (New York: Praeger, 1990); Tony Schwartz, *Guerrilla Media*; David Protess

and Maxwell McCombs, *Agenda Setting* (Hillsdale, N.J.: Lawrence Erlbaum Associates, 1991); Tony Schwartz, *Media in Politics*, video-recording (Princeton, N.J.: Films for the Humanities, 1989); Kathleen Hall Jamieson, *Dirty Politics: Deception, Distraction, and Democracy* (New York: Oxford University Press, 1992); Garth Jowett and Victoria O'Donnell, *Propaganda and Persuasion*, 2d ed. (Newbury Park, Calif.: Sage, 1992); Jacques Ellul, *Propaganda: The Formation of Men's Attitudes* (New York: Vintage, 1965); Joel Swerdlow, *Media Technology and the Vote: A Sourcebook* (Washington, D.C.: Annenberg Washington Program, 1988).

7. In a "zero-sum" game, a gain for one group implies a corre-sponding loss for others competing for the same resources. Political action is therefore likely to be based on exclusive, narrowly defined interests rather than on any inclusive societal interest.

8. In a "non–zero-sum" game, mutual cooperation and compro-mises are seen as possible goals in which several or all involved par-ties may gain without anyone necessarily losing.

Bibliography

Achenbaum, W. Andrew. 1974. "The Obsolescence of Old Age in America, 1865–1914." *Journal of Social History* 8: 45–64.

———. 1978. *Old Age in a New Land: The American Experience since 1790.* Baltimore: Johns Hopkins University Press.

———. 1980. "Did Social Security Attempt to Regulate the Poor?" *Research on Aging* 2: 270–88.

———. 1983. *Shades of Gray: Old Age, American Values, and Federal Policies since 1920.* Boston: Little, Brown.

———. 1986. *Social Security: Visions and Revisions.* Cambridge: Cambridge University Press.

———. 1987. "Reconstructing the Gerontological Society of America's History." *Gerontologist* 27: 21–29.

———. 1993. "Generational Relations in Historical Context." In *The Changing Contract across Generations*, edited by Vern Bengston and W. Andrew Achenbaum, 25–41. New York: Aldine de Gruyter.

Achenbaum, W. Andrew, and P. N. Stearns. 1978. "Essay: Old Age and Modernization." *Gerontologist* 18: 307–12.

Adams, J. S. 1965. "Inequity in Social Exchange." In *Advances in Experimental Social Psychology*, vol. 2, edited by Leonard Berkowitz, 267–99. New York: Academic Press.

Alsop, Joseph, and Robert Kintner. 1939. "Merchandizing Miracles: Sheridan Downey and the Pension Business." *Saturday Evening Post*, 16 September, 5–7, 85–87, 89–90.

Altmeyer, Arthur J. 1966. *The Formative Years of Social Security.* Madison: University of Wisconsin Press.

Amenta, Edwin, and Theda Skocpol. 1988. "Redefining the New Deal: World War II and the Development of Social Provision in the United States." In *The Politics of Social Policy in the United States,* edited by Margaret Weir, Ann Shola Orloff, and Theda Skocpol, 81–122. Princeton: Princeton University Press.

Amenta, Edwin, and Yvonne Zylan. 1991. "It Happened Here: Political Opportunity, the New Institutionalism, and the Townsend Movement." *American Sociological Review* 56: 250–65.

American Labor Legislation Review (ALLR). For the years 1922–40. Vols. 12–31. New York: American Association for Labor Legislation.

Ansolabehere, Stephen, Roy Behr, and Shanto Iyengar. 1993. *The Media Game: American Politics in the Television Age*. New York: Macmillan.

Arieff, Irwin. 1981. "Claude Pepper: Champion of the Aged." *Congressional Quarterly Weekly Report* 39(48): 2342.

Atchley, Robert C. 1989. "Retiree Bashing: No Good Deed Goes Unpunished." *Generations* 13, no. 2: 21–22.

Austin, William, and Elaine Hatfield. 1980. "Equity Theory, Power, and Social Justice." In *Justice and Social Interaction: Experimental and Theoretical Contributions from Psychological Research*, edited by Gerold Mikula, 25–61. New York: Springer-Verlag.

Axinn, June, and H. Levin. 1975. *Social Welfare: A History of the American Response to Need*. New York: Harper & Row.

Axinn, June, and M. Stern. 1988. *Dependency and Poverty: Old Problems in a New World*. Lexington, Mass.: Lexington Books.

Bachrach, Peter. 1967. *The Theory of Democratic Elitism: A Critique*. Boston: Little, Brown.

Bagdikian, Ben H. 1992. *The Media Monopoly*. 4th ed. Boston: Beacon Press.

Ball, Robert M. 1988. "Social Security across Generations." In *Social Security and Economic Well-Being across Generations*, edited by John R. Gist, 11–38. Washington, D.C.: American Association of Retired Persons.

Barnouw, Erik. 1990. *Tube of Plenty: The Evolution of American Television*. 2d ed. New York: Oxford University Press.

Barone, Michael, and Grant Ujifusa. 1982. *The Almanac of American Politics*. Washington, D.C.: Barone & Co.

Barringer, F. 1993. "'Lead . . . or Leave' Asks: Who's Spending Our Inheritance?" *New York Times*, 14 March, 32.

Barry, Robert L., and Gerard V. Bradley, eds. *Set No Limits: A Rebuttal to Daniel Callahan's Proposal to Limit Health Care for the Elderly*. Urbana: University of Illinois Press.

Beman, Lamar T. 1927. *Selected Articles on Old-Age Pensions*. New York: H. W. Wilson.

Bennett, W. Lance. 1975. *The Political Mind and the Political Environment*. Lexington, Mass.: D. C. Heath.

———. 1988. *News: The Politics of Illusion*. 2d ed. New York: Longman.

———. 1992. *The Governing Crisis: Media, Money, and Marketing in American Elections*. New York: St. Martin's Press.

Berger, Peter, and T. Luckmann. 1966. *The Social Construction of Reality: A Treatise on the Sociology of Knowledge*. New York: Doubleday.

Berkowitz, Edward, ed. 1987. *Social Security after Fifty: Success and Failure.* Westport, Conn.: Greenwood Press.

Bethel, Tom. 1981. "Social Security: Permit for Idleness?" *Journal of the Institute of Socioeconomic Studies* 6 (3 Autumn): 40–50.

Betten, Neil. 1973. "American Attitudes toward the Poor: A Historical Overview." *Current History* 65 (July): 1–5.

Biden, Joseph R. 1981. "Congressional Address by Senator Joseph R. Biden." *Congressional Digest* 60: 203, 205, 207. Washington, D.C.

Binney, Elizabeth A., and Carroll L. Estes. 1988. "The Retreat of the State and Its Transfer of Responsibility: The Intergenerational War." *International Journal of Health Services* 18(1): 83–96.

———. 1990. "Setting the Wrong Limits: Class Biases and the Biographical Standard." In *A Good Old Age? The Paradox of Setting Limits,* edited by P. Homer and M. Holstein. New York: Simon & Schuster.

Binstock, Robert. 1969. "The Gerontological Society and Public Policy: A Report." *Gerontologist* 9: 69.

———. 1972. "Interest Group Liberalism and the Politics of Aging." *Gerontologist* 12: 265–80.

———. 1974. "Aging and the Future of American Politics." *Annals of the American Academy of the Political and Social Sciences,* September, 199–212.

———. 1981. "The Politics of Aging Interest Groups." In *The Aging in Politics: Process and Policy,* edited by Robert B. Hudson. Springfield, Ill.: Charles C. Thomas.

———. 1983a. "The Aged as Scapegoat." *Gerontologist* 23: 136–43.

———. 1983b. "The Oldest Old: A Fresh Perspective on Compassionate Ageism Revisited." *Milbank Memorial Fund Quarterly/Health and Society* 63: 420–51.

———. 1991. "From the Great Society to the Aging Society: 25 Years of the Older Americans Act. *Generations* 15, no. 3: 11–18.

Bladen, Ashby. 1980. "The Shocking Shape of Things to Come." *Forbes,* 26 May, 39–40.

Blumer, Herbert. 1951. "Collective Behavior." In *New Outline of the Principles of Sociology,* 2d ed., ed. A. M. Lee. New York: Barnes & Noble.

———. 1969. *Symbolic Interactionism: Perspective and Method.* Englewood Cliffs, N.J.: Prentice-Hall.

Board of Guardians. [1827] 1971. "Report of the Board of Guardians of the Poor of the City and Districts of Philadelphia." Reprinted in *The Historical Record: The Almshouse Experience,* edited by David J. Rothman. New York: Arno Press and the New York Times.

Bodo, John R. 1954. *The Protestant Clergy and Public Issues, 1812–1848.* Princeton, N.J.: Princeton University Press.

Boorstin, Daniel. 1962. *The Image; or, What Happened to the American Dream.* New York: Antheneum.

Boskin, Michael J. 1977. "Social Security: The Alternative before Us." In *The Crisis in Social Security: Problems and Prospects*, edited by Michael J. Boskin, 173–86. San Francisco: Institute for Contemporary Studies.

————. 1986. *Too Many Promises: The Uncertain Future of Social Security.* Homewood, Ill.: Dow Jones-Irwin.

————. 1988. "The Financial Impact of Social Security by Cohort under Alternative Financing Assumptions." In *Issues in Contemporary Retirement*, edited by R. Ricardo-Campbell and E. P. Lazear, 207–32. San Francisco: Institute for Contemporary Studies.

Bowler, M. Kenneth. 1987. "Changing Politics of Federal Health Insurance Programs." *Political Science and Politics*, Spring, 202–11.

Brinton, J. W. 1936. *The Townsend National Recovery Plan.* 3d ed. Chicago: Townsend National Weekly.

Branco, Kenneth J., and John B. Williamson. 1982. "Stereotyping and the Lifecycle: A Focus on Views of the Aged." In *In the Eye of the Beholder*, edited by Arthur G. Miller, 411–65. New York: Praeger.

Burghardt, Steve, and Michael Fabricant. 1987. *Working under the Safety Net: Policy and Practice with the New American Poor.* Newbury Park, Calif.: Sage Publications.

Burke, Kenneth. 1969. *A Grammar of Motives.* Berkeley: University of California Press.

Burnham, Walter Dean. 1981. "The 1980 Earthquake: Realignment, Reaction, or What?" In *The Hidden Election: Politics and Economics in the 1980 Presidential Campaign,* edited by T. Ferguson and J. Rogers, 98–140. New York: Pantheon.

Business Week. 1978. "The Social Security Time Bomb Is Still Ticking." 9 January, 79, 82.

Business Week. 1981. "The Battle over Repairing Social Security." 28 September, 116.

Butler, Robert N. 1969. "Ageism: Another Form of Bigotry." *Gerontologist* 9: 243–46.

————. 1975. *Why Survive? Being Old in America.* New York: Harper & Row.

————. 1983. "A Generation at Risk." *Across the Board*, July–August, 37–45.

Callahan, Daniel. 1987. *Setting Limits: Medical Goals in an Aging Society.* New York: Simon & Schuster.

Canterbury, John. 1938. "'Ham and Eggs' in California." *Nation* 147 (17): 408–10.

Cantril, Hadley. 1948. *The Psychology of Social Movements.* 7th ed. New York: John Wiley & Sons.

————. 1952. *Public Opinion: 1935–1946.* Princeton: Princeton University Press.

Carey, Matthew. 1835. *Letters on the Condition of the Poor.* Philadelphia: Hasswell & Barringon.

Carlie, Michael K. 1969. "The Politics of Age: Interest Group or Social Movement?" *Gerontologist* 9: 259–63.

Carlson, Elliot. 1987. "The Phony War: Exploding the Myth of Generational Conflict between Young and Old." *Modern Maturity,* February, 34–46.

Cates, Jerry R. 1983. *Insuring Inequality: Administrative Leadership in Social Security, 1935–54.* Ann Arbor: University of Michigan Press.

Chakravarty, Subrata, and K. Weisman. 1988. "Consuming Our Children: The Intergenerational Transfer of Wealth." *Forbes,* 14 November, 222–32.

Chambers, Clarke A. 1963. *Seedtime of Reform: American Social Service and Social Action, 1918–1933.* Minneapolis: University of Minnesota Press.

Chen, Yung-Ping. 1988. "Making Assets Out of Tomorrow's Elderly." In *Retirement Reconsidered: Economic and Social Roles for Older People,* edited by Robert Morris and Scott A. Bass, 73–88. New York: Springer.

City of New York. 1917. "Minutes of the Common Council of the City of New York, 1734–1831." New York: New York City Council.

Clair, Jeffrey M., David A. Karp, and William C. Yoels. Forthcoming. *Experiencing the Life Cycle.* 2d ed. Springfield, Ill.: Charles C. Thomas.

Clark, R., and D. Barker. 1981. *Reversing the Trend toward Early Retirement.* Washington, D.C.: American Enterprise Institute.

Clark, Timothy B. 1981. "Saving Social Security—Reagan and Congress Face Some Unpleasant Choices." *National Journal,* 13 June, 1052–57.

Clement, Priscilla Ferguson. 1985. *Welfare and the Poor in the Nineteenth-Century City: Philadelphia 1800–1854.* Cranbury, N.J.: Associated University Presses.

Clinton, De Witt. 1793. "Address Delivered before Holland Lodge." New York, 24 December.

Cohen, Richard. 1981. "For Spending Cuts, Only the Beginning." *National Journal,* 8 August, 13: 1414.

Cohen, Wilbur J. 1978. "Social Security: Focusing on the Facts." *American Federationist,* April, 6.

———. 1981. "The Threat to Social Security: What to Do about It." *New Leader,* 1 June, 5–7.

———. 1983. "The Bipartisan Solution: Securing Social Security." *New Leader,* 7 February, 5–8.

Cole, Thomas R. 1991. "The Specter of Old Age: History, Politics, and Culture in an Aging America." In *Growing Old in America,* edited by Beth Hess and Elizabeth Markson, 23–37. New Brunswick, N.J.: Transaction Books.

———. 1992. *The Journey of Life: A Cultural History of Aging in America.* Cambridge: Cambridge University Press.

Coll, Blanche D. 1969. *Perspectives in Public Welfare: A History.* Washington, D.C.: U.S. Government Printing Office.

———. 1972. "Public Assistance in the U.S.: Colonial Times to 1860." In

Comparative Development in Social Welfare, edited by E. W. Martin. London: Allen & Unwin.

Committee on Economic Security. 1937. *Social Security in America.* Washington, D.C.: U.S. Government Printing Office.

Cooley, Charles Horton. 1902. *Human Nature and Social Order.* New York: Charles Scribner's Sons.

Coolidge, John B. 1961. "Hingham Builds a Meeting House." *New England Quarterly* 34: 435–61.

Cooperider, Jay. 1987. "Lines Drawn for Generational Battle: Elderly Are Richer, Younger Are Poorer." *Lafayette Journal and Courier,* 26 April, A13.

Coulson, Crocker. 1987. "Geezer Sleaze: FDR's Son and the Ultimate Interest Group." *New Republic,* 20 April, 21–23.

Crowther, Samuel. 1930a. "The Need for Old-Age Pensions." *Forbes* 25 (8): 15–34.

———. 1930b. "Insure Your Child for Old Age." *Forbes* 25 (12): 23–40.

Crystal, Stephen. 1982. *America's Old Age Crisis: Public Policy and the Two Worlds of Aging.* New York: Basic Books.

Cummings, John. 1895. *Poor Laws of Massachusetts and New York.* New York: Macmillan.

Dalleck, Robert. 1984. *Ronald Reagan: The Politics of Symbolism.* Cambridge, Mass.: Harvard University Press.

Davis, K., and P. Van De Oever. 1981. "Age Relations and Public Policy in Advanced Industrial Societies." *Population and Development Review* 7: 1–18.

Day, Christine. 1990. *What Older Americans Think: Interest Groups and Aging Policy.* Princeton, N.J.: Princeton University Press.

de Beauvoir, Simone. 1972. *The Coming of Age,* translated by P. O'Brien. New York: G. P. Putnam's Sons.

Dearing, Mary R. 1951. *Veterans in Politics: The Story of the G.A.R.* Baton Rouge: Louisiana State University Press.

Demos, John. 1978. "Old Age in Early New England." In *The American Family in Social-Historical Perspective,* ed. Michael Gordon, 220–56. New York: St. Martin's Press.

Denton, Robert E. 1988. *The Primetime Presidency of Ronald Reagan.* New York: Praeger.

Derthick, Martha. 1975. *Uncontrollable Spending for Social Services.* Washington, D.C.: Brookings Institute.

———. 1979. *Policymaking for Social Security.* Washington, D.C.: Brookings Institute.

DeSario, Jack. 1987. "Health Issues and Policy Options." *Political Science and Politics,* Spring, 226–31.

Devine, Donald J. 1972. *The Political Culture of the United States: The*

Influence of Member Values on Regime Maintenance. Boston: Little Brown & Co.

Diamond, Edwin, and Stephen Bates. 1992. *The Spot: The Rise of Political Advertising on Television.* Cambridge, Mass.: MIT Press.

Dill, Clarence C. 1930. "What Senator Dill Said." *Old Age Security Herald* 4(5).

Douglas, Paul H. 1936. *Social Security in the United States: An Analysis of the Federal Social Security Act.* New York: Whittlesey House.

Downey, Sheridan. 1939. *Pension or Penury?* New York: Harper.

Eagle Magazine. For the years 1922–26. Vols. 10–14. Chicago: Fraternal Order of the Eagles.

Easton, David. 1965. *A Framework for Political Analysis.* Englewood Cliffs, N.J.: Prentice-Hall.

Edelman, Murray. 1964. *The Symbolic Use of Politics.* Urbana: University of Illinois Press.

———. 1971. *Politics as Symbolic Action.* Chicago: Markham.

———. 1977. *Political Language: Words that Succeed and Policies that Fail.* New York: Academic Press.

———. 1985. "Political Language and Political Reality." *Political Science and Politics* 18(1): 10–19.

———. 1988. *Constructing the Political Spectacle.* Chicago: University of Chicago Press.

Edsall, Thomas Byrne. 1984. *The New Politics of Inequality.* New York: W. W. Norton.

Ellul, Jacques. 1965. *Propaganda: The Formation of Men's Attitudes.* New York: Vintage.

Epstein, Abraham. 1922. *Facing Old Age.* New York: Alfred Knopf.

———. 1926. *The Problems of Old Age Pensions in Industry.* Harrisburg: Pennsylvania Old Age Commission.

———. 1928. *The Challenge of the Aged.* New York: Vanguard.

———. [1938] 1968. *Insecurity, a Challenge to America: A Study of Social Insurance in the United States and Abroad.* New York: Agathon Press.

Estes, Carroll L. 1979. *The Aging Enterprise: A Critical Examination of Social Policies and Services for the Aged.* San Francisco: Jossey-Bass.

———. 1983. "Social Security: The Social Construction of a Crisis." *Milbank Memorial Fund Quarterly/Health and Society* 61(3): 445–61.

———. 1984. "Austerity and Aging: 1980 and Beyond." In *Readings in the Political Economy of Aging,* edited by Meridith Minkler and Carroll Estes, 241–53. Farmingdale, N.Y.: Baywood.

———. 1988. "Cost Containment and the Elderly: Conflict or Challenge?" *Journal of the American Geriatric Society* 36: 68–72.

———. 1990. "The Reagan Legacy: Privatization, the Welfare State and Aging." In *Old Age and the Welfare State,* edited by Jill Quadagno and John F. Myles. Philadelphia: Temple University Press.

———. 1993. "The Aging Enterprise Revisited." *Gerontologist* 33: 292–98.

Etzioni, Amitai. 1976. "Old People and Public Policy." *Social Policy* 6: 21–29.

———. 1988. "Spare the Old: Health Care Generation War." *Nation*, 11 June.

Evans, Linda, and J. B. Williamson. 1981. "Social Security and Social Control." *Generations* 6: 18–20.

Fairlie, H. 1988. "Greedy Geezers: Talkin' bout My Generation." *New Republic*, 28 March, 19–22.

Feagin, Joe R. 1975. *Subordinating the Poor*. Englewood Cliffs, N.J.: Prentice-Hall.

Feagin, Joe R., and C. B. Feagin. 1978. *Discrimination American Style*. Englewood Cliffs, N.J.: Prentice-Hall.

Feingold, Eugene. 1966. *Medicare: Policy and Politics: A Case Study and Policy Analysis*. San Francisco: Chandler & Sharp.

Feldstein, Martin. 1974. "Social Security, Induced Retirement, and Capital Formation." *Journal of Political Economy* 82: 905–26.

———. 1975. "Toward a Reform of Social Security." *Public Interest* 40: 75–95.

———. 1977. "Facing the Social Security Crisis." *Public Interest* 47: 88–100.

Feldstein, Martin, and Anthony Pellechio. 1979. "Social Security Wealth: The Impact of Alternative Inflation Adjustments." In *Financing Social Security*, edited by Colin Campbell, 99–117. Washington: American Enterprise Institute.

Ferguson, Thomas, and Joel Rogers. 1981. "The Reagan Victory: Corporate Coalitions in the 1980 Campaign." In *The Hidden Election: Politics and Economics in the 1980 Presidential Campaign*, edited by T. Ferguson and J. Rogers, 3–64. New York: Pantheon.

———. 1986. *Right Turn: The Decline of the Democrats and the Future of American Politics*. New York: Hill & Wang.

Ferrara, Peter J. 1980. *Social Security: The Inherent Contradiction*. San Francisco: Cato Institute.

———. 1982. *Social Security: Averting the Crisis*. Washington, D.C.: Cato Institute.

———. 1985. "Social Security and the Super IRA: A Populist Proposal." In *Social Security: Prospects for Real Reform*, edited by Peter J. Ferrara, 193–220. Washington, D.C.: Cato Institute.

Fine, Sidney. 1956. *Laissez-Faire and the General Welfare State: A Study of Conflict in American Thought, 1865–1901*. Ann Arbor: University of Michigan Press.

Fischer, David Hackett. 1977. *Growing Old in America*. New York: Oxford University Press.

———. 1979. "The Politics of Aging: A Short History." *Journal of the Institute for Socioeconomic Studies* 4: 51–66.

———. 1980. "Growing Old in America." In *Aging: The Individual and Society*, 34–49. New York: St. Martin's Press.

Fisher, Irving. 1932. "The Stamped Scrip Plan." *New Republic,* 21 December, 163–64.

———. 1933. *Stamp Scrip.* New York: Adelphi.

Fisher, Jan. 1986. "Maggie Kuhn's Vision: Young and Old together." *Fifty-Plus* 26 (7): 22–23.

Flanagan, William G. 1980. "Social Security: Don't Count on It." *Forbes,* 8 December, 161–62.

Flint, J. 1980. "The Old Folks: Can We Afford Them?" *Forbes,* 18 February, 51–56.

Franklin, Benjamin. [1768] 1971. "On the Laboring Poor—Communicated to the Editor of a Newspaper, April, 1768." In *Essays on General Politics, Commerce, and Political Economy,* vol. 2, edited by James Sparks, 367–71. New York: Augustus M. Kelley.

Friedan, Betty. 1993. *The Fountain of Age.* New York: Simon & Schuster.

Friedman, Milton. 1978. "Payroll Taxes, No; General Revenues, Yes." In *Financing Social Security,* edited by C. Campbell, 25–30. San Francisco: Institute for Contemporary Studies.

Galbraith, John Kenneth. 1984. "The Heartless Society." *New York Times Magazine,* 2 September.

———. 1985. "How to Get the Poor off Our Conscience." *Harper's,* November, 17–20.

Gallup, George H. 1965. "Majority Backs Medical Care of Aged through Social Security." *Public Opinion News Service,* 3 January.

Gallup, George H. 1972. *The Gallup Poll: Public Opinion, 1935–1971,* 9, 76. New York: Random House.

Gamson, William. 1975. *The Strategy of Social Protest.* Homewood, Ill.: Dorsey Press.

———. 1988. "Political Discourse and Collective Action." In *Social Movement Participation across Cultures,* edited by B. Klandermans, H. Kriesi, and S. Tarrow, 219–44. Greenwich, Conn.: JAI Press.

———. 1992. *Talking Politics.* Cambridge: Cambridge University Press.

Gamson, William, and K. Lasch. 1983. "The Political Culture of Social Welfare Policy." In *Evaluating the Welfare State: Social and Political Perspectives,* edited by S. Spiro and E. Yuchtman-Yaar, 397–415. New York: Academic Press.

Gamson, William, and Andre Modigliani. 1989. "Media Discourse and Public Opinion on Nuclear Power: A Constructionist Approach." *American Journal of Sociology* 95: 1–37.

Gamson, William, and David Stuart. 1992. "Media Discourse as a Symbolic Contest: The Bomb in Political Cartoons." *Sociological Forum* 7: 55–86.

Garnham, N. 1979. "Toward a Political Economy of Mass Communications." *Media, Culture, and Society* 2: 123–46.

Geertz, Clifford. 1973. *The Interpretation of Cultures.* New York: Basic Books.

Gelfand, Donald E., and Alfred J. Kutzik, eds. 1979. *Adulthood and Aging.* Vol. 5, *Ethnicity and Aging: Theory, Research, and Policy.* New York: Springer Publishing Co.

Gelfand, Donald E., and William Bechild. 1991. "The Evolution of the Older Americans Act: A 25-Year Review of Legislative Changes." *Generations,* Summer–Fall, 19–22.

Georges, Christopher. 1992. "Old Money: Why the Mighty AARP Spends as Much Furnishing Its Offices as It Does on Programs to Help the Elderly." *Washington Monthly,* June, 16–21.

Gergen, David. 1990. "Sixtysomething: Part III." *U.S. News & World Report,* 14 May, 82.

Ginsberg, Benjamin. 1986. *The Captive Public: How Mass Opinion Promotes State Power.* New York: Basic Books.

Gist, J. R. 1988. *Social Security and Well-Being across Generations.* Washington, D.C.: Public Policy Institute, American Association of Retired Persons.

———. 1993. *Entitlements and the Federal Budget Deficit: Setting the Record Straight.* Washington, D.C.: AARP Public Policy Institute.

Glasson, William. 1902. "The South and the Service Pension Laws." *South Atlantic Quarterly* 1 (October): 351–60.

———. 1918. *Federal Military Pensions in the United States.* New York: Oxford University Press.

Goffman, Erving. 1959. *The Presentation of Self in Everyday Life.* Garden City, N.Y.: Doubleday.

———. 1961. *Asylums.* Garden City, N.Y.: Doubleday.

———. 1963. *Stigma: Notes on the Management of Spoiled Identity.* Englewood Cliffs, N.J.: Prentice-Hall.

———. 1974. *Frame Analysis.* Cambridge, Mass.: Harvard University Press.

Goodman, J. C. 1985. "Private Alternatives to Social Security." In *Social Security: Prospects for Real Reform,* edited by Peter J. Ferrara, 103–12. Washington, D.C.: Cato Institute.

Gough, Ian. 1975. "State Expenditures in Advanced Capitalism." *New Left Review* 92: 53–92.

Graebner, William. 1978. "Retirement and the Corporate State, 1885–1935: A New Context for Social Security." Paper presented at the annual meeting of the Organization of American Historians. New York, April.

———. 1980. *A History of Retirement: The Meaning and Function of an American Institution, 1885–1978.* New Haven, Conn.: Yale University Press.

Gray Panther Movement. 1974. *Gray Panthers Pamphlet.* Philadelphia: Gray Panthers.

Green, William. 1931. "The Nation's Obligation." Excerpts from a May 1931 address to the Fourth Annual National Conference on Old Age Security. *Old Age Security Herald* 5: 3.

Greider, William. 1981. "The Education of David Stockman." *Atlantic Monthly,* December.

Haber, Carole. 1983. *Beyond Sixty-five: The Dilemma of Old Age in America's Past.* Cambridge: Cambridge University Press.

Hamby, Alonzo. 1985. *Liberalism and Its Challengers: F.D.R. to Reagan.* New York: Oxford University Press.

Hamilton, Phil. 1938. "$30 a Week for Life!" *California: Magazine of the Pacific* 36 (August): 12–13.

Harris, Herbert. 1936. "Dr. Townsend's Marching Soldiers." *Current History,* February, 455–62.

Harris, Louis. 1975. *The Myth and Reality of Aging in America.* Washington, D.C.: National Council on Aging.

Harris, Richard. 1966. *A Sacred Trust.* New York: New American Library.

Hartz, Louis. 1955. *The Liberal Tradition in America.* New York: Harcourt Brace.

Havighurst, Robert J. 1963. "Successful Aging." In *Processes of Aging,* vol. 1, edited by R. Williams, C. Tibbitts, and W. Donahue, 299–320. New York: Atherton.

Heclo, Hugh. 1988. "Generational Politics." In *The Vulnerable,* edited by John L. Palmer, Timothy Smeeding, and Barbara Torrey, 381–411. Washington, D.C.: Urban Institute Press.

Heffernan, Robert, and Charles Maynard. 1977. "Living and Dying with Dignity: The Rise of Old Age and Dying as Social Problems." In *This Land of Promises,* edited by A. Mauss and J. Wolfe, 73–111. Philadelphia: J. B. Lippincott.

Heisler, Martin, and Robert Kvavik. 1974. "Patterns of European Politics: The European Polity Model." In *Politics in Europe: Structures and Processes in Some Post-Industrial Democracies,* edited by Martin Heisler, 27–89. New York: David McKay.

Hering, Frank E. 1922–23. "Awakening Interest in Old Age Protection." *American Labor Legislation Review* 12–13.

Herman, Edward, and Noam Chomsky. 1988. *Manufacturing Consent: The Political Economy of the Mass Media.* New York: Pantheon.

Hess, Beth. 1974. "Stereotypes of the Aged." *Journal of Communication* 24: 76–85.

Hess, John L. 1988. "Social Security Is for Everybody." *Nation,* 16 January, 52–53.

———. 1990. "Social Security Wars: Confessions of a Greedy Geezer." *Nation,* 2 April, 1, 452–53.

Hessel, Dicter. 1977. *Maggie Kuhn on Aging.* Philadelphia: Westminster Press.

Hewitt, Paul. 1986. *A Broken Promise*. Washington, D.C.: Americans for Generational Equity.

Hewitt, Paul, and Neil Howe. 1988. "Generational Equity and the Future of Generational Politics." *Generations* 12: 10–13.

Hildreth, James M., 1981. "The Great COLA War—What's at Stake." *U.S. News & World Report*, 26 April, 90.

———. 1982. "Those Fouled-up Social Security Checks." *U.S. News & World Report*, 1 February.

Hofstadter, Richard. 1944. *Social Darwinism in American Thought, 1860–1915*. London: Oxford University Press.

Holtzman, Abraham. 1952. "The Townsend Movement: A Study in Old Age Pressure Politics." Ph.D. diss. Harvard University.

———. 1954. "Analysis of Old Age Politics in the United States." *Journal of Gerontology* 9: 56–66.

———. 1963. *The Townsend Movement*. New York: Bookman Associates.

Hudson, Robert B. 1978. "The Graying of the Federal Budget and Its Consequences for Old-Age Policy." *Gerontologist* 18: 428–40.

———. 1981 (editor). *The Aging in Politics: Process and Policy*. Springfield, Ill.: Charles C. Thomas.

———. 1981. "The Graying of the Federal Budget and It's Consequences for Old-Age Policy." In *The Aging in Politics: Process and Policy*, edited by Robert B. Hudson, 261–81. Springfield, Ill.: Charles C. Thomas.

———. 1988. "Social Policy and Aging: Renewing the Federal Role." *Generations* 13: 23–26.

Hutton, William R. 1989. "The Young and the Old Are Not Enemies." *USA Today Magazine*, March, 63–65.

Independent Opinions. 1913. *Independent* 75 (August): 504.

Iyengar, Shanto. 1991. *Is Anybody Responsible? How Television Frames Political Issues*. Chicago: University of Chicago Press.

Iyengar, Shanto, and Donald Kinder. 1987. *News that Matters*. Chicago: University of Chicago Press.

Jacobs, Ruth H., and Beth Hess. 1978. "Panther Power: Symbol and Substance." *Long-Term Care and Health Services Quarterly*, Fall, 238–43.

Jamieson, Kathleen Hall. 1992. *Dirty Politics: Deception, Distraction, and Democracy*. New York: Oxford University Press.

———. 1992. *Packaging the Presidency: A History and Criticism of Presidential Campaign Advertising*. 2d ed. New York: Oxford University Press.

Jannson, Bruce S. 1988. *The Reluctant Welfare State: A History of American Social Welfare Policies*. Belmont, Calif.: Wadsworth.

Jowett, Garth, and Victoria O'Donnell. 1992. *Propaganda and Persuasion*. 2d ed. Newbury Park, Calif.: Sage Publications.

Kaim-Caudle, Peter R. 1973. *Comparative Social Policy and Social Security*. London: Martin Robertson.

Kaplan, J. 1982. "Three Perspectives on the 1981 White House Conference on Aging." *Gerontologist* 22: 125–28.

Karp, David A., and William C. Yoels. 1982. *Experiencing the Life Cycle: The Social Psychology of Aging.* Springfield, Ill.: Charles C. Thomas.

Keen, Sam. 1986. *Faces of the Enemy: Reflections of the Hostile Imagination.* San Francisco: Harper & Row.

Kellner, Douglas. 1990. *Television and the Crisis of Democracy.* Boulder, Colo.: Westview Press.

Kelly, James. 1981. "A Slash at Social Security: The Beefs Are Loud as Budget Cutters Attack a 'Sacred Cow.'" *Time*, 25 May, 24–25.

Kelso, Robert W. 1969. *The History of Public Poor Relief in Massachusetts: 1620–1920.* 2d ed. Montclair, N.J.: Patterson Smith.

Kennedy, John Fitzgerald. 1963. "Elderly Citizens of Our Nation: Presidential Address to Congress." *Congressional Record*, 21 February, 2693.

Keyfitz, Nathan. 1980. "Why Social Security Is in Trouble." *Public Interest* 58: 102–19.

Kingson, Eric R. 1984. "Financing Social Security: Agenda Setting and the Enactment of the 1983 Amendments to the Social Security Act." *Policy Studies Journal* 13: 131–55.

———. 1988. "Generational Equity: An Unexpected Opportunity to Broaden the Politics of Aging." *Gerontologist* 28(6): 765–72.

———. 1989. "Understanding and Learning from the Generational Equity Debate." *The Aging Connection* 198, no. 13 (October–November).

Kingson, Eric R., B. A. Hirshorn, and L. K. Harootyan. 1986. *The Common Stake: The Interdependence of Generations—a Policy Framework for an Aging Society.* Washington, D.C.: Gerontological Society of America.

Kingson, Eric R., Barbara A. Hirshorn, and John M. Cornman. 1986. *Ties that Bind: Interdependence of Generations.* Washington, D.C.: Seven Locks Press.

Kingson, Eric R., and John B. Williamson. 1991. "Generational Equity or Privatizing Social Security?" *Society* 28 (6): 38–41.

Klebaner, B. J. 1952. *Public Poor Relief in America, 1790–1860.* New York: Columbia University.

Kleyman, Paul. 1974. *Senior Power: Growing Old Rebelliously.* San Francisco: Glide Publications.

Knepper, Max. 1939. "Scrambled Eggs in California." *Current History*, October, 58–64.

Kosterlitz, Julie. 1988. "Catastrophic Coverage a Catastrophe." *National Journal* 20 (19 November): 2949–52.

Kosterlitz, Julie. 1988. "Young v. Old." *National Journal* 20 (10 December): 3160.

Kotlikoff, Laurence. 1992. *Generational Accounting: Knowing Who Pays, and When, for What We Spend.* New York: Free Press.

Kudrle, Robert T., and Theodore Marmor. 1981. "The Develpment of the Welfare State in North America." In *The Development of Welfare States in Europe and North America*, edited by Peter Flora and Arnold Heidenheimer, 67–80. New Brunswick, N.J.: Transaction Books.

Kuhn, Maggie. 1976. "What Old People Want for Themselves and Others in Society." In *Advocacy and Age: Issues, Experiences, Strategies*, edited by Paul A. Kerschner, 87–96. Los Angeles: University of Southern California Press.

———. 1978. "Open Letter." *Gerontologist* 18(5): 422–24.

———. 1979. "Advocacy in this New Age." *Aging* 297–98: 2–5.

———. 1991. *No Stone Unturned: The Life and Times of Maggie Kuhn*. New York: Ballantine.

Kuhn, Maggie, and J. E. Bader. 1991. "Old and Young Are Alike in Many Ways." *Gerontologist* 31 (2): 273–74.

Kuttner, Robert. 1980. *The Revolt of the Haves: Tax Rebellions and Hard Times*. New York: Simon & Schuster.

———. 1982. "The Social Security Hysteria." *New Republic*, 27 December, 17–21.

Kutzik, Alfred J. 1979. "American Social Provision for the Aged: An Historical Perspective." In *Ethnicity and Aging*, edited by Donald Gelfand and Alfred Kutzik, 32–65. New York: Springer.

Laffer, E., and D. Ranson. 1977. "A Proposal for Reforming Social Security." In *Income Support for the Aged,* edited by G. S. Trolley and R. V. Burhauser, 130–50. Cambridge, Mass.: Ballinger.

Lamm, Richard D. 1985. *Mega-Traumas at the Year 2000*. Boston: Houghton Mifflin.

———. 1987. *The Ten Commandments of an Aging Society*. Denver: Center for Public Policy and Contemporary Issues.

Lammers, William W. 1983. *Public Policy and Aging*. Washington, D.C.: Congressional Quarterly Press.

Laslett, Peter, and James Fiskin, eds. 1992. *Justice between Age Groups and Generations*. New Haven, Conn.: Yale University Press.

Leotta, Louis. 1975. "Abraham Epstein and the Movement for Old Age Security." *Labor History* 16 (3): 359–77.

Lerner, M. J. 1977. "The Justice Motive: Some Hypotheses as to Its Origins and Forms." *Journal of Personality* 45: 1–52.

Levin, Jack, and William Levin. 1980. *Ageism: Prejudices and Discrimination against the Elderly*. Belmont, Calif.: Wadsworth.

Levine, R., and D. Campbell. 1972. *Ethnocentrism: Theories of Conflict, Ethnic Attitudes, and Group Behavior*. New York: Wiley.

Light, Paul. 1985. *Artful Work: The Politics of Social Security Reform*. New York: Random House.

Lindsey, Robert. 1980. "Inflation and a Demographic Shift Pose Huge Problem for U.S. Pension System." *New York Times*, 18 May, 48.

Linsky, M. 1986. *Impact: How the Press Affects Federal Policymaking*. New York: W. W. Norton.

Literary Digest. 1935. "Current Opinion: By Switching to Conservatives, Justice Roberts Gives New Dealers Chills." 18 May, 12.

Longman, Phillip. 1982. "Taking America to the Cleaners." *Washington Monthly*, November, 25–30.

———. 1985. "Justice between Generations." *Atlantic Monthly* 256: 73–81.

———. 1986a. "Age Wars: The Coming Battle between Young and Old." *Futurist* 20 (1): 8–11.

———. 1986b. "The Youth Machine vs. the Baby Boomers: A Scenario." *Futurist* 20 (1): 9.

———. 1987. *Born to Pay: The New Politics of Aging in America*. Boston: Houghton Mifflin.

———. 1989. "Catastrophic Follies: The Old Folks Outfox Themselves." *New Republic*, 21 August, 16–17.

Lowi, Theodore. 1964. "American Business, Public Policy, and Political Theory." *World Politics* 16: 676–715.

Lubove, Roy. 1968. *The Struggle for Social Security: 1900–1935*. Cambridge, Mass.: Harvard University Press.

Lyman, Francesca. 1988. "Maggie Kuhn: A Wrinkled Radical's Crusade." *Progressive* 52 (January): 29–31.

McAllister, Eugene J. 1980. *Agenda for Progress*. Washington, D.C.: Heritage Foundation.

MacPherson, C. B. 1962. *The Political Theory of Possessive Individualism: Hobbes to Locke*. London: Oxford University Press.

Magnuson, Ed. 1983. "Champion of the Elderly: At 82, Claude Pepper Is at the Peak of His Career." *Time*, 25 April, 21–29.

Margolis, Michael, and Gary Mauser. 1989. *Manipulating Public Opinion: Essays on Public Opinion as a Dependent Variable*. Pacific Grove, Calif.: Brooks Cole.

Marmor, Theodore R. 1969. "The Congress: Medicare Politics and Policy." In *American Political Institutions and Public Policy*, edited by Allan Sindler, 3–66. Boston: Little, Brown.

———. 1973. *The Politics of Medicare*. Chicago: Aldine.

———. 1981. "Enacting Medicare." In *The Aging in Politics: Process and Policy*, edited by Robert Hudson, 105–34. Springfield, Ill.: Charles C. Thomas.

Marmor, Theodore R., and J. L. Mashaw. 1988. *Social Security: Beyond the Rhetoric of Crisis*. Princeton, N.J.: Princeton University Press.

Mather, Cotton. 1690. *Address to Old Men and Young Men and Little Children*. Boston: R. Pierce.

———. [1713] 1912. *Diary of Cotton Mather, Vol. II*. Boston: Massachusetts Historical Society.

Mather, Increase. 1716. *Two Discourses Shewing, I, That the Lord's Ears Are*

Open to the Prayers of the Righteous, and II, The Dignity and Duty of Aged Servants of the Lord. Boston: B. Green.

Mauser, Gary. 1989. "Marketing and Political Campaigning: Strategies and Limits." In *Manipulating Public Opinion*, edited by Michael Margolis and Gary Mauser, 19–46. Pacific Grove, Calif.: Brooks Cole.

Mauss Armand, 1971. "On Being Strangled by the Stars and Stripes: The New Left, the Old Left, and the Natural History of American Radical Movements." *Journal of Social Issues* 27: 102–85.

————. 1975. *Social Problems as Social Movements.* Philadelphia: J. B. Lippincott.

Mead, George Herbert. 1934. *Mind, Self, and Society: From the Standpoint of a Social Behaviorist.* Chicago: University of Chicago Press.

Milne, Richard. 1935. *That Man Townsend.* Indianapolis: Prosperity.

Minkler, Meredith. 1991. "Generational Equity and the New Victim Blaming." In *Critical Perspectives on Aging: The Political and Moral Economy of Growing Old*, edited by Meredith Minkler and Carroll L. Estes, 67–80. Amytiville, N.Y.: Baywood.

Minkler, Meredith, and Ann Robertson. 1991. "The Ideology of 'Age/Race Wars': Deconstructing a Social Problem." *Ageing and Society* 11: 1–22.

Mitchell, Greg. 1992. *The Campaign of the Century: Upton Sinclair's Race for Governor of California and the Birth of Media Politics.* New York: Random House.

Mitroff, Ian, and Warren Bennis. 1993. *The Unreality Industry: The Deliberate Manufacturing of Falsehood.* New York: Oxford University Press.

Modern Crusader. For the years 1934–35. Long Beach, Calif.: C. J. McDonald.

Mohl, Raymond A. 1971. *Poverty in New York: 1783–1825.* New York: Oxford University Press.

————. 1973. "Three Centuries of American Public Welfare: 1600–1932." *Current History* 65: 6–10.

Moody, H. R. 1988a. *Abundance of Life: Human Development Policies for an Aging Society.* New York: Columbia University Press.

————. 1988b. "The Contradictions of an Aging Society: From Zero Sum to Productive Society." In *Retirement Reconsidered: Economic and Social Roles for Older People*, edited by Robert Morris and Scott A. Bass, 15–34. New York: Springer.

Moore, Winston. 1939. *Out of the Frying Pan.* Los Angeles: De Vorss.

Morgenthau, Tom, and Mary Hager. 1983. "Legions of the Old." *Newsweek*, 24 January, 23.

Morris, J. 1983. "Social Security: The Phony Crisis." *Monthly Review* 34: 1–13.

Morris, Robert. 1967. "Reality or Illusion: The Gerontological Society's Contribution to Public Policy." *Gerontologist* 7: 229–33.

Morris, Robert, and Scott A. Bass. 1988. "Toward a New Paradigm about

Work and Age." In *Retirement Reconsidered: Economic and Social Roles for Older People*, edited by Robert Morris and Scott A. Bass, 3–14. New York: Springer.

Myles, John F. 1981. "The Trillion-Dollar Misunderstanding." *Working Papers* 8: 29–30.

———. 1983. "Conflict, Crisis, and the Future of Old Age Security." *Milbank Memorial Fund Quarterly/Health and Society* 61 (3): 463–72.

———. 1984. *Old Age in the Welfare State: The Political Economy of Public Pensions.* Boston: Little, Brown.

———. 1985. "The Trillion-Dollar Misunderstanding." In *Growing Old in America*, edited by Beth Hess and Elizabeth Markson, 507–23. New Brunswick, N.J.: Transaction Books.

———. 1991. "Postwar Capitalism and the Extension of Social Security into a Retirement Wage." In *Critical Perspectives on Aging: The Political and Moral Economy of Growing Old*, edited by Meredith Minkler and Carroll L. Estes, 293–309. Amityville, N.Y.: Baywood.

Myles, John F., and Jill S. Quadagno. 1992. *States, Labor Markets, and the Future of Old-Age Policy.* Philadelphia: Temple University Press.

Nation. 1990. "Gray Power." 28 May.

National Ham and Eggs. For the years 1938–41. Los Angeles: Retirement Life Payments Association.

National Townsend Weekly. For the years 1935–40. Los Angeles: Prosperity Publishing Co.

Neuberger, Richard, and Kelley Loe. 1936. *An Army of the Aged: A History and Analysis of the Townsend Old-Age Pension Plan.* Caldwell, Id.: Caxton.

Neugarten, Bernice L. 1982. "Policy for the 1980's: Age or Need Entitlement?" In *Age or Need? Public Policies for Older People*, edited by Bernice L. Neugarten. Beverly Hills, Calif.: Sage Publications.

New England Almanack 1872, January, 22.

New York Daily Gazette 1791, 4 January.

New York Evening Post 1810, 5 January.

New York State Senate. [1857] 1938. "Report of the Select Senate Committee to Visit Charitable and Penal Institutions, 1857." New York Senate Document No. 8 of 1857. In *Public Welfare Administration in the United States: Selected Documents*, ed. S. P. Breckinridge. Chicago: University of Chicago Press.

New York Times. 1988. "Aid to Elderly Divides Young, Old, and Politicians." 23 June, 1A.

Newsweek. 1979. "A Growing Disillusion with Social Security." 12 March.

———. 1982. "The Third Rail of Politics." 24 May, 24–26.

———. 1983. "The Social Security Crisis/Legions of the Old." 24 January, 18–28.

————. 1990. "Blaming the Voter: Hapless Budgeteers Single Out 'Greedy Geezers.'" 29 October, 36.

Novack, Phillip. 1989. "Strength from Its Gray Roots." *Forbes*, 25 November, 89–94.

O'Byrne, Arthur C. 1953. *The Political Significance of the Townsend Movement in California, 1934–1950*. Ph.D. diss. University of Southern California.

O'Connor, J. 1973. *The Fiscal Crisis of the State*. New York: St. Martin's Press.

Offen, C. 1972. "Profile of a Gray Panther." *Retirement Living*, December, 33.

Old Age Security Herald/Social Security (OASH). For the years 1930–34. Vols. 4–7. New York: American Association for Social Security.

Old Age Security Herald. 1931. "Coolidge and Self-Respecting Security." 5 (4): 2.

Oliver, John W. 1917. "History of the Civil War Military Pensions, 1861–1885." *Bulletin of the University of Wisconsin*, No. 844. Madison: University of Wisconsin.

Olson, Laura Katz. 1982. *The Political Economy of Aging: The State, Private Power, and Social Welfare*. New York: Columbia University Press.

O'Reilly, J. Fanning. 1904. *The History of the Fraternal Order of Eagles*. New York: Schlesinger.

Oriol, William E., compiler. 1987. *Bibliographies and Indexes in Gerontology*. Vol. 5, *Federal Public Policy on Aging since 1960: An Annotated Bibliography*. New York: Greenwood Press.

Orloff, Ann Shola, 1988. "The Political Origins of America's Belated Welfare State." In *The Politics of Social Policy in the United States*, edited by Margaret Weir, Ann Orloff, and Theda Skocpol, 37–80. Princeton, N. J.: Princeton University Press.

————. 1993. *The Politics of Pensions*. Madison: University of Wisconsin Press.

Orloff, Ann Shola, and Theda Skocpol. 1984. "Why Not Equal Protection? Explaining the Politics of Public Social Spending in Britain, 1900–1911, and the United States, 1880s–1920s." *American Sociological Review* 49 (December): 726–50.

Owen, Russell. 1935. "Townsend Talks of His Plans and Hopes." *New York Times Magazine*, 29 December, 3, 15.

Ozawa, Martha N. 1976. "Income Redistribution and Social Security." *Social Service Review* 50: 216–17.

————. 1984. "The 1983 Amendments to the Social Security Act: The Issue of Intergenerational Equity." *Social Work* 29 (2): 131–37.

Paine, Thomas. [1792] 1967. *The Writings of Thomas Paine, 1779–1792*, vol. 2, edited by Moncure D. Conway. New York: AMS Press.

Parenti, Michael. 1993. *Inventing Reality: The Politics of News Media*. 2d ed. New York: St. Martin's Press.

Pascall, Glenn. 1985. *The Trillion-Dollar Budget: How to Stop the Bankrupting of America*. Seattle: University of Washington Press.

Pepper, Claude. 1980. "Older Americans Are the Poorest Americans." *New York Times*, 29 February, A10.

Peterson, Peter G. 1982a. "The Salvation of Social Security." *New York Review of Books*, 16 December.

———. 1982b. "Social Security: The Coming Crash." *New York Review of Books*, 2 December.

Peterson, Peter G., and N. Howe. 1988. *On Borrowed Time: How the Growth in Entitlement Spending Threatens America's Future*. San Francisco: Institute for Contemporary Studies.

Petit, C. 1985. "Experts Say an Older America Needs New Definition of Age." *San Francisco Chronicle*, 11 October, 24.

Pfau, Michael. 1990. *Attack Politics: Strategy and Defense*. New York: Praeger.

Phillips, Kevin. 1990. *The Politics of Rich and Poor: Wealth and the American Electorate in the Reagan Aftermath*. New York: Random House.

Pierce, Lloyd F. 1953. *The Activities of the American Association for Labor Legislation in Behalf of Social Security and Protective Legislation*. Ph.D. diss. University of Wisconsin.

Piven, Frances Fox, and Richard A. Cloward. 1982. *The New Class War: Reagan's Attack on the Welfare State and Its Consequences*. New York: Pantheon.

Piven, Frances Fox, and Richard A. Cloward. 1971. *Regulating the Poor: The Functions of Public Welfare*. New York: Pantheon.

———. 1977. *People's Movements, Why They Succeed, How They Fail*. New York: Pantheon.

Pollack, Ronald F. 1988. "Serving Intergenerational Needs, Not Intergenerational Conflict." *Generations* 12 (2): 14–18.

Postman, Neil. 1984. *Amusing Ourselves to Death: Public Discourse in the Age of Show Business*. New York: Viking Penguin.

Powell, Lawrence A. 1985. "Mass Media as Legitimizers of Control." In *Aging and Public Policy: Social Control or Social Justice?* edited by John Williamson, Judith Shindul, and Linda Evans, 180–205. Springfield, Ill.: Charles C. Thomas.

———. 1995a. "The American Association of Retired Persons." In *United States Health Interest Groups*, edited by Craig Ramsay. Westport, Conn.: Greenwood Press.

———. 1995b. "The National Council of Senior Citizens." In *United States Health Interest Groups*, edited by Craig Ramsay. Westport, Conn.: Greenwood Press.

Powell, Lawrence A., and John B. Williamson. 1985. "Mass Media and the Aged." *Social Policy* 16 (1): 38–49.

———. 1985. "The Reagan-Era Shift toward Restrictiveness in Old Age Policy in Historical Perspective." *International Journal of Aging and Human Development* 21 (2).

244   *Bibliography*

Powell, Lawrence A., and Cherylon Robinson. 1996. "The Postmodern Politics of Context Definition." *Sociological Quarterly* 37 (2): 201–27.

Pratt, Henry J. 1974. "Old Age Associations in National Politics." *Annals of the American Academy of Political and Social Science* 415: 106–19.

———. 1976. *The Gray Lobby.* Chicago: University of Chicago Press.

———. 1978. "Symbolic Politics and White House Conferences on Aging." *Society,* July–August, 67–72.

———. 1983. "National Interest Groups among the Elderly: Consolidation and Constraint." In *Aging and Public Policy: The Politics of Growing Old in America,* edited by William Browne and Laura Katz Olson, 145–79. Westport, Conn.: Greenwood Press.

———. 1992. "Senior Organizations and Senior Empowerment: An International Perspective." Paper presented at the Conference on Population and Ageing, sponsored by the International Federation on Ageing, San Diego, 17–19 September.

———. 1993. *Gray Agendas.* Ann Arbor: University of Michigan Press.

Protess, David, and Maxwell McCombs. 1991. *Agenda Setting.* Hillsdale, N.J.: Lawrence Erlbaum Associates.

Pumphrey, Ralph E., and Muriel W. Pumphrey, eds. 1961. *The Heritage of American Social Work.* New York: Columbia University Press.

Putnam, Jackson K. 1970. *Old-Age Politics in California: From Richardson to Reagan.* Stanford, Calif.: Stanford University Press.

Quadagno, Jill S. 1984a. "From Poor Laws to Pensions: The Evolution of Economic Support for the Aged in England and America." *Milbank Memorial Fund Quarterly* 62 (3): 417–46.

———. 1984b. "Welfare Capitalism and the Social Security Act of 1935." *American Sociological Review* 49: 632–47.

———. 1988a. "From Old-Age Assistance to Supplemental Security Income: The Political Economy of Relief in the South, 1935–1972." In *The Politics of Social Policy in the United States,* edited by Margaret Weir, Ann Shola Orloff, and Theda Skocpol, 235–63. Princeton, N.J.: Princeton University Press.

———. 1988b. *The Transformation of Old Age Security: Class and Politics in the American Welfare State.* Chicago: University of Chicago Press.

———. 1989. "Generational Equity and the Politics of the Welfare State." *Politics and Society* 17 (3): 353–76.

———. 1992. "Interest Group Politics and the Future of U.S. Social Security." In *States, Labor Markets and the Future of Old-Age Policy,* edited by John F. Myles and Jill S. Quadagno. Philadelphia: Temple University Press.

Qualter, Terence H. 1985. *Opinion Control in Democracies.* New York: St. Martin's Press.

Quincy J. [1821] 1971. "Report of the Committee to Whom Was Referred the Consideration of the Pauper Laws of the Commonwealth." In *The

Almshouse Experience: Collected Reports, 7–9. New York: Arno Press and New York Times.

Rabushka, Alvin, and Bruce Jacobs. 1980. "Are Old Folks Really Poor? Herewith a Look at Some Common Views." *New York Times*, 15 February, A29.

Reagan, Ronald. 1981. "President Reagan's Address to a Joint Session of Congress, February 18, 1981." *Congressional Quarterly*, 21 February, 361.

———. 1982. Televised presidential address on the economy, 24 September 1981. Reprinted in *Reagan's First Year*, 125–28. Washington, D.C.: Congressional Quarterly.

Reeves, Richard. 1985. *The Reagan Detour*. New York: Simon & Schuster.

Ricardo-Campbell, R. 1977a. "The Problem of Fairness." In *The Crisis in Social Security: Problems and Prospects*, edited by Michael J. Boskin, 124–45. San Francisco: Institute for Contemporary Studies.

———. 1977b. *Social Security: Promise and Reality*. Stanford, Calif.: Hoover Institution Press.

Ricardo-Campbell, R., and E. P. Lazear, eds. 1988. *Issues in Contemporary Retirement*. Stanford, Calif.: Hoover Institution Press.

Rich, Bennett M., and Martha Baum. 1984. *The Aging: A Guide to Public Policy*. Pittsburgh: University of Pittsburgh Press.

Rimlinger, Gaston V. 1971. *Welfare Policy and Industrialization in Europe, America, and Russia*. New York: Wiley.

Rogers, E. M., and J. W. Dearing. 1988. "Agenda-Setting Research: Where Has It Been, Where Is It Going?" In *Communication Yearbook 11*, edited by J. Anderson, 555–94. Newbury Park, Calif.: Sage Publications.

Roosevelt, Franklin Delano. 1934. *Review of Legislative Accomplishments of the Administration and Congress*. H. Doc. 397. 73rd Cong., 2d Sess., 4. Washington, D.C.: U.S. Government Printing Office.

Rose, Arnold M. 1963. "Organizations for the Elderly: Political Implications." In *Politics of Age*, edited by Wilma Donahue and Clark Tibbitts, 135–45. Philadelphia: F. A. Davis.

———. 1965. "Group Consciousness among the Aging." In *Older People and Their Social World*, edited by Warren A. Peterson and Arnold M. Rose, 19–36. Philadelphia: F. A. Davis.

Rothman, David J. 1971. *The Discovery of the Asylum*. Boston: Little, Brown.

Rothmyer, Karen. 1981. "Citizen Schaife." *Columbia Journalism Review*, July–August.

Rubinow, I. M. 1913. *Social Insurance with Special Reference to American Conditions*. New York: Henry Holt.

Sabato, Larry. 1981. *The Rise of Political Consultants*. New York: Basic Books.

Sabato, Larry, and David Beiler. 1988. "Magic . . . or Blue Smoke and Mirrors? Reflections on New Technologies and Trends in the Political

Consultant Trade." In *Media Technology and the Vote: A Sourcebook*, edited by Joel Swerdlow, 3–17. Washington, D.C.: Annenberg Washington Program.

Saloma, John S. 1983. *Omnibus Politics: The New Conservative Labyrinth*. New York: Hill & Wang.

Samuelson, Robert J. 1978. "Busting the U.S. Budget: The Costs of Aging in America." *National Journal* 10 (18 February): 256–60.

———. 1990a. "Pampering the Elderly." *Newsweek*, 29 October, 61.

———. 1990b. "Pampering the Elderly II." *Newsweek*, 2 November, 58.

———. 1992. "The Future Be Damned." *Newsweek*, 6 January, 36.

Sanders, Daniel S. 1973. *The Impact of Reform Movements on Social Policy Change: The Case of Social Insurance*. Fair Lawn, N.J.: R. E. Burdick.

Sanders, Heywood T. 1980. "Paying for the 'Bloody Shirt': The Politics of Civil War Pensions." In *Political Benefits*, edited by Barry S. Rundquist. Lexington, Mass.: Lexington Books.

Schiller, Herbert I. 1989. *Culture, Incorporated: The Corporate Takeover of Public Expression*. New York: Oxford University Press.

Schiltz, Michael. 1970. *Public Attitudes toward Social Security, 1935–1965*. Washington, D.C.: U.S. Department of Health, Education, and Welfare.

Schlesinger, Arthur M. 1958. *The Coming of the New Deal*. Boston: Houghton Mifflin.

———. 1960. *The Politics of Upheaval*. Boston: Houghton Mifflin.

Schneider, David M. 1938. *The History of Public Welfare in New York State, 1609–1866*. Chicago: University of Chicago Press.

Schobel, Bruce D. 1992. "Sooner than You Think: The Coming Bankruptcy of Social Security." *Policy Review*, Fall, 41–43.

Schottland, Charles I. 1970. *The Social Security Program in the United States*. 2d ed. New York: Appleton-Century-Crofts.

Schwartz, Tony. 1989a. *Guerrilla Media: A Citizen's Guide to Using Electronic Media for Social Change*. Videorecording. Princeton, N.J.: Films for the Humanities.

———. 1989b. *Media in Politics*. Videorecording. Princeton, N.J.: Films for the Humanities.

Schwarz, John. 1988. *America's Hidden Success*. New York: W. W. Norton.

Scull, A.T. 1977. *Decarceration: Community Treatment and the Deviant—a Radical View*. Englewood Cliffs, N.J.: Prentice-Hall.

Seager, Henry R. 1930. "Need of Provision for the Aged in New York." *American Labor Legislation Review* 20 (March): 68.

Sears, David O., and Jack Citrin. 1985. *Tax Revolt: Something for Nothing in California*. Cambridge, Mass.: Harvard University Press.

Shirbman, D. 1985. "Senior Citizens Mobilize." *Wall Street Journal*, 17 April, 56.

Sinclair, Upton. 1934a. *EPIC Answers: How to End Poverty in California*. Los Angeles: End Poverty League.

————. 1934b. *I, Candidate for Governor, and How I Got Licked: The Inside Story of a Political Campaign, the EPIC Plan, and How Big Business Raised Millions of Dollars and Beat It by Millions of Lies.* Pasadena, Calif.: Sinclair.

Skidmore, Max J. 1970. *Medicare and the American Rhetoric of Reconciliation.* University: University of Alabama Press.

Skocpol, Theda, and John Ikenberry. 1983. "The Political Formation of the American Welfare State in Historical and Comparative Perspective." *Comparative Social Research* 6: 87–148.

Smelser, Neil J. 1962. *Theory of Collective Behavior.* New York: Free Press.

Smith, Lee. 1992. "The Tyranny of America's Old." *Fortune,* 13 January, 68–72.

Social Security (formerly *Old Age Security Herald*). For the years 1939–42. New York: American Association for Social Security.

Social Security. 1942. "Life of Abraham Epstein: An American Epic." September–October, 5.

Spencer, Herbert. 1868. *Social Statics.* London: Williams & Norgate.

Stewart, Kenneth. 1934. "Upton Sinclair and His EPIC Plan for California." *Literary Digest,* 25 August, 10.

Stockman, David. 1986. *The Triumph of Politics: Why the Reagan Revolution Failed.* New York: Harper & Row.

Stone, Marvin. 1981. "The Social Security Flare-Up." *U.S. News & World Report,* 8 June, 92.

Storey, James R. 1983. *Older Americans in the Reagan Era: Impacts of Federal Policy Changes.* Washington, D.C.: Urban Institute.

————. 1986. "Policy Changes Affecting the Older Americans during the First Reagan Administration." *Gerontologist* 26: 27–31.

Sulvetta, Margaret B., and Katherine Swartz. 1986. *The Uninsured and Uncompensated Care: A Chartbook.* Washington, D.C.: National Health Policy Forum.

Taylor, Paul. 1986. "The Coming Conflict as We Soak the Young to Enrich the Old." *Washington Post,* 5 January, D1, D4.

Thurow, Lester. 1980. *The Zero-Sum Society: Distribution and Possibilities for Economic Change.* New York: Basic Books.

————. 1981. "Saving Social Security." *Newsweek,* 26 October, 71.

Time. 1982. "A Partisan Clash at the Bipartisan Commission." 24 May, 27.

Tishler, Hace S. 1971. *Self-Reliance and Social Security, 1870–1917.* Port Washington, N.Y.: Kennikat Press.

Tobin, James. 1988. "Reaganomics in Retrospect." In *The Reagan Revolution?,* edited by B. B. Kymlicka, 85–103. Chicago: Dorsey Press.

Torrey, B. 1982. "Guns vs. Canes: The Fiscal Implications of an Aging Population." *American Economic Review* 72 (2): 309–13.

Townsend, Francis E. 1943. *New Horizons: An Autobiography.* Chicago: J. L. Stuart.

Townsend Plan. 1934. "The Townsend Plan Song." In *The Records of the Committee on Economic Security*, vol. 43, 47. Washington, D.C.: National Archives.

Trattner, Walter I. 1974. *From Poor Laws to Welfare State*. New York: Free Press.

Tropman, J. E. 1987. *Public Policy Opinion and the Elderly, 1952–1978*. New York: Greenwood Press.

Tufte, Edward R. 1978. *Political Control of the Economy*. Princeton, N.J.: Princeton University Press.

U.S. Department of Commerce, Bureau of the Census. 1960. *Historical Statistics of the United States: Colonial Times to 1957*. Washington, D.C.: U.S. Government Printing Office.

U.S. Department of Health, Education, and Welfare. 1972. "Higher Social Security Payments." Letter. *DHEW Publication* No. (SSA)73-10322 (October). Washington, D.C.: Social Security Administration.

U.S. House of Representatives, Committee on Labor. 1930. *Old Age Pensions: Hearings before the Committee on Labor*. 71st Cong., 2d Sess. Washington, D.C.: U.S. Government Printing Office, 20, 21, 28 February.

U.S. House of Representatives, Select Committee on Aging. 1977. "Public Hearing on Fragmentation and Proliferation of Services." Testimony presented by Maggie Kuhn of the Gray Panthers. 4 April.

U.S. News & World Report. 1976. "Fresh Scare over Social Security." 16 February, 68–70.

———. 1981a. "The Battle to Save Social Security: The Nation's Premier Pension System Is in Danger of Going Broke, Warns a Bleak New Report." 20 July, 41–43.

———. 1981b. "Senior Citizens Put on the War Paint." 27 July, 33–34.

———. 1982a. "Limit Increases in Social Security? Pro and Con." 10 May, 81–82.

———. 1982b. "Will Social Security Go Broke Soon?" 15 February, 35–36.

———. 1983. "The Great Debate over Social Security." 21 February, 31–32.

U.S. Senate, Committee on Finance. 1935. *Economic Security Act: Hearings on S.1130, a Bill to Alleviate the Hazards of Old Age Unemployment, Illness, and Dependency*. 74th Cong., 1st Sess. Washington, D.C.: U.S. Government Printing Office.

U.S. Senate, Committee on Pensions. 1931. *Old Age Pensions: Hearings before the Committee on Pensions*. 72nd Cong., 1st Sess. Washington, D.C.: U.S. Government Printing Office.

Waldo, Daniel R., and Helen Lazenby. 1984. "Demographic Characteristics and Health Care Use and Expenditures by the Aged in the United States, 1977–1984." *Health Care Financing Review* 6 (1): 1–29.

Waldo, Daniel R., Katherine Levit, and Helen Lazenby. 1986. "National Health Care Expenditures." *Health Care Financing Review* 8 (1): 14.

Wallace, Steven P., John B. Williamson, and Rita Gaston-Lung. 1992. *The Senior Movement: References and Resources.* New York: G. K. Hall.

Walsh, David I. 1926–27. "Justice to Veterans of Industry: Calls for Old Age Pensions." *American Labor Legislation Review* 16–17: 224.

Wattenberg, B. J. 1987. *The Birth Dearth: What Happens When People in Free Countries Don't Have Enough Babies.* New York: Pharos Books.

Weaver, Carolyn. 1982. *The Crisis in Social Security: Economic and Political Origins.* Durham, N.C.: Duke Press Policy Studies.

Weaver, W. 1982. "Age Discrimination Charges Found on Sharp Rise in U.S." *New York Times,* 22 February.

Wells, Robert V. 1975. *The Population of the British Colonies in North America before 1776.* Princeton, N.J.: Princeton University Press.

White, Theodore H. 1961. *The Making of the President, 1960.* New York: Antheneum.

Wildavsky, Aaron. 1962. *Dixon-Yates: A Study in Power Politics.* New Haven, Conn.: Yale University Press.

Willard, Samuel. 1726. *A Compleat Body of Divinity in Two Hundred and Fifty Expository Lectures on the Assembly's Shorter Catechism.* Boston: B. Elliot & D. Henchman.

Williamson, John B., Linda Evans, and Lawrence A. Powell. 1982a. "The Political Influence of Older Americans." *Journal of Sociology and Social Welfare* 8: 771–95.

———. 1982b. *The Politics of Aging: Power and Policy.* Springfield, Ill.: Charles C. Thomas.

———. 1984. "Old Age Relief Policy prior to 1900: The Trend toward Restrictiveness." *American Journal of Economics and Sociology* 43: 369–84.

Williamson, John B., and Fred C. Pampel. 1993. *Old-Age Security in Comparative Perspective.* New York: Oxford University Press.

Williamson, John B., Judith A. Shindul, and Linda Evans. 1985. *Aging and Public Policy: Social Control or Social Justice?* Springfield, Ill.: Charles C. Thomas.

Wise, Stephen S. 1930. "What Rabbi Wise Said." *Old Age Security Herald* 4 (5): 12.

Witte, Edwin E. 1936. "Are Old Age Pensions Worth Their Cost?" *American Labor Legislation Review* 26 (1): 7–14.

———. 1963. *The Development of the Social Security Act.* 2d ed. Madison: University of Wisconsin Press.

Woodsworth, J. S. 1934. "Social Insurance in Canada: Program and Prospects." *American Labor Legislation Review* 24 (1): 61–66.

Workman, Janet. 1924–25. "Old Age Assistance Laws Superior to Almshouse System." *American Labor Legislation Review* 14–15: 302.

Yates, J. V. N. [1824] 1971. "Report of the Secretary of State in 1824 on the Relief and Settlement of the Poor." In *The Almshouse Experience: Collected Reports*, 942, 951–52, 958. New York: Arno Press and New York Times.

Zinsser, John. 1986. "Gray Panthers: Fighting the Good Fight for 15 Years." *Fifty-Plus* 26 (3): 12–13.

Index

Achenbaum, W. Andrew, 20, 21, 37, 43, 97, 140, 214
Adams, J. S., 76
Administration on Aging, 16, 129, 147, 149–50
AFL–CIO. *See* American Federation of Labor
Age Discrimination in Employment Act, 140
age wars. *See* intergenerational warfare
ageism, 138–40
aging enterprise, 129, 149, 210
Agricultural Adjustment Act, 104
Allen, Lawrence, 46
Allen, Willis, 46
almshouses. *See* poorhouses
Altmeyer, Arthur, 44, 94, 99, 103, 104
American Association for Labor Legislation (AALL), 15, 41, 44, 49, 52, 97, 106–7, 114–15, 142
American Association for Social Security (AASS), 15, 41, 49–52, 61–62, 76, 97, 106–7, 142
American Association of Retired Persons (AARP), 16, 57, 111, 114, 117, 134–35, 138, 143, 150, 159, 184, 186, 194, 202, 205
American Enterprise Institute, 154
American Federation of Labor (AFL), 43, 112; AFL–CIO, 114, 117–18, 143, 161, 163
American Geriatrics Society, 118
American Hospital Association, 118, 122
American Labor Legislation Review, 44, 61, 66, 72, 75
American Legion, 118
American Medical Association, 78, 108, 114–23
Americans for Generational Equity (AGE), 150, 167, 180–82, 186, 208
Anderson, Clinton, 122, 126
Andrews, John, 44
Andrus, Ethel Percy, 114, 134
Ansolabehere, Stephen, 222
Arrears of Pension Act, 32
Austin, William, 76
Axinn, June, 112, 113

baby boomers, 2, 182
Bachrach, Peter, 10
Bagdikian, Ben, 222
balanced budget, 153
Barnouw, Erik, 223
Barone, Michael, 132
Barringer, F., 2
Barry, Robert L., 218
Bates, Stephen, 222
Baudrillard, Jean, 212
Baum, Martha, 148, 162
Beibel, Fredo, 88
Bennett, W. Lance, 201, 204, 205, 222
Bennis, Warren, 205, 222
Berger, Peter, 8, 9
Bethel, Tom, 157, 169, 178
Biden, Joseph, 184
big business, 68–69; opposition to old-age pensions, 69, 72
big government, 81, 83, 210

251

The Authors

Lawrence Alfred Powell received his Ph.D. from MIT in 1987 and is currently assistant professor of political science at the University of Texas–San Antonio. His published works include *The Politics of Aging: Power and Policy* and numerous articles and book chapters on aging, mass media, and political psychology. He is currently director of the Crossnational Variations in Distributive Justice Perception project, a 10-nation comparative study of citizen attitudes toward equity and social justice in Europe, Australia, New Zealand, Canada, and the United States.

Kenneth J. Branco is director of the Martin Institute for Law and Society and associate professor of sociology at Stonehill College. He is adjunct associate professor at the Center for Gerontology and Health Care at Brown University and lecturer at the Graduate School of Social Work at Boston College. He received his B.A. from the University of Massachusetts at Amherst and his M.S.W. and Ph.D. from Boston College. His recent publications focus on psychosocial functioning and advance care planning in long-term care.

John B. Williamson is professor of sociology at Boston College. He received his B.S. from MIT and his Ph.D. from Harvard University. He is author or co-author of 15 books, including *Old-Age Security in Comparative Perspective* (1993), *The Senior Movement* (1992), *Age, Class, Politics, and the Welfare State* (1989), *Aging and Public Policy* (1985), and *The Politics of Aging* (1982).